AF598818

Heroines *of* Horticulture

A CELEBRATION OF WOMEN WHO SHAPED NORTH AMERICA'S GARDENING HERITAGE

STEFAN WHITE

4880 Lower Valley Road • Atglen, PA 19310

Library of Congress Control Number: 2024932650

Edited by Ian Robertson
Designed by Danielle D. Farmer
Cover design by Ashley Millhouse
Type set in Bodoni Std/Ainslie Sans

ISBN: 978-0-7643-6549-2
978-1-5073-0392-4 (Epub)
Printed in China

Published by Schiffer Publishing, Ltd.
4880 Lower Valley Road
Atglen, PA 19310
Phone: (610) 593-1777; Fax: (610) 593-2002
Email: info@schifferbooks.com
Web: www.schifferbooks.com
For our complete selection of fine books on this and related subjects, please visit our website at www.schifferbooks.com. You may also write for a free catalog.

Schiffer Publishing's titles are available at special discounts for bulk purchases for sales promotions or premiums. Special editions, including personalized covers, corporate imprints, and excerpts, can be created in large quantities for special needs. For more information, contact the publisher.

Contents

Appendixes:

Introduction

This book tells the stories of 100 key, trailblazing women who established themselves as real contributors to America's horticulture heritage, as founders of the evolution of gardening in North America, and to the very development of the USA and Canada.

They needed courage and determination to overcome the many difficulties and obstacles placed in their way, including the attitude of men with strong prejudices, who considered their professions to be a male right protected from the incursion of women. These women were stubborn, determined, obsessive, and sometimes eccentric—perhaps what is needed to be a pioneer?

You will read tales of invention, determination, creativity, dogged research, innovation, perspiration, and inspiration that helped shape North America. We owe them a great deal, but their work and achievements have been virtually forgotten and ignored. The focus of this book is to give these forgotten, deserving women horticulturists in North America the recognition and thanks that they fully deserve.

The 100 women featured in this book changed the face of American history and its landscape, using their broad range of skills as landscape architects, naturalists, botanists, writers, plant hunters and collectors, garden designers, botanical artists, journalists, nursery women, plant breeders, landscape photographers, business women, horticultural school founders, conservationists, ecologists, broadcasters, and botanical scientists. The range of accomplishments of these selected women is vast and the variety of their talents is amazing. These stories show just how important women have been to North America's horticultural heritage, to its love of nature, its environment, its development, and its landscape.

In addition to being of interest to gardeners, this book is an insight into the history of the emerging, developing nations of the USA and Canada. It is also a celebration of how women met and overcame challenges and obstacles to achieve equality with men. Gender equality remains a fight to this day, and you will read about how in the past men often deliberately prevented women from contributing to horticultural work and study in an attempt to preserve their dominance.

When American lifestyles changed, so did private gardens. Perhaps the biggest change came when the vast estates of the wealthy in the 1920s gave way to increasing urbanization and the need for designing gardens for much smaller spaces. Pioneering women gardeners, especially landscape architects, took all these evolutions in their stride. This book gives insight into how gardening has changed in North America over the centuries and how critical these pioneering women have been.

In the past, traditional gardening history tended to focus on famous male landscape designers, plant hunters, and grand estates and has often forgotten the contributions made by women. One of the great experts on garden history and on garden writing, Eleanour Sinclair Rohde (1881–1950), noted that over the 600 years of garden writing that she had examined, she had encountered a great shortage of books written by, and for, women gardeners:

> All the more remarkable because, since Medieval days, the garden has been regarded as the special province of the housewife. The history of women in the garden is a history of women's lives. Ask most people to name women gardeners and most can only come up with two or three women. There are many, mostly unrecognized, who deserve appreciation and acknowledgment of their work.

Women gardeners with plows and hand tools for gardens, Atlanta, Georgia, 1910. Photograph originally published in Horace Edward Stockbridge's *Land Teaching* (Southern Ruralist Company, 1910). *Library of Congress*

Each of the selected 100 pioneers has their biography summarized in chapter 4, in the heart of this book. They are listed in chronological order according to the year of their birth.

Many simply ignored difficulties placed in their way and plowed their own path. Some of them have been included for their infectious enthusiasm for gardening and their ability to spread this joy to others, encouraging people to enjoy the outdoors, appreciate nature, and love gardening. A good example of this is Thalassa Cruso (see 4.92), a television presenter, author, and newspaper columnist. In her case, she succeeded in educating others about the joys of gardening and the pleasures it can bring in her television programs and writing in the 1960s and '70s. Others, such as Beatrix Farrand (see 4.42), are hugely influential figures in their chosen field—in her case landscape architecture. She was commissioned to design more than 110 important gardens and public spaces across North America and Europe. Her career included commissions to design gardens for private residences, estates, and country homes; public parks; botanical gardens; college campuses; and the White House.

Others, such as Ellen Biddle Shipman (see 4.38), have designed as many as 1,000 gardens of varying size across the continent. Some, like Kate Sessions (see 4.21), confined their work to a very small geographic area, in her case San Diego, California, and largely to just one area within the city limits, Balboa Park.

Some have concentrated their work on a single species of plant, like Hulda Klager, the Lilac Lady (see 4.31). Others have dedicated their lives to creating a notable private garden and, upon their death, have generously donated their garden to local authorities to open it to the public, sometimes with a large monetary endowment to maintain it. Lady Bird Johnson (see 4.96) used her status and influence as first lady to beautify the nation's cities and highways; more than 200 laws related to the environment were passed during the Johnson administration, many of which are credited to her enthusiastic support and work. Influential women pioneers who were Native American and African American are included.

The women authors that have been selected—18 out of the 100—have written seminal works on gardening, often passing on practical advice gleaned from their own experiences, and, by doing so, have increased interest in gardening and converted many to the joys of gardening. By the mid-nineteenth century there were enough women eager for advice about gardening to make books bestsellers, because those who could not afford a gardener needed to do the hard work themselves, and they were eager buyers of instructional books. The printed word gave them access to horticultural knowledge and advice on many aspects of gardening.

Two of the women are included because, in addition to creating worthwhile gardens, they were delightfully and joyfully eccentric. Another two of the selected women (among the most praiseworthy and deserving of inclusion in the book) encouraged children to love gardening, plants, and nature by establishing children's gardens and parks, particularly for youngsters living in deprived areas that would otherwise not have had access to the outdoors and the joys and challenges of nature and gardening. Others used their particular skills as botanic artists to record plants in all their glory for posterity. Some ensured the survival of important records of earlier gardens by photographing them for posterity. Others encouraged gardeners through establishing garden clubs and horticultural societies.

Some of North America's most impressive, larger gardens were created during the Gilded Age, when wealthy industrialists wanted to create magnificent estates with exceptional gardens. This was the era during the late nineteenth century (1870s to about 1900), a time of rapid economic growth, especially in the northern and western United States. While many of the wives of newly wealthy industrialists may not have been involved in the initial design of large estate gardens (prominent landscape architects were normally commissioned to do this), some of them did become involved with their suggestions as to format, theme, and style of the gardens. The depth of their contribution to their gardens depended on their level of interest in gardening. Some, like Clara Ford (see 4.34), wife of automobile pioneer Henry Ford, were enthusiasts of a particular element; in her case her love of roses, which resulted in the creation of a spectacularly significant rose garden in her estate in Fair Lane, Wisconsin. She is also included in the book to represent a number of women in a particular category—the wives of wealthy industrialists who used their riches to build magnificent mansions that needed grand, impressive gardens and landscapes to set them in. Several donated their estates, and a legacy to manage them, so that the public could enjoy them after they left. Sadly, many of these grand estates became impossibly expensive to maintain and were sold off to developers, who razed the gardens to build housing developments. Some, once their children had left the family home and their motherly duties were over, became interested in occupying their time with an interest, and they became more involved with gardening. Few, if any, of this exclusive band of women would have gotten their hands dirty in the soil—they had a small army of gardeners employed to do all the manual work, and in the house they had servants to perform household tasks, so they had time on their hands. They were similar to British ladies who accompanied their husbands in the nineteenth century to remote countries overseas like India to govern the British Empire. Apart from organizing social events and dinner parties, they had little to occupy their time, and, to avoid boredom, many took an interest in overseeing the development and upkeep of the garden and in researching, finding, and cultivating plants.

The Roaring Twenties was another period of economic prosperity. This period saw the large-scale development and use of automobiles, telephones, movies, radio, and electrical appliances. This was another period of rapid industrial and economic growth and accelerated consumer demand, and it introduced significantly new changes in lifestyle and culture. It was a time when many people moved to the newly developed suburbs and garden cities. Through this, an explosion in gardening occurred, bringing the joys and challenges of gardening to a massive new audience. Women were at the forefront of taking advantage of this social revolution, and several women were closely involved in designing gardens for these new suburban housing developments.

Each woman's entry includes, where available, a portrait or photograph of the subject and a summary of her qualifications, her achievements, anecdotes about her career, her contribution to gardening history, and occasional quotations. It would have been appropriate to have a portrait of every one of the women featured but, sadly, although images, including photographs, do exist of practically every one of them, a good number of them are so early that the clarity, quality, and resolution simply means that they cannot be reproduced in this book because the parameters for printing on the page are not met. In cases where the resolution does not enable

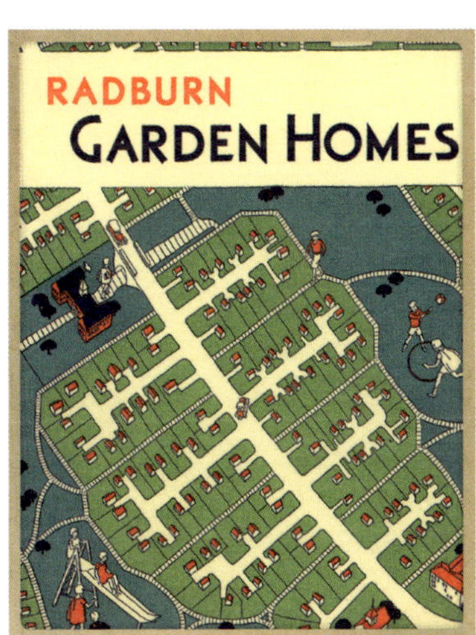

Cover for a brochure advertising a suburban housing project in Radburn, New Jersey, a planned model community developed by the City Housing Corporation in the late 1920s. Marjorie Sewell Cautley (see 4.69) was appointed landscape architect for the project. Radburn was intended to provide families with modest incomes and limited resources the opportunity to live in healthful, pleasing conditions rather than in crowded, urban apartments. John D. Rockefeller Jr. was a substantial investor, putting in more than $1.5 million. Eleanor Roosevelt served as a member of the advisory committee. *Historic New England*

the photograph to be printed on the page, I have commissioned an artist to create a line drawing to provide a portrait. The work of this talented individual, Pablo Jose Martinez, is featured in the portraits in the 100 biographies, and his work is an integral part of describing their lives. Please see appendix E for his biography.

My selection of these pioneering American women gardeners has been made on the basis that the individual left a legacy that has somehow benefited gardeners, the North American landscape, its heritage, or horticulture in general. These brief biographies tell how each woman has contributed to America's great gardening heritage and legacy. Finding, researching, and writing about these talented, brave, and determined women has been a long and rewarding journey, and I hope that you enjoy the result. They are an extraordinary collection with varied talents but with one common theme: they have contributed to North America's gardening heritage, helped develop emerging nations, brought joy to garden lovers, and ensured their place in history—true heroines of horticulture.

CHAPTER
1

How Women Were Restricted *by* Educational Opportunities

– 1 –

Any examination of the role of women in the evolution of the USA and Canada cannot ignore the fact that women had very restricted educational opportunities until the late nineteenth century. One of the joys of basic gardening is that it requires no formal training. A lot of it is common sense, and the basic skills and tips can easily be passed on from generation to generation. However, the sciences involved with horticulture, such as botany, landscape architecture, and garden design, need higher education and degrees from colleges or universities. Quite simply, women were not admitted to these for more than 200 years after the arrival of Pilgrims on the *Mayflower* in 1620. They were deliberately excluded, largely because they were deemed unsuitable for the sciences and because men wanted to preserve their dominance over women. The views of society, which were also the views of most women assimilated in the process of socialization, made marriage and children the raison d'être of a woman's existence. Consequently female education in North America in the early nineteenth century was either inferior or nonexistent.

In colonial America, elementary education became widespread in New England but was still limited elsewhere. New England Puritans believed it was necessary to study the bible, so boys and girls were taught to read at an early age. It was also required that each town pay for a primary school. About 10 percent enjoyed secondary schooling. Few girls attended formal schools, but most were able to get some education at home, or at so-called *dame schools*, where women taught basic reading and writing skills in their own houses.

A New England dame school in colonial times, 1713. Engraving. Unknown author.
Bettman Archive

Campaigning for school reform began in the 1830s, and attitudes began to change. Girls were starting to be regarded as capable and deserving of common school education to become good citizens and better contributors to community life. The increasing acceptance and the provision of education for girls resulted in a dramatic rise of female enrolments in schools of all levels.

By 1750, nearly 90 percent of New England's women and almost all of its men could read and write. The percentage of literate women then doubled in the sixty years between 1780 and 1840. Tax-supported schooling for girls had begun as early as 1767 in New England. It was optional, and some towns proved reluctant. Northampton, Massachusetts, for example, was a late adopter because it had many rich families who dominated the political and social structures, and they did not want to pay taxes to schools or aid poor families. Northampton assessed taxes on all households, rather than only on those with children, and used the funds to support a grammar school to prepare boys for college. Not until after 1800 did Northampton educate girls with public money. In contrast, the town of Sutton, Massachusetts, at the time was diverse in terms of social leadership and religion. Sutton paid for its schools by means of taxes on households with children only, thereby creating an active constituency in favor of universal education for boys and girls. However, there were absolutely no higher educational opportunities for women.

Historians point out that reading and writing were different skills in the colonial era. School taught both, but in places without schools, writing was taught mainly to boys and only to a few privileged girls. The prevailing attitude was that men handled worldly affairs and needed to read and write, but girls only needed to read (especially religious materials). This educational disparity between reading and writing explains why nearly all colonial women could read but could not write and could not sign their names—they used an *X*.

Across the South there was very little public schooling. Most parents either homeschooled their children or, if they could afford the cost, used tutors or sent them to small local private schools. A study of women's signatures in Georgia

Seminary Building, Mount Holyoke Female Seminary, ca. 1880s. *Archives and Special Collections Mount Holyoke College*

indicates a high degree of literacy in areas with schools. In South Carolina, scores of school projects were advertised in the *South Carolina Gazette* beginning in 1732.

In first half of the nineteenth century, before the emergence of high schools (which did not become widespread in the USA until after the Civil War ended in 1865), academies and seminaries were established as a transition from grammar school for those who wanted to prepare for college work and as a form of higher education for the many who would not advance to college. The founding of female academies was a new opportunity for women seeking higher learning. As an example, in New York State thirty-two new academies were incorporated between 1819 and 1853 with the prefix *female* in the title. *Female seminaries* began to offer higher education to women, such as that started in Middlebury, Vermont (1814), the Troy Female Seminary (1821), and the Hartford Female Seminary (1828). Other colleges founded before the Civil War with all-female student bodies included Mount Holyoke College of South Hadley, Massachusetts, founded in 1837 by Mary Lyon as Mount Holyoke Female Seminary; Wesleyan College of Macon, Georgia, founded in 1836 as Georgia Female College, which is the first college in the world chartered to grant degrees to women; Queens College (now Queens University) of Charlotte, North Carolina, founded in 1857 as Charlotte Female Institute; Averett College (now Averett University) of Danville, Virginia, founded in 1859 as Union Women's College; and Vassar College, founded in Poughkeepsie, New York, in 1861.

Prior to the American Civil War, few colleges admitted women. Founded in 1772 as a primary school, Salem College is the oldest female educational establishment. Some were founded as coeducational institutions. Other early coeducational schools included Hillsdale College, founded as Michigan Central College in Spring Arbor, Michigan, in 1844, and Antioch College, founded by noted educator Horace Mann in 1852 in Yellow Springs, Ohio. Hollins University was founded as Valley

Union Seminary in Roanoke, Virginia, in 1842 as a coeducational institution but became all-female in 1952. With the start of the Civil War in 1861, many males were away fighting, so more opportunities arose for women to fill the empty space in schools, and universities became more willing to admit women.

During the 1830s and 1840s, especially in the South, the female seminary or academy quickly became en vogue. In Alabama twenty-seven academies for girls were founded between 1822 and 1861. These schools trained girls in domestic, literary, and religious matters, as well as in mathematics, philosophy, and history, providing the first higher education for females in the United States.

An engraved print by Henry Howe depicting collegiate buildings on the campus of Oberlin College, Ohio, as they appeared in 1846. This print was an illustration in the 1847 edition of *Historical Collections of Ohio* by Henry Howe. *Oberlin College Archives*

In 1835 Oberlin Collegiate Institute in Oberlin, Ohio, became the first predominantly white collegiate institution to admit African American male students, and, two years later it opened its doors to all women, becoming the first coeducational college in the country. In 1862, Mount Allison University in New Brunswick was the first university to allow female students in Canada. The struggle over access to education lies at the heart of why women's participation in science has been delayed compared to that of men. Universities were restricted to male students in most countries until the latter part of the nineteenth century.

The world of horticultural academia believed that, for instance, botany was a science, and worthwhile research could not be performed by people without higher education, such as a degree from a recognized university or college. Many enthusiastic women were undertaking significant projects, particularly in the study of plants, but they were not *qualified* and were often dismissed without their work being studied. The men dominating the world of horticulture despised amateurs entering their domain and dismissed women's efforts as *drawing room science*, believing that botany had been debased by becoming, as one academic put it, *an amusement for ladies rather than the occupation for the serious thoughts of man.*

The Ichabod Crane schoolhouse is a nineteenth-century building (ca. 1850) that served as a local single-room public school into the 1940s. Recently awarded a "Legends & Lore" marker by the New York Folklore Society & William G. Pomeroy Foundation, honoring Washington Irving's *Sleepy Hollow* character Ichabod Crane, who was patterned after the original Kinderhook schoolteacher, Jesse Merwin—hence the schoolhouse name. Collection of the Columbia County Historical Society, acquired in 1974. *Vaaltje*

Women were forced to look for chinks in the armor that allowed some women to break through and take part in the ongoing work of science. However, the lack of higher education immediately and effectively excluded women from the world of botany until the end of the nineteenth century. The wonder is not so much that there were so few women scientists prior to 1900, but that there were any at all.

When a ban on women entering universities was lifted, the world of academia opened up and they were able to present their research as serious scientific achievements. Until the last quarter of the century it was not possible for a woman to support herself as a botanist, except perhaps by writing textbooks. Botany is a science that was largely beyond the reach of women until the late nineteenth century, and, when higher education was made available, of the listed pioneering American women gardeners, a fifth of them made their mark by their research and other contributions.

Before the education reform that occurred during the Progressive Era (1890s to the 1920s), boys and girls often had different course programs of study. It was not uncommon for girls to be educated toward the jobs that society deemed appropriate, such as secretary, journalist, or social service worker. The idea of a *differentiated curriculum* between boys and girls was common throughout schools in the United States. This caused the high school education system to become a more *efficient site for the construction of gender*. When women's education was approved at all, it was often thought that its value lay in the education of future sons. Even such highly successful women as Almira Phelps (see 4.8) supported the *separate spheres* doctrine in her writings. During this time there was a push to make women a better *domesticated citizen* rather than a scholar. The voices of many women were just beginning to be heard in society, as well as the education system, but there was still opposition from some as to the credibility of their words. Girls of different races and ethnicities were also entering the public school system at this time.

The Progressive Era was a period of widespread social activism and political reform across the United States that spanned the 1890s to the 1920s. The main objectives of the Progressive movement included addressing problems caused by industrialization, urbanization, immigration, and political corruption. Many activists joined efforts to reform local government, public education, medicine, finance, insurance, industry, railroads, churches, and many other areas. Initially the movement operated chiefly at the local level, but later it expanded to state and national levels. Progressives drew support from the middle class, and supporters included many lawyers, teachers, physicians, ministers, and business people. Progressives supported reforms in modernizing approaches to economics, government, industry, finance, medicine, theology, and even the family. They also achieved significant reforms in schooling and education in general.

The University of Pennsylvania permitted women to attend with nondegree status in the late 1870s. They were admitted formally as graduate students when the graduate program was established in 1882, and as undergraduates when the school of education (now a graduate school) opened in 1914. The remainder of the Ivy League were disgracefully slow in accepting women: the years that they allowed women to enroll are as follows:

Yale: 1969
Princeton: 1969
Cornell: technically 1872, but as a practical matter in 1970
Brown: 1971 (when its women's college, Pembroke, merged with Brown)
Dartmouth: 1972
Harvard: 1977 (when Harvard and Radcliffe merged)
Columbia: 1981 (although Barnard students were allowed to attend certain Columbia courses as early as 1955)

These dates should be 100 years earlier, but they are not misprints. It was not until 1969 that the Ivy League permitted women to enroll and effectively enjoy the same facilities as men.

In the late nineteenth and early twentieth centuries opportunities grew in North America for women to study horticulture. New schools were established for women and many of the women in this book studied at these. They include new gardening schools for women such as the Pennsylvania School of Horticulture for Women; Lowthorpe School of Landscape Architecture, Gardening, and Horticulture for Women; the California School of Gardening for Women at the University of

California; and similar training for women offered by Cornell University and the University of Illinois.

In 1915, the Cambridge School of Architecture and Landscape Architecture for Women was founded in Massachusetts, a direct response to the fact that women were not permitted to attend classes in these fields at Harvard and elsewhere. Several alumni of the schools for women who wished to study horticulture are featured in this book.

Coinciding with the beginnings of the first wave of feminism in the twentieth century came the attempt by women to gain equal rights to education in the United States. After long battles against gender oppression, women finally obtained the right to be educated through several government acts and conventions, the opening of facilities willing to educate them, and the opportunity to continue into higher education.

When higher education became available to women, it opened up a wide range of opportunities for women interested in all aspects of gardening, including horticulture, landscape architecture, garden design, botanical research, plant breeding, conservation, ecology, and scientific research.

Largely because of the restriction of educational opportunities, only seventeen of the 100 women featured in this book were born before 1850, but, as society developed in the latter part of the nineteenth century, the role of women was redefined. New freedoms and education denied them previously opened up many new horizons and career opportunities. The twentieth century was the real heart of the emergence and recognition of women in the world of horticulture, and in the twenty-first century, gender equality ensures that women have the same opportunities as men (although the pay gap still exists in many areas).

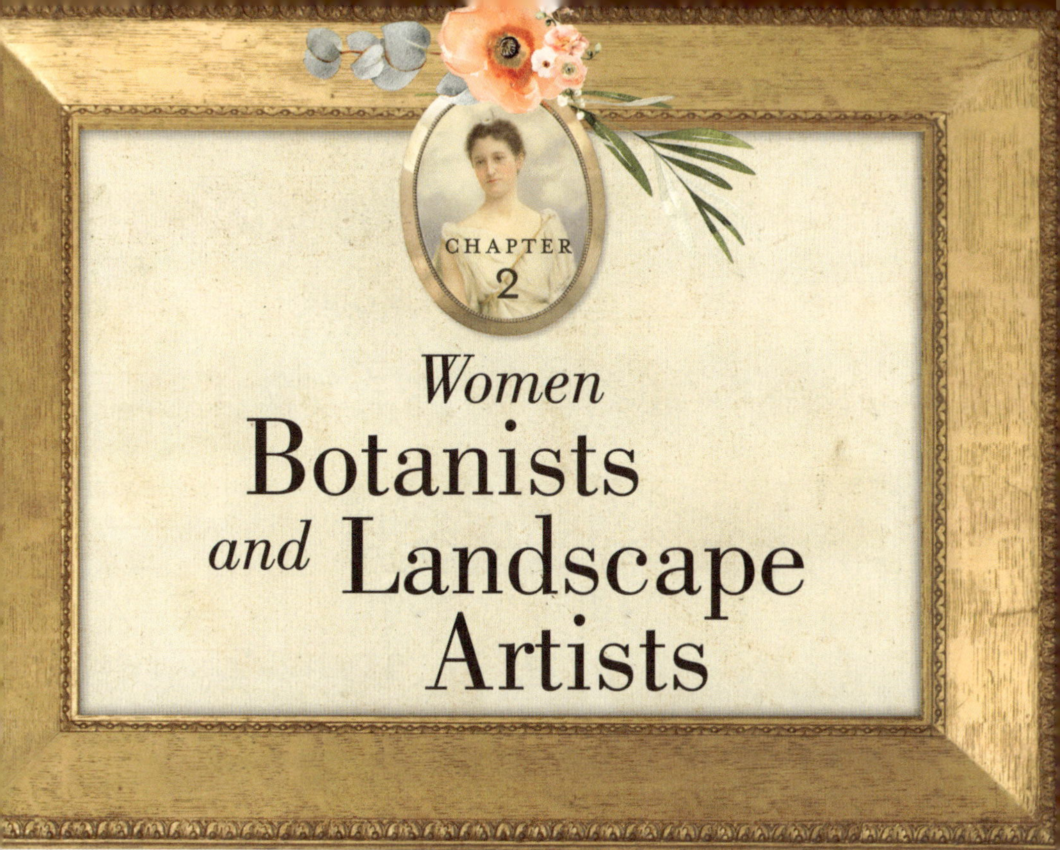

Women Botanists and Landscape Artists

One-fifth of the pioneering American women gardeners featured in this book are identified as involved with the science of botany, and they had to overcome many challenges and obstacles to achieve their goals. In this chapter the lack of educational opportunities for women is highlighted, in particular the fact that higher education was not available to them until around 1840. This prevented women from studying the sciences, including botany. It was considered *a suitable and elevating subject for women* in the latter part of the nineteenth century. Before that, in an article about nineteenth-century American botany by C. Earle Smith, not a single woman is mentioned. Harry Baker Humphrey in his *Makers of North American Botany* (which covered 250 years) included only two women: Jane Colden (see 4.3) and Elizabeth Gertrude Britton (see 4.22). To the extent that a career implies paid employment, this was not possible in American botany for women (or men) until the mid-nineteenth century. By the end of that century,

American botany had become largely professionalized: positions were available at universities and in government agencies, botanical societies had been formed (and were increasingly excluding amateurs), and the PhD was becoming a standard qualification. In addition, several botanical journals were available for publications of research. All the women botanists included published either botanical books or articles in botanical journals, meeting at least one requirement of the twentieth-century definition of a professional with a career. Many of them had neither advanced degrees nor paid employment. Elizabeth Britton, the most eminent woman botanist of her period, had neither. The responsibilities of marriage, including the care of children, made original work in sciences, especially in botanical research, nearly impossible.

Early Woman Botanist, 1835, by John Lee Comstock (1789–1858). *Science History Institute*

Women might collect and examine flowers or perhaps make herbaria of their dried specimens. A few married women managed the writing of botanical books, and some were able to work with their husband at home, or in their husband's laboratory. Until the late nineteenth century a single woman rarely had a room of her own or the financial security to do her own work. A father or other male relative sometimes provided the security or mentorship, but only until marriage. Not until the founding of women's colleges, largely in the 1870s and 1880s, was it possible for a single woman to support herself in botany. Limited work opportunities for women in botany also became available at agricultural experimental stations by the 1890s. Many of the notable women in botany born after 1850 remained single. Most of the botanical women in the generation born in the decade after 1900 were professional botanists with PhDs and academic positions (largely at women's colleges) and chose to remain single.

Much of what we now know about women botanists in the USA comes from research by Emmanuel David Rudolph. He was the first botanist to research the vegetation of Antarctica. He made five field trips there in the 1960s. Later he was known for his interest and research into the history of nineteenth- and early-twentieth-century biology and botany. He provides us with statistical information about women botanists. He writes that botany in the USA did not really take off until after the Civil War, which ended in 1865. There followed a *period of rapid expansion in women's education and the interest of women in plants*, writes Rudolph. Still, very few of the women in Rudolph's list of women botanists got PhDs. The barriers against women, simply for being women, in academia were extremely high. He counted only seventeen PhDs in the world for women botanists by 1899. Five of these had their degrees granted by the University of Zürich, Switzerland, and five by the University of Pennsylvania, which had opened a graduate department for women in 1892.

The first women to receive PhDs in botany from American universities were Alice Carter (Syracuse University) and Mary E. Holmes (University of Michigan), both in 1888. Carter became a high school teacher and Holmes an editor. Rudolph stated that 1,185 American women were actively engaged in botany in the nineteenth century. Most of these belonged to botanical clubs or made plant collections, but only nine were listed as having made scientific contributions *on a par with those made by men*. Rudolph notes that at the turn of the twentieth century, increased professionalism resulted in *a belittling of amateurs* across the board. Women would have been particularly hit by such attitudes, which served to reinforce their segregation in academia. Nevertheless, he concludes: *It is remarkable that so many women in nineteenth-century America were seriously interested in plants. They did make a difference that only now is beginning to be noted.*

The largest category of the chosen 100 by profession is landscape architecture—twenty-six out of the 100. What is a landscape architect? The terminology has evolved to include those once known as landscape gardeners, landscape designers, architects, surveyors, or civil engineers, particularly those from the nineteenth century who practiced before the term *landscape architect* was coined. The phrase excludes gardeners, botanists, writers, theoreticians, ecologists, artists, and others who did not practice landscape design at a site scale and were not trained as a historical *landscape gardener* or contemporary *landscape architect*. Women have contributed in many ways to the evolution of landscape architecture in North America. The biographies of twenty-six of them in this book attest to their skills, aptitude, and determination to overcome the prejudices of men, who were reluctant at first to admit them into their profession. In her book *Vocation for the Trained Woman*, Beatrix Farrand (see 4.42) wrote that landscape gardening was

a profession that no women should attempt who is not above, rather than below, the average strength and endurance, as the work swings from one extreme to another, sometimes meaning 8 hours or more office work like making plans, drawing specifications, and draughting – and this continue for several days, followed by the entire change which field work means. This is not infrequently involving a week's continuous work in which the average day, including times and travelling, is 12 hours or over. No one can be a landscape gardener who has not an eye... This means the appreciation of the texture as well as the color of the landscape, the peculiar quality of each individual and its adaptation to the specific treatment; for it cannot be too strongly borne in mind that landscaping gardening is the profession of a painter built on the substructure of that of an engineer.

Before 1800, landscape gardening in Europe (later called landscape architecture) largely concerned master planning and garden design for large projects, such as palaces and royal properties, religious complexes, manor houses, and centers of government. The term "landscape architecture" was invented by Gilbert Laing Meason (1769–1832), a Scottish merchant, estate owner, and agricultural improver. He was interested in art history and wrote a book titled *On The Landscape Architecture of the Great Painters of Italy*. It was printed in 1828 by C. Hullmandel in London, England, in an edition of just 150 copies. It was not a commercial success. It covered the way that buildings and structures were sited within landscapes in paintings to produce beautiful compositions. It included thoughts on the placing of buildings in their surroundings—a concept that forms a central part of the landscape architect's work today. The term would probably have died out if it had not been taken up by horticulturalist and planner John Claudius Loudon (1783–1843). He was a Scottish botanist, garden designer, and prolific horticultural and landscape design writer. Through his publications he hoped to spread his ideals of the creation of common space and the improvement of city planning, and he wanted to develop an appreciation and interest in agriculture and horticulture. He was a city planner and designed many garden projects, including parks, stately homes, cemeteries, and botanical gardens. He thought that the term "landscape architect" had a wider application outside art theory, and explained this view in an article in the contemporaneous *Gardener's Magazine* (which he had founded). He felt that landscape architect aptly described the composition of created landscapes, and he was instrumental in the adoption of the term "landscape architecture" by the profession. He took the term from Meason's book and gave it publicity in his *Encyclopedias*, in his 1840 book on landscape gardening, and in his book about one of England's premier garden designers, *Landscape Architecture of the Late Humphry*

Repton. The term was picked up by Loudon's American admirer Andrew Jackson Downing (1815–1852). He was an American landscape designer, horticulturist, writer, and editor of *The Horticulturist* magazine. Downing is considered to be a founder of American landscape architecture. In 1841 his first book, *A Treatise on the Theory and Practice of Landscape Gardening, Adapted to North America*, was published to great success; it was the first book on the subject in the United States.

Humphry Repton's business card, depicting him measuring distances for a garden design. Repton was an eminent English landscape designer whose work influenced several early American garden designers.

gardenhistorymatters.com

During the latter nineteenth century the term "landscape architect" began to be used by professional landscape designers and was firmly established after Frederick Law Olmsted (1822–1903) first used the term to describe his profession. With Beatrix Farrand and others he founded the American Society of Landscape Architects (ASLA) in 1899.

Landscape architecture is a multidisciplinary field, incorporating aspects of botany, horticulture, the fine arts, architecture, industrial design, soil sciences, environmental psychology, geography, ecology, civil engineering, and urban design. The activities of a landscape architect can range from the creation of public parks and parkways to site planning for campuses and corporate office parks, from the design of residential estates to the design of civil infrastructure and the management of large wilderness areas or reclamation of degraded landscapes such as mines or landfills. Landscape architects work on structures and external spaces with limitations toward the landscape or park aspect of the design—large or small, urban, suburban, and rural—while integrating ecological sustainability. The most valuable contribution can be made at the first stage of a project to generate ideas with technical understanding and creative flair for the design, organization, and use of spaces. The landscape architect can conceive the overall concept and prepare the master plan from which detailed design drawings and technical specifications are prepared. They can also review proposals to authorize and supervise contracts for the construction work. Other skills include preparing design impact assessments, conducting environmental assessments and audits, and serving as an expert witness at inquiries on land use issues. Landscape architects focus on planning the gardens, and on how they will look and what will have to be done.

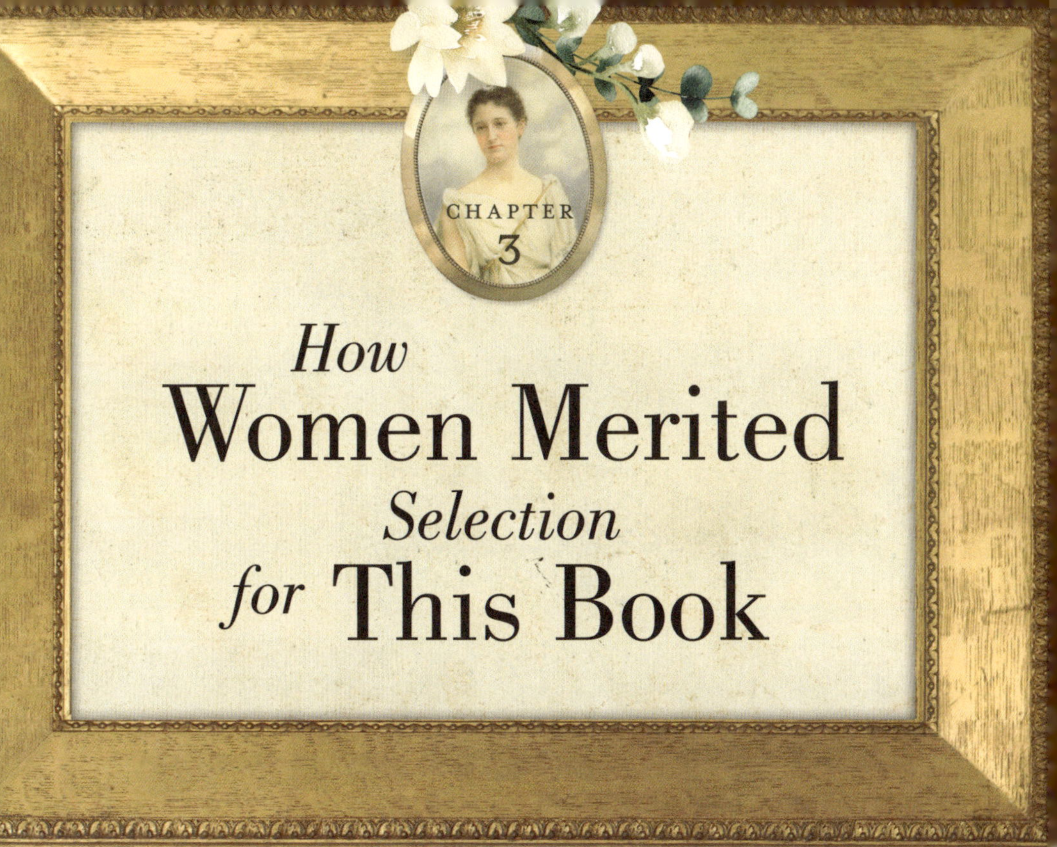

How Women Merited *Selection for* This Book

The women selected represent those that have made the most significant contributions to America's gardening evolution. They are listed in chronological order of their date of birth. There are many who have made worthwhile contributions to America's gardening heritage and who are alive today. In the belief that their work is perhaps not ended, they are not included in this book. Some of the pioneering women are selected because of their scientific expertise—one was even awarded the prestigious Nobel Prize for her botanical work. Others are here because, even without any horticultural training, they created significant gardens. Yet more merited inclusion because they left their gardens, after passing on, for the benefit of the public by arranging for them to be open to visitors, often financed by trusts set up by them to fund the running costs. Some were trained landscape architects of skill and renown who were commissioned to design large estate gardens and public parks, but also smaller suburban gardens.

You will read of women who refused to be cowed by men putting obstacles in their way to preserve their dominance of their vocations. This was particularly relevant in the world of academia. As outlined in chapter 1, educational opportunities were very restricted for women until the late nineteenth century. They were denied entry into universities and colleges, but nevertheless many overcame this obstacle to achieve advances in horticultural fields. Those who did eventually find it possible to obtain higher education and were awarded qualifications often found that job opportunities were scarce. This was especially so in the Great Depression, which started in the United States after a major fall in stock prices that began around September 1929.

Another reason it was often difficult to find work, despite being qualified, was because of the prejudice against women entering what was regarded as the domain of men. Some of the brave women featured in this book simply ignored difficulties placed in their way and plowed their own path. Determination and perseverance is a common theme of pioneering women gardeners.

Books on gardening by, and for, women were rare until the mid-nineteenth century. Today there are websites, magazines, catalogs, books, and TV programs to give advice on practically all aspects of cultivating flowers, shrubs, trees, fruit, and vegetables. Because of the lack of information about gardening, eighteen of these 100 pioneering women saw this as an opportunity as a career and became authors, sharing and passing on their knowledge and experience to women who needed to know the essentials. These were among the bestselling books of their day, and, as well as specialist gardening writers, many other women wrote gardening books as a sideline to their successful careers in other directions, such as landscape architecture and as garden designers.

By no means did all the women featured in this book get their hands dirty in the garden. Their achievements may have been through botanical artistry, broadcasting, photography of gardens, writing articles or books about gardening, or designing gardens, parks, and public spaces. Some landscape gardeners and garden designers did combine their office work with practical digging, weeding, and landscaping, and others who did indeed dirty their hands might have felt as English garden designer Vita Sackville-West wrote: *I am not the armchair, library fireside gardener . . . for the last 40 years of my life I have broken my back, my finger nails and sometimes my heart, in the practical pursuit of my favourite* [*sic*] *occupation.*

In this volume, the choice of these pioneering American women was made on the basis that the individual left a legacy that has somehow benefited gardeners, the North American landscape, its heritage, or horticulture in general. Those that were omitted were cut for a variety of reasons; for instance, that their work benefited agriculture but not horticulture. These talented women included Marjorie Hoy, an entomologist and geneticist best known for her work on pest management and biological control in agriculture, and Mary-Dell Chilton, called the *Queen of Agrobacterium*, who produced the first transgenic plants. Virginia Walbot's discoveries in developmental biology helped change how corn is grown, and greatly assist boosting yields by the eradication of the disease called corn smut. These women's work is of great benefit to farmers and agriculture in general, but not specifically to gardening, so these otherwise deserving women were omitted.

Author's note: I have disciplined myself to focus on the core elements and not to veer too far from the theme of this book. The women selected were a personal choice, and I have no doubt whatsoever that there are some women deserving of inclusion whom I have (unintentionally) omitted. The author invites readers, should they have any suggestions of women who deserve to be included, to write to the publisher for consideration in future editions of this book.

Much of what is written in the biographies is from existing research, but it is the first time that the contributions by these selected women to North America's gardening heritage have been collated in one book. For the first time, the stories of 100 of the most significant and deserving women pioneering gardeners are collected together, and their contributions to the evolving nations of the USA and Canada are detailed in the biographies. These tell how each woman has contributed to America's great gardening heritage and legacy. Many of the women featured are little known and hardly recognized, which makes this book an overdue opportunity to acknowledge their work and celebrate their achievements.

CHAPTER 4

The Heroines *of* Horticulture:

Biographies of the 100 Brave, Determined, Creative Women Who Have Shaped North America's Heritage and Its Gardening Landscape

4.1 MARTHA DANIELL LOGAN (1704–1779)

Horticulturist and the first person to publish a gardening calendar in colonial America.

Martha was born in 1704 in St. Thomas Parish, South Carolina, the second child of Robert Daniell and his second wife, Martha Wainwright. Her father came to South Carolina from Barbados in 1679. When he arrived he was already wealthy, and he increased his holdings in real estate, slaves (as was usual for landholders of the time), and ships over the years. He owned 48,000 acres. In 1704 and 1705 he had a stormy term as lieutenant governor of North Carolina; he served twice in the same capacity in South Carolina from 1715 through to 1717. Martha's upbringing was influenced by her father's nursery business, and she learned how to cultivate plants.

In May 1718, when she was thirteen, her father died, leading Martha to marry George Logan Jr. in 1719. They spent their early married years on a plantation 10 miles up the Wando River from Charleston, on land Martha had inherited from her father. There, between 1720 and 1736, Martha gave birth to eight children.

Colonists at this time relied on a productive kitchen garden to provide food for the family table. Their gardens were usually the domain of the woman of the house. Initially Martha lived a somewhat privileged life and would have had servants to perform the household and gardening tasks, which would, unlike most women of the early colonial days, have given her leisure time to devote to her interests. In her case this included gardening and the cultivation of plants.

Illustration from *It's About Time: Early America—Planning an 18th Century Garden with Martha Daniell Logan*. The picture is by Richard Houston (c. 1721–1775). Some sources maintain that this is a depiction of Martha Logan, but it is more likely a nonspecific portrayal of an eighteenth-century woman gardening.

It appears the family finances became stretched, leading Martha to supplement their income; she taught and boarded students at her Wando River house. She paid for advertisements describing her services in the *South Carolina Gazette*.

By 1749, an advertisement was published featuring the Logan house and properties for sale. In the early 1750s the Logan family sold and moved to Charleston.

According to the *South Carolina Gazette* of December 6, 1751, Martha maintained a well-known garden and plant nursery on the Green, near Trott's Point in Charleston. Her garden was a business and a source of income, and gardening dominated Martha's life from there on.

The *South Carolina Gazette* of November 5, 1753, stated that Daniell Logan, her son, sold imported seeds, flower roots, and cuttings at his *mother's house on the Green near Trott's Point*. Martha also advertised her plants and related products in the same newspaper.

A 1753 advertisement told customers that she had *a parcel of very good seed, flower roots, and fruit stones*. She offered plant products *just imported from London* and *flouring* [*sic*] *shrubs and box edging beds*.

Her acquaintance with a fellow gardener, Elizabeth Lamboll (see 4.4), increased Martha's skills in cultivating plants. Other Charleston gardeners willingly gave or swapped seeds and roots with her, although it is recorded that she was disappointed when Dr. Alexander Garden, a respected and gifted gardener, ignored her requests for specimens of unusual plants from his garden.

John Bartram (1699–1777) was sometimes called the Father of American Botany. He was an early and respected American botanist, horticulturist, and explorer, particularly instrumental in sending seeds from the New World to European gardeners. Many North American trees and flowers were first introduced into cultivation in Europe by him. His botanical career started with a small area of his farm devoted to growing plants he found interesting, and he developed his hobby into a thriving business. John's 8-acre botanic garden, Bartram's Garden, in Kingsessing, was situated on the west bank of the Schuylkill about 3 miles from the center of Philadelphia. Today it is part of a 45-acre national historic landmark operated by the John Bartram Association in cooperation with Philadelphia Parks and Recreation.

John Bartram met Martha Logan in 1760, and, for at least five years, they carried on an eager exchange of letters, seeds, and plants. They used a silk bag to send seeds and lists of available plants, along with lists of plants that each wanted from the other's geographical area. Martha shipped and received tubs of cuttings and roots on ships traveling between Charleston and Philadelphia. *Her garden is her delight*, wrote Bartram to his London correspondent Peter Collinson.

In the 1750s, gardening had become a favored pastime among wealthy Charlestonians, and they especially sought landscaping with rare plants. Martha saw an opportunity when she realized that professional gardeners and written advice were scarcely available to amateur gardeners, so she started to supplement her nursery business income with horticultural writing.

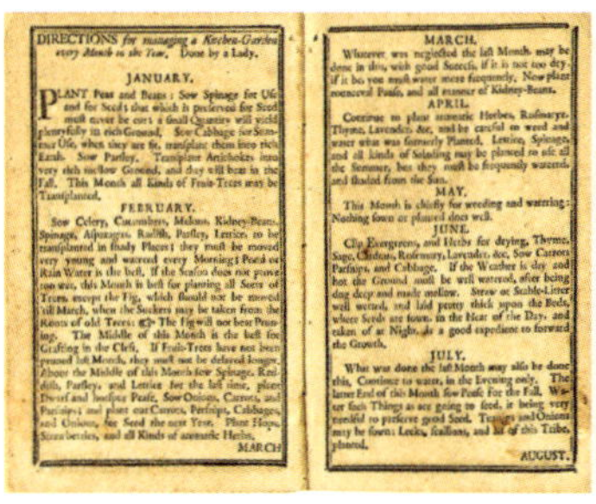
DIRECTIONS *for managing a Kitchen-Garden every Month in the Year.* Done by a Lady.

JANUARY.

FEBRUARY.

MARCH.

APRIL.

MAY.

This Month is chiefly for weeding and watering: Nothing sown or planted does well.

JUNE.

JULY.

AUGUST.

There is no known, proven portrait of Martha Daniell Logan, but a copy of her 1757 *Almanack Gardener's Calendar* survives. Two pages are pictured here. *South Carolina Historical Society, Charleston*

Martha published the *Gardener's Kalendar*, which became a standard text for colonial South Carolina gardeners, and wrote a gardening guide for John Tobler's 1752 *South Carolina Almanack*. She slightly changed and enlarged the calendar over subsequent decades. She also wrote a series of gardening advice articles, including *Directions for Managing a Kitchen Garden Every Month of the Year. Done by a Lady*. Her byline did not appear until after her death, although the calendar was published intermittently for more than fifty years in various almanacs. As an example of her advice she counseled:

> *In November, trim your monthly roses; and, at the full moon, open their roots and dung them. For April: Now you may plant out orange trees, etc. but let it be done at the change of the moon, watering them well, until they have taken root. She dismisses the month of May, saying: This month is chiefly for weeding and watering. Nothing sown or planted does well.*

One bit of her advice that is still appreciated is *What was neglected last month may be successfully done in this.*

Martha's husband died in 1764 and she lived for another fifteen years, continuing her nursery business and writing. Martha Daniell Logan died in

Charleston in 1779 and was buried in the family vault, sadly since destroyed, in St. Phillip's churchyard, Charleston. She is one of the earliest recorded North American women gardeners who supplemented the income from her plant nursery with writing gardening guides. She left us a valuable insight into gardening practices in the eighteenth century and a glimpse into the challenges faced by women of that era.

4.2 ELIZA LUCAS PINCKNEY (1722–1793)

Managing three plantations, Eliza had a major influence on the colonial economy. She changed agriculture in the area that would become the state of South Carolina, developing indigo as one of the most important cash crops.

Eliza (Elizabeth) Lucas was born December 19, 1722, on the island of Antigua, in the colony of the British Leeward Islands in the Caribbean. She grew up on Poorest, one of her family's three sugarcane plantations on the island. She was the eldest child of Lt. Colonel George Lucas, of Dalzell's Regiment of Foot in the British army, and his wife, Ann Lucas. Eliza was said to have treasured her education at boarding school, where studies included French and music. However, her favorite subject was botany.

In 1738 Col. Lucas moved his family from Antigua to South Carolina. Eliza's grandfather John Lucas had acquired three tracts of land there: Garden Hill on the Combahee River (1,500 acres), another 3,000 acres on the Waccamaw River, and Wappoo Plantation (600 acres) on Wappoo Creek, a tidal creek that connected the

Eliza Pinckney by Edward Greene Malbone (1777–1807). Watercolor on ivory.
Gibbes Museum of Art, Charleston, South Carolina

Ashley and Stono Rivers. They chose to reside at Wappoo, which was 17 miles by land to Charleston (then known as Charles Town) and 6 miles by river.

In 1739 Col. Lucas had to return to Antigua to deal with the political conflict between England and Spain. He was appointed lieutenant governor of the island. England's involvement in the War of the Austrian Succession thwarted his attempts to move back to South Carolina with his family. Eliza's letters to him show that she regarded her father with great respect and deep affection, and she wrote that she acted as head of the family by managing the plantations. Her mother had died shortly after they moved to Antigua.

Eliza was only sixteen years old when she became responsible for managing Wappoo Plantation and its twenty slaves, in addition to supervising overseers at two other Lucas plantations: one inland that produced tar and timber and a 3,000-acre rice plantation on the Waccamaw River.

On May 27, 1744, Eliza Lucas married attorney Charles Pinckney, a childless widower more than twenty years her senior. He built a house on Charleston's waterfront for his bride.

From Antigua, her father, Col. Lucas, sent Eliza various types of seeds for trial on the plantations. Like other plantation owners, the family was eager to find crops for the uplands that could supplement their cultivation of rice. First Eliza tried ginger, cotton, and alfalfa.

Starting in 1739, she began experimenting with cultivating and improving strains of the indigo plant, the dye of which in the expanding textile market had created demand. When Col. Lucas sent Eliza *Indigofera* seeds in 1740, she expressed her *greater hopes* for them. After three years of persistence and many failed attempts, Eliza proved that indigo could be successfully grown and processed in South Carolina.

"On Manufacturing Indigo into a Dye" in *Gentleman's Magazine* (June 1755): 256–59. Attributed to "C.W." (Charles Woodmason). *Charleston County Public Library*

The 1744 indigo crop was a success. Six pounds from Wappoo were sent to England and *found better than the French indigo*. Seed from this crop was distributed to many Carolina planters, who were soon profiting from Carolina's new staple export product.

Eliza had proven that colonial planters could make a profit in an extremely competitive market. Due to her successes, the volume of indigo dye exported to Europe increased dramatically from 5,000 pounds in 1745 to 130,000 pounds by 1748.

It was Eliza's perseverance that brought success to experiments in growing this crop, which had been tried and then discarded near Charleston seventy years earlier.

Indigo became second only to rice as the South Carolina colony's commodity cash crop and contributed greatly to the wealth of its plantation owners. It accounted for more than one-third of the total value of exports from the colony. Indigo sales sustained the Carolina economy for three decades, until the War of Independence in 1776 cut off trade with England.

Eliza carefully copied all the letters she wrote to her family, friends, and acquaintances into a *letter book*. This is one of the most complete collections of writing from eighteenth-century America and provides a valuable glimpse into the life of an elite colonial woman living during this period. Eliza's writings detail goings-on at the plantations, her pastimes, social visits, and even her experiments with indigo over several years. It describes everyday life over an extended period of time, rather than a singular event in history. The letter book was passed down from mother to daughter well into the twentieth century, at which point the Lucas-Pinckney family donated the letter book to the South Carolina Historical Society.

In 1758 Charles Pinckney contracted malaria and died. Widowed, Eliza continued to manage their extensive plantations. She wrote to her friend Mrs. Boddicott in England in May 1740:

> I have the business of three plantations to transact which requires much writing and more business and fatigue of other sorts than you can imagine. But lest you should imagine it too burthensome to a girl at my early time of life, give me leave to assure you I think myself happy.

After her husband's death Eliza spent thirty years overseeing the management of seven plantations. She invested monies she earned from exporting indigo into her children's education.

Eliza Lucas Pinckney died of breast cancer on May 26, 1793, in Philadelphia, where she had gone for treatment. At her funeral, President George Washington, then presiding over the United States government in Philadelphia, served as one of her pallbearers.

In the twentieth century, Eliza Lucas Pinckney was the first woman to be inducted into South Carolina's Business Hall of Fame. She is a fine example of a determined early colonial woman succeeding in business and overcoming challenges and prejudices that many would see as insurmountable.

4.3 JANE COLDEN (1724–1766)

Early adopter of the Linnaean system of plant identification and the first botanist of her sex in her country, according to nineteenth-century botanist Asa Gray

Born in New York City in 1724, Jane grew up in the Hudson Valley on the estate of her father, Cadwallader Colden, who held the important post of lieutenant governor of New York. The land was part of Ulster County at the time, situated 9 miles west of what was then the small riverside settlement of Newburgh. Today it lies within the hamlet of Coldenham, in the Orange County town of Montgomery, 60 miles northwest of New York City.

Jane was taught by her father, who was a physician and a scientist. He noted her interest in botany and focused her education on the study of plants using the system of scientific classification and nomenclature that had been recently devised by Swedish botanist Carolus Linnaeus (1707–1778). Linnaeus's classification remains the basis for naming and describing plant species to this day.

Of his daughter, Cadwallader wrote in a 1755 letter to Dr. John Frederic Gronovius, a patron of Linnaeus, that she possessed *a natural inclination to reading and a natural curiosity for natural philosophy and natural history*. He wrote that Jane

Jane Colden

was already writing descriptions of plants, using Linnaeus's classification, and taking impressions of leaves by using a press.

Cadwallader also wrote that he thought the study of botany was particularly well suited to women:

> *Their natural curiosity and the pleasure they take in the beauty and variety of dress seems to fit them for it. The chief reason that few or none of them have hitherto applied themselves to this study, I believe, is because all the books of any value are wrote [sic] in Latin and so filled with technical words that obtaining the necessary knowledge is so tiresome and disagreeable that they are discouraged at the first set out and give it over before they can receive any pleasure in the pursuit. He added: I have a daughter who has an inclination to reading and a curiosity for natural philosophy or natural history, and a sufficient capacity for attaining a competent knowledge.*

Noting that she applied the Linnaean system of plant identification to the American flora she collected and studied, botanist John Ellis wrote to Carl Linnaeus of her work. He wrote: "She deserves to be celebrated."

She was eventually regarded as a respected botanist by many prominent botanists of her era, including John Bartram, Peter Collinson, Alexander Garden, and Carolus Linnaeus himself.

Jane married Scottish widower Dr. William Farquhar on March 12, 1759, but before that, between 1753 and 1758, Jane quietly cataloged New York's flora. Americans did not become aware of Jane's manuscript until many years after her death. She had compiled specimens and information on more than 300 species of plants from the lower Hudson River valley and classified them according to the Linnaean system. She developed a technique for making ink impressions of leaves and was also a skilled illustrator, doing ink drawings of 340 different leaves. To many drawings she added pieces of folklore and suggested medicinal uses for the plant. Some of the descriptions include the month of flowering and the habitat a plant could be found in.

Jane's life as a botanical forerunner did not come to light until 1895, when James Britten published her biography *Jane Colden and the Flora of New York* in the *Journal of Botany, British and Foreign*.

British scientist Peter Collinson was an avid gardener and the middleman for an international exchange of scientific ideas in mid-eighteenth-century London. He is best known for his correspondence with Benjamin Franklin about electricity. On January

20, 1756, he wrote to American botanist John Bartram: *Our friend Colden's daughter has, in a scientific manner, sent over several sheets of plants, very curiously anatomized after this* [Linnaeus's] *method. I believe she is the first lady that has attempted anything of this nature.* In this instance Jane was recognized as what she is known as today by the *Dictionary of American Biography: the first female botanist in America*. Collinson corresponded with Jane and wrote to Linnaeus in 1758: *As this accomplished lady is the only one of the fair sex that I have heard of, who is scientifically skillful in the Linnaean system, you, no doubt, will distinguish her merits, and recommend her example to the ladies of every country.*

Jane participated in the local Natural History Circle, where she exchanged seeds and plants with other plant collectors in the American colonies and in Europe. Contemporary botanists in England and the colonies discussed her in their correspondence, describing her with such accolades as *assiduous*, *accomplished*, *scientifically skilful*, and *ingenious*. In view of the limited educational opportunities available to women in the eighteenth century, Jane Colden's acceptance by eminent naturalists and botanists is remarkable.

Jane Colden died giving birth to her first child in 1766 at age forty-one. A plant sanctuary in her honor was established in the late 1990s at Knox's Headquarters State Historic Site in New Windsor, near where she lived and worked.

Asa Gray, considered the most important American botanist of the nineteenth century, described her in 1843 as the *first botanist of her sex in her country*.

4.4 ELIZABETH LAMBOLL (1725–1760)

One of the first colonial horticulturalists, Elizabeth contributed greatly to the establishment and advancement of scientific gardening in South Carolina.

Elizabeth Lamboll house at 19 King Street, Charleston. *Lamboll House Bed and Breakfast*

Elizabeth was probably born in 1725, most likely in Charleston, South Carolina, although an accurate record of her birth does not exist. In addition, there does not appear to be any portrait of her. Historians surmise that she was the daughter of a Charleston silversmith, Richard Pitts. She married Thomas Lamboll in November 1743. He was thirty years her senior, and she was his third wife. The couple had one daughter.

Elizabeth lived in a house on the northwest corner of King and Lamboll Streets, near the Ashley River in Charleston. Her garden was landscaped directly south of the residence. As an enthusiastic and skilled amateur gardener, she created one of Charleston's earliest gardens, planted primarily with indigenous flowers, vegetables, shrubs, and trees.

She actively shared her horticultural knowledge and techniques and swapped seeds and roots with local gardening enthusiasts, one of which was Martha Daniell Logan (see 4.1). Elizabeth's friendship with Philadelphia naturalist John Bartram (1699–1777) helped him become the premier botanist, horticulturist, and explorer in the American colonies. Swedish botanist Carl Linnaeus said he was the *greatest natural botanist in the world*. Elizabeth introduced Bartram to previously unknown plant species, which he described and documented for botanical publications.

While Elizabeth enthusiastically engaged in her gardening, her husband, Thomas, wrote to Bartram, telling him about the plants she was collecting and intending to ship to him, and also describing her cultivation methods. In a letter dated February 16, 1761, he revealed how his wife carefully managed and controlled her gardens. He detailed the steps that she diligently followed to prepare plant beds with mold and how she raised or flattened the ground, as needed, to ensure adequate moisture for healthy growth. It is recorded that Elizabeth carefully saved rainwater for her plants and covered her garden beds with leaves in winter. During planting she cleaned the roots, removed any insects, and used her fingers to dig holes in the soil to plant roots and seeds.

In 1760 Bartram wrote that Elizabeth had sent him *two noble cargoes* that initiated a regular exchange of plants such as the *Magnolia tripetala*, or umbrella tree, indigenous to South Carolina. On April 30, 1761, Thomas Lamboll sent Bartram a list of *Flowers & Herbs* that his wife was *fond of procuring*, including tulips, aniseed, and peonies. In 1762 he provided another detailed list of the contents of his wife's shipments to Bartram. Included in this were oaks, roses, lilies, honeysuckle, asters, and holly.

Accompanied by his son William, John Bartram visited the Lambolls' garden in August 1765 when en route to Florida. William Bartram settled in Florida to grow indigo, and Elizabeth gathered and sent him horticultural plants and supplies there. She extended her courteous treatment to Bartram's wife, as indicated by Thomas Lamboll in a letter about harvesting pomegranates in which he wrote: *Mrs Lamboll chose to send Mrs Bartram a Bisket Cagg full (say 51) of the best she could Pick.*

Elizabeth Lamboll died in Charleston in October 1770. Her daughter, Mary Lamboll Thomas, continued to ship plants to William Bartram, just as her mother had sent specimens to his father.

4.5 MARGARET TILGHMAN CARROLL (1742–1817)

This pioneer of the greenhouse helped design George Washington's notable gardens at Mount Vernon.

Margaret Tilghman, the daughter of Matthew Tilghman and Anne Lloyd, was born in Talbot County, Maryland, in 1742. At age twenty-one she married Charles Carroll, a barrister and a distant cousin of Charles Carroll, a signer of the Declaration of Independence. In 1756 Charles began building Mount Clare in Baltimore, a Georgian-style mansion on property inherited from his father. He named it Mount Clare in honor of his grandmother Mary Clare Dunn. The house was built with soft pink brick, most of which would have been made on the plantation. A series of grass ramps led from a bowling green down to terraces, offering a sweeping view across the lower fields to the waters of the Patapsco River about a mile away.

Margaret Tilghman Carroll by Charles Willson Peale, 1770.
Mount Clare Museum House

While her husband was busy with affairs of state, serving in the legislature and on the Committee of Correspondence and the Council of Safety, Margaret, a skilled and keen gardener, delighted in planning and designing the grounds of Mount Clare.

She is perhaps best remembered for her orangery or greenhouse, where orange, lemon, and peach trees bloomed. She is also known for helping George Washington design his own greenhouse for his garden in Mount Vernon, 13 miles south of Washington, DC, and situated on the banks of the Potomac River in Fairfax County, Virginia.

Eighteenth-century colonial greenhouses were glass-windowed structures of wood, or brick, or stone in which tender plants were protected, cultivated, and preserved. Later, iron and glass greenhouses would appear in the first half of the nineteenth century, allowing more light into the structures. The price of glass in colonial and early America remained high until nearly the middle of the nineteenth century, so early greenhouses were essentially a luxury for the wealthy, who could grow exotic fruits and plants in a heated, protected environment.

In addition to her greenhouse, Margaret also had built a 39-by-24-foot brick structure at Mount Clare that she called a "Stove House." This featured an intricate air heating system for growing plants indoors, such as pineapples, all year round.

Because of her expertise and skill as a horticulturist, George Washington asked Margaret for advice on how to build and heat a greenhouse and what plants to grow at his house, Mount Vernon.

George Washington wrote a letter to Margaret's cousin, Col. Tench Tilghman, in August 1784:

> I shall essay the finishing of my greenhouse this fall, but find that neither myself, nor any person about me is so well skilled in the internal constructions as to proceed without a probability at least of running into errors. Shall I for this reason, ask the favor of you to give me a short description of the greenhouse at Mrs Carroll's? I am persuaded, now that I planned mine on too contracted a scale. My house is (of Brick) 40 ft by 24, in the outer dimensions.

On September 16, 1789, Washington wrote to Margaret:

> Madam. A Person having been lately sent to me from Europe in the capacity of a Gardner, who professes a knowledge in the culture of rare plants and care of a greenhouse, I am desirous to profit of the

> very obliging offer you were pleased some time ago to make me. In availing myself of your goodness I am far from desiring that it should induce any inconvenience to yourself but, reconciling your disposition to oblige, with your convenience, I shall be happy to receive such aids as you can well spare, and as will not impair your collection.

Margaret was certainly happy to oblige. For example, it is recorded that on October 29, 1789, she sent twenty pots of lemon and orange trees, plus five boxes of assorted other greenhouse plants, by boat to George Washington at the harbor in Alexandria. Margaret also supplied Washington, at his specific request, with saplings from her own greenhouse.

Margaret survived her husband by more than thirty years and never remarried. She devoted herself to her garden and to remodeling Mount Clare. Margaret Tilghman Carroll died in 1817 and is buried with her husband at St. Anne's Churchyard in Annapolis, Maryland.

4.6 LADY JEAN SKIPWITH (1748–1826)

This Virginia plantation owner and manager is known for her considerable gardens, her botanical manuscript notes, and having an extensive library. Her garden was built by enslaved laborers.

Jean Miller was born in 1748. Her father was Hugh Miller, a Scottish tobacco merchant who had emigrated and lived in Elm Hill plantation, near Baskerville, Mecklenburg County, Virginia, from 1746 to 1760. On his wife's death in 1760, he returned to

Glasgow, Scotland, with his five children and died there in 1762. Jean lived in Scotland until around 1786, then moved briefly to Liverpool, England, before returning to the Elm Hill plantation, which she had inherited from her father.

Sir Peyton Skipwith lived close to Elm Hill. He was one of the wealthiest men in Virginia, who resided in the Georgian-style mansion that he had built, Prestwould Plantation, sited high above where the Dan and Stanton Rivers merge. It was a working tobacco plantation with farm and livestock, and thoroughbred horses were raised there. It had a mill, blacksmith shop, store, and a ferry. He had previously been married to Jean's sister Anne, who died in childbirth in 1779. He met Jean and wrote to her on September 7, 1788, stating his wish *to complete a union on which my future happiness so much and so immediately depends*. They were married on September 25, 1788, in Granville, North Carolina.

Lady Jean gave birth to four children in five years (all after the age of forty). By 1797 she had moved her family from Elm Hill to Prestwould. Lady Jean kept detailed notes, including records of household purchases and copious garden jottings.

It was at Prestwould that Lady Jean created the garden based on the traditional, classic English design. It was enslaved laborers, overseen by Samuel Dedman, who built her garden, but Dedman worked closely with Lady Jean to carry out her design. Sketches in Lady Jean's hand detail several different garden plots. Her sketches show highly organized plots crisscrossed by "boardwalks," some wide enough for wheelbarrows, pony carts, or couples taking exercise to pass across. The plans also indicate where Lady Jean planned to plant verbena, strawberry, crocus, phlox, violets, pansies, and portulaca, as well as annuals and shrubbery.

She located the garden to the east of the entrance to the house. Its prominent position emphasized to visitors that the gardens were important at Prestwould. She designed terraced garden beds that fell toward the family cemetery. The gardens included an orangery, a bee house, and special beds where she could observe and make meticulous notes about the growth habits of particular plants.

Lady Jean often corresponded with neighbors, requesting cuttings of plants she could add to her own collections or offering gardening advice of her own. She ordered plants from Prince Nurseries on Long Island (as did George Washington and Thomas Jefferson). She collected specimens locally and traded seeds with other gardeners in the United States and overseas.

Lady Jean was also an avid keeper of lists. One read *Shrubs to be got when I can*. The archives include records of Lady Jean's orders for vegetables, roots, and bulbs, which she grew in raised beds. Among the houseplants that she itemized were oleander, dwarf myrtle, rose geranium, and chrysanthemum, observing that those would *live in the garden through the winter, though the first frost would destroy the flower*. Her *wintering plants* included *oranges, lemons, and limes* and were grown in a glass-walled orangery.

Her detailed botanical notes describe where each kind of plant was grown at Prestwould, what the ideal conditions for its growth were, and how it should be cared for. She listed the many wildflowers she collected, including trillium and viola. She also kept records of her fruit crops, notes on how to raise trees from cuttings, and lists of what she had planted. Today her notes continue to be a valuable resource for historians and botanists in documenting early North American gardens.

Lady Jean procured and planted varieties of roses, lilacs, jasmine, honeysuckle, and mock orange. She had a wildflower garden with bloodroot, monkshood, wolfsbane, ladies' slipper, asters, violets, columbine, liverwort, and a plant called Carolina-kidney-bean-tree. Her gardening notes were extensive and demonstrated a woman well educated in gardening and botany. She sometimes included the Latin name for a plant. She grafted fruit trees and listed the dates when the fruit trees would be ripe. These trees included several kinds of cherry, peach, pear, plumb, nectarine, and apple. There were also strawberry and raspberry bushes. The bananas may have been grown in a small conservatory, the foundation of which is to one end of the garden.

By her death Lady Jean had acquired a library of more than 850 books, perhaps the largest library assembled by an American woman of that time. Her collection, the product of an independent and curious mind, reflected her interests in botany, gardening, travel, geography, and history.

Lady Jean Skipwith died on May 19, 1826. She is buried in the Skipwith Family Cemetery at Prestwould, Mecklenburg County, Virginia. Prestwould Plantation, its outbuildings, and its grounds are now a national historic landmark and are open to the public.

4.7 FRANCES "FANNY" PENNIMAN (1760–1834)

Frances Montresor Buchanan Allen Penniman is known for her link to the American Revolution, as well as being a botanist and skilled gardener.

Frances, called Fanny by her family and friends, was born in 1760, the illegitimate daughter of British military engineer John Montresor and Anna Schoolcraft of Schoharie, New York. Her mother died in childbirth, and Fanny was raised by her aunt Margaret.

In 1766 Margaret married Crean Brush (1725–1778), Irish born and known for his participation in loyalist armies during the American War of Independence. He moved the family to Westminster, Vermont, in 1776. The same year, sixteen-year-old Fanny married John Buchanan, a retired British military officer. He was killed while fighting as a member of the King's Loyal Rangers, and Fanny's child with him died young. Fanny was twenty-four and a widow when she met Ethan Allen, an American Revolutionary War leader who fought for Vermont's independence.

They married in 1784, settled on a farm in Burlington, and had three children together. Fanny was noted to be attractive and well educated. She had a love of science—botany in particular—and was a gifted musician. In spring 1787 the Allens moved to Burlington, Vermont, having purchased a farm in the Winooski River Intervale north of the city. Today it has been converted into Ethan Allen Park.

Ethan Allen made a very significant contribution to the early history of Vermont (at that time called the New Hampshire Grants). The territory constituted the northern frontier of the New England colonies. He is best known for the capture of Fort Ticonderoga at the outbreak of the War of Independence and his leadership of the Green Mountain Boys.

In 1789 Gen. Allen died suddenly, stricken with apoplexy while bringing a load of hay across the lake from South Hero. Fanny was widowed again at age twenty-nine. Financially ill prepared to look after herself and her three children (and two of Gen. Allen's daughters still living at home), she left Burlington to live in Westminster, Windham County, Vermont, with her aunt Margaret, where she remained until 1792.

In 1793 she married Dr. Jabez Penniman, and they moved back to the Allen farm, living there from 1794 to 1800. Debts later forced them to give up the farm and return to Westminster. In 1803 her husband became US customs collector for Vermont, and the family relocated to Swanton. During the War of 1812 they took up residence in Burlington and Colchester, and he served as Colchester town clerk and Chittenden County probate judge.

Fanny's descendants owned some interesting Allen family relics, including two beautiful portraits by John Singleton Copley (1738–1815), a well-established portrait painter in colonial New England. They were of Fanny and of Mrs. Crean Brush. Fanny was painted in 1771, when she was eleven years old.

The Pennimans lived in a house formerly standing opposite St. Michael's College, at the top of the hill, just above the High Bridge. Here Fanny gave birth to four children. It was here that Fanny's keen interest in nature blossomed and resulted in a large collection of local flowers. She established two herbaria in 1814. The location was familiar to Burlington people, as they passed the house on the way out of town to what was to become known as Fort Ethan Allen.

Fanny was admired for her skill in gardening, and her garden was stocked with a rare variety of plants and shrubs, mostly transplanted from local flora. Botany was said to be Fanny's *favorite amusement*. The region around High Bridge was noticed by a Massachusetts botanist, who explored the west side of Vermont in 1829. He described the area as *a remarkable region, rich in rare and interesting plants*. A part of this land was the Penniman farm, and here, starting in 1814, Fanny, helped by her daughter Adelia (1801–1884), found and preserved their specimens. They foraged on the banks of the river in both directions and searched the woods, then the site of the fort, for wildflowers. They pressed flowers to preserve them for display in the herbaria, but they also dug up and carried home plants from their native sites and cultivated and improved them by planting them in the home garden. They achieved this before any manual of botany or horticultural textbooks had been published, so identification and the accurate recording of specimens were largely self-taught.

It is likely that specimens in these small herbaria are the oldest in the state, because the oldest in the herbaria of the University of Vermont are dated 1819. There were eighty or ninety specimens in each herbarium, although quite a number of cultivated plants are included. Many of the botanical names have long since been changed, and one at least, the ground or moss pink, had not been listed in *Vermont Flora*. The 200 sheets of wild and cultivated plants from around the Penniman home in Colchester are labeled with Latin and common names, as well as the coded meanings of flowers popular at that time. The first *Flora of North America* was published in London, England, in 1814, and the expensive book was unlikely to have reached the colonial frontier quickly. It remains something of a mystery how Fanny and Adelia accurately identified the wild plants they collected.

A historian named Hall, quoting from one who knew her well, said this of Fanny: *She was a fascinating woman, endowed with an ease of manner which she had acquired from intercourse with the polite society of the day, in which she had been brought up; possessed of a refined taste and many accomplishments.*

Frances *"Fanny"* Allen Penniman died in 1834 and was buried in Elmwood Cemetery, Burlington, Vermont. She was an important, early pioneer of plant collecting, and her determination, passion, and dedication to botany was a fine example to others who followed her plant hunting, preserving, and recording local wild flora.

4.8 ALMIRA HART LINCOLN PHELPS (1793–1884)

Teacher, writer, and publisher Almira was a pioneer of women's education. As well as a lover of botany, she strove to raise the academic standards of education for girls.

Almira was born on July 15, 1793, in Berlin, Connecticut. The youngest of seventeen children, Almira was raised in a household that encouraged reading and discussion. She studied at various New England boarding schools, including Middlebury Academy and Pittsfield Female Academy. At age sixteen she went to live in Vermont with her sister, Emma. John Willard, a student at Middlebury College, boarded at their home and tutored Phelps on his lessons from the all-male college. This experience showed Almira the disparity between educational opportunities available for males and females, and she spent the rest of her life fighting to close the educational gap between genders.

In 1817 she married Simeon Lincoln, editor of the *Connecticut Mirror of Hartford*. After his death in 1823 she became a teacher in New York in her sister's Troy Female Seminary, where she remained for eight years. While teaching at Female Seminary her interests in science increased, and her botanical career began under the influence of Amos Eaton, a professor of botany. While under the direction of Eaton she found her passion in botany and the lack of introductory textbooks for secondary and beginning college-level students. In 1829 this led Almira to write and publish her first and most famous textbook, *Familiar Lectures on Botany. . . a Flora for Practical Botanists* (1839).

It enjoyed wide use and went through nine editions in ten years. She married a prosperous lawyer, John Phelps, in 1831. Over the following several years she published *Lectures to Young Ladies* (1833), *Botany for Beginners* (1833), *Geology for Beginners* (1834), *Chemistry for Beginners* (1834), *Natural Philosophy for Beginners* (1836), *Lectures on Natural Philosophy* (1836), and *Lectures on Chemistry* (1837).

Almira also wrote a novel, *Caroline Westerly* (1833). In 1838 she became principal of the Young Ladies' Seminary in West Chester, Pennsylvania. When the school closed the following year, she became head of the Female Institute of Rahway, New Jersey. With each new publication and her continuing teaching lectures, Almira's fame grew, and she was asked to head many female seminaries.

Between 1828 and 1837 she had established herself as a reputable author, publishing ten textbooks, most focusing on botany and the education of young women. Her books, such as *Familiar Lectures on Botany*, received praise as excellent educational tools for women. They became the standard textbooks across the United States and Canada, selling more than 3,500 copies. Almira was now a household name.

In 1841 Almira became principal and her husband the business manager of the Patapsco Female Institute in Ellicott's Mills, Maryland. Later, in 1849, her husband died. In her fifteen years at that school, Almira created an institution of high academic standards, with a curriculum rich in the sciences, mathematics, and natural history. The school was designed in particular to train highly qualified teachers. She raised the curriculum to make it a nationally renowned school for girls, increasing enrollment to 150. She loaned selected deserving students some money from her own pocket to attend the school.

In 1856, at age sixty-two, Almira retired from the institute after transforming the school into a successful enterprise and her entire life improving educational opportunities for young women. She settled in Baltimore. In her remaining years she wrote frequently for national periodicals. Her other books include the novel *Ida Norman* (1848), *Christian Households* (1858), and *Hours with My Pupils* (1859).

In 1859 Almira was the third woman elected as a member of the American Association for the Advancement of Science. After gaining her membership she continued to write, lecture, and revise her textbooks.

Almira Hart Lincoln Phelps died on her ninety-first birthday on July 15, 1884. She is remembered for being only the third woman elected as a member of the American Association for the Advancement of Science.

4.9 CATHARINE PARR TRAILL (1802–1899)

English Canadian Catharine is known for her work on Canadian flora and writings on life in the colony of Upper Canada (now Ontario).

Catharine Parr Traill. Illustration from her book (February 1884).
Topley Studio, Library and Archives, Canada, PA-802715

Catharine Parr Strickland was born in 1802 in Rotherhithe, Southwark, England, the fifth daughter of Thomas Strickland and Elizabeth Homer. After her father died in 1818, Catharine and her other unmarried sisters turned to writing and editorial work as the main source of family income. Catharine began with children's stories, her first titled *The Tell Tale: An Original Collection of Moral and Amusing Stories*. This appeared anonymously in 1818, when she was just sixteen years old.

A prolific author until her marriage, Catharine averaged one book per year. In 1832 she was joined with L. Thomas Traill, a retired officer of the Napoleonic Wars, and they soon immigrated to Upper Canada, settling near Peterborough, on the Otonabee River in central Ontario, Canada, where her brother Samuel was a surveyor.

Catharine is considered important because she pioneered investigations into Canada's natural history. Also, in her writing she described her experiences of life in the colony, detailing local flora and the natural environment of the land. Chronicling her new life in letters and journals, she collected these into a volume called *The Backwoods of Canada*, which was published in 1836. Even today this book is regarded as an important source of information about early colonial Canada. In it can be found descriptions of everyday life in the community; the relationships among Canadians, Americans, and Indigenous peoples; and details on the local climate, flora, and fauna.

More of Catharine's observations about Canada were included in a novel called *Canadian Crusoes* (1851). She also collected information and advice about skills necessary for a new settler, which was published in 1854 as *The Female Emigrant's Guide* (later retitled *The Canadian Settler's Guide*).

After suffering through the depression of 1836, her husband, Thomas, joined the militia in 1837 to fight against the Upper Canada Rebellion. In 1840, dissatisfied with life in the backwoods, the Traills moved to the city of Belleville, at the mouth of the Moira River on the Bay of Quinte in Ontario. Catharine spent her years in Belleville writing about the natural environment. After twenty-seven years, in 1859 Lt. Thomas Traill died, leaving Catharine the sole provider for herself and her seven surviving children.

One of the most widely read Canadian authors in the 1860s, Catharine maintained a collection of dried plant specimens that she called her *Hortus siccus* (i.e., herbarium). She kept detailed notes about all the native flowers, shrubs, and trees that she saw and collected. She quickly set about organizing her botanical notes into book form, and she asked her niece, Agnes Dunbar Fitzgibbon (1833–1913), to supply illustrations for the book to increase the chance of finding a publisher. At the time Agnes was the busy wife of a Toronto barrister, but when he died in February 1865, thirty-two-year-old Agnes agreed to help her aunt. She, too, was now a widow and had six children to support. After receiving some praise and some encouragement from several professors at the University of Toronto, Catharine began to offer her manuscript to various publishers.

In November 1866, a Montreal firm agreed to publish her book on wildflowers, with the condition that Catharine and Agnes would personally supply the illustrations. There were to be ten illustrated, full-page (14 × 11 in.) plates in each book, but because the publisher could not print color images, each lithographed plate had to be hand-painted. This amounted to 5,000 hand-painted plates for a run of 500 books.

From July 1867 to December 1868, with the help of three of her daughters, Agnes painted the 5,000 lithographed plates while Catharine further edited the text and wrote the preface. The finished book, *Canadian Wild Flowers*, went on sale in January 1869 and was sold out within six weeks. It was especially praised for Agnes Fitzgibbon's beautiful and accurate illustrations, which evoke Ontario's wild woodland and meadow flora. In 1894 biologist James Fletcher praised Catharine's plant descriptions as *one of the greatest botanical triumphs*. She focused on celebrating endangered habitats.

In 1885, the full text of Catharine's original *Hortus siccus* was published in Ottawa as *Studies of Plant Life in Canada: Gleanings from Forest, Lake and Plain*. Once again her niece (by now Mrs. Agnes Chamberlin) hand-painted all the illustrations from her own lithographs.

Nearing the end of her life, Catharine published *Pearls and Pebbles* (1894), a collection of writings from her pioneering days, including the many changes she had witnessed over sixty years. She also tried her hand at a collection of children's tales called *Cot and Cradle Stories* (1895), published in Toronto by William Briggs.

Catharine Parr Traill died at her residence in Westove, in Lakefield, Ontario, on August 28, 1899. Her many albums of plant collections are currently housed in the National Herbarium of Canada at the Canadian Museum of Nature. Trent University, Peterborough, Ontario, paid tribute to Catharine by naming their downtown campus for her. Catharine Parr Traill College is the university's main college for graduate studies.

4.10 MARY RIGGS COLLINS (1808–1872)

An avid gardener, Mary planted flowers from around the world at her home, Somerset Place, in North Carolina, although the plantation relied heavily on its slave population to clear and cultivate the land.

Mary was the wife of Josiah Collins III. They were married on August 9, 1829, in Newark, New Jersey, and by 1830 they had moved to Somerset Place in Washington County, one of North Carolina's largest plantations. Sited on the shores of Lake Phelps, it originally consisted of more than 100,000 acres of land. However, this had been divided among the children of Josiah's father, Josiah Collins II, upon his death in 1839. By the 1860s the census of the day records that Somerset Place comprised 14,500 acres (of which about 2,000 acres were cultivated). Records also showed that 328 slaves worked on the property.

By the mid-1800s Somerset Place included more than fifty structures, including three large barns, stables, sawmills, gristmills, twenty-six slave houses, a kitchen complex, a laundry, a dairy, a storehouse, a smokehouse, a salting house, and homes for overseers. The primary crop grown was corn, but the plantation also produced wheat, peas, beans, potatoes, sweet potatoes, oats, flax, wool, butter, milk, and silk.

Somerset Place relied heavily on its slave population to clear and cultivate the land. About 60 percent of Somerset's field hands are recorded as being women. In the winter, women and the older children cleaned out ditches, weeded fields, cleared the roads, repaired old fences and built new ones, and chopped wood and burned wood to make charcoal. In the spring men, women, and children all helped in the preparation of the fields for planting crops.

Women slaves who were too old for work in the fields were given jobs such as weeding the gardens, milking the plantation's fifty-two cows, shepherding the 225 sheep, cleaning out the chicken yard and the pig pens, or caring for the children of younger mothers who worked in the fields.

One of Mary's greatest pleasures was the flower garden that she designed and developed near the main house, alongside the canal. She had built a greenhouse near the house's kitchen, where she could plant new varieties of the more delicate flowers for her garden. Once her neighbor, Caroline Pettigrew, asked Mary for some ivy. Caroline assumed she would send one of the three slaves who helped her in the garden, but Mary shocked her by personally bringing the cuttings and planting them herself.

The flower and vegetable gardens that bordered the main house impressed visitors, leaving little doubt that the gardens were the visible expressions of Mary's personal tastes, values, and attitudes. In April 1856 her neighbor remarked *Mrs. Collins's garden is bringing out all its treasures. . .*

This image of Mary, by an unknown photographer, was probably taken shortly after the sudden death of her husband. It was the custom for nineteenth-century widows to dress in black for at least a year after their husband's death, including black-trimmed head coverings. *Somerset Place State Historic Sites*

After the Civil War the family was left without unpaid slave labor, and the land could not be profitably cultivated. The Collins family unsuccessfully attempted to restore Somerset Place, but they were forced to sell the property to creditors in 1867 and relied on Josiah's training as a lawyer to support them. Eventually Somerset Place was acquired by the State of North Carolina. The mansion and outbuildings were restored and are now open as a state historic site that emphasizes the role of enslaved laborers on southern plantations.

Mary Riggs Collins died in 1872. She is buried in Saint Paul's Episcopal Churchyard, Edenton, Chowan County, North Carolina. Despite having no formal horticultural training, using her personal preferences and values she designed, landscaped, and created one of North Carolina's earliest distinctive gardens, featuring extensive flower garden areas and a greenhouse to protect her tender plants.

4.11 JANE LORING GRAY (1821–1909)

Wife and secretary to eminent botanist Asa Gray, Jane was a keen botanist in her own right.

Jane was born in 1821, the daughter of a Boston lawyer, Charles Greely Loring. In 1847 she agreed to marry Asa Gray, fisher professor of natural history at Harvard University and already one of America's most famous and accomplished botanists. They were married on May 4, 1848, and lived in a house in the Botanic Garden, Cambridge, Massachusetts. Jane accompanied her husband on most of his voyages and plant-hunting expeditions and chronicled them in her letters to her family. Evidence suggests that she took a very active interest in the scientific pursuits of her husband and his friends. As well as providing companionship on his travels, importantly it is recorded that Jane often acted as a secretary for her husband. Her keen interest in plants and involvement in her husband's work was a huge asset to botanical progress.

The 1840s was a time of military expeditions, railroad surveys, and governmental and other explorations of untamed wilderness. This resulted in a large number of botanical specimens from collectors that needed to be classified and named. Thousands of collected dried and pressed new plant samples needed identification and botanical naming. Gray is credited by the *International Plant Names Index* with 752 records. Herbarium sheets and reference books were Gray's tools of his trade, and he would have been greatly helped in classifications and recording data by Jane. In 1865, it was estimated that his herbarium collection contained 200,000 specimens, and, at the time of his death in 1888, it was estimated to be twice that size. Today Harvard University's Gray Herbarium includes more than five million specimens.

This photograph, dated 1877, is from the archives of the Gray Herbarium, Harvard University. It was taken by William Henry Jackson (1843–1942) at La Veta Pass, Colorado. It pictures the US geological survey of the territories under the direction of Ferdinand Vanderveer Hayden (1829–1887). *From left to right (mostly seated):* Sir Joseph Dalton Hooker (1817–1911), Asa Gray (1810–1888, *seated on the ground*), Mrs. Strachey, Jane Loring Gray (*in white hat*, 1821–1909), Captain Stevenson, Dr. Lanborn, General Strachey (*standing, in black hat*), and Ferdinand Vanderveer Hayden (1829–1887). *oeb.harvard.edu*

Just as Emma Darwin helped Charles Darwin with his correspondence, Jane often acted as a secretary for her husband and assisted him on his many travels. She also corresponded, in her own name, with eminent botanists like George Bentham and Francis Boott. After Asa Gray's death Jane published a selection of Bentham's letters.

Aided by Jane, Asa Gray identified many hundreds of new plant species over his career, and numerous others have been named in his honor, including the genus *Grayia* of the amaranth family. Asa Gray died on January 30, 1888, and was buried at Mount Auburn Cemetery in Cambridge, Massachusetts. The cemetery's Asa Gray Garden, with a central fountain and numerous unusual tree varieties, is named in his honor. After Asa Gray's death, Jane contributed funds toward the establishment of the Asa Gray Professorship. Her legacy was greater than the important work that she did to support Asa Gray during his life. She strove diligently to preserve his scientific contributions, and as a part of her efforts to memorialize him through preserving and chronicling his life's work, she organized his correspondence, manuscripts, and papers, and deposited them at Harvard as a tribute to his work and as an archive for study in the future.

Jane transcribed and edited a book of important Gray correspondence titled *Letters of Asa Gray*, published in 1893. She sent gift copies of this book to major university and garden libraries all over the world.

Jane Loring Gray died in 1909 and is also buried in Mount Auburn Cemetery in Cambridge, Massachusetts. She was married to one of North America's most prominent botanists, and her life was largely devoted to assisting her husband. *Gray's Manual* remains a standard work on botany, and, aided by Jane, he identified many hundreds of new plant species.

4.12 SUSAN HALLOWELL (1835–1911)

A trailblazer in the higher education of women, Susan was the first woman in North America to create, organize, and maintain a botany department. She resided over Wellesley College, Massachusetts, for some twenty-five years.

A lover of nature from childhood, Susan was born in Bangor, Maine, in 1835. She began her career as a teacher as soon as she graduated from local Colby College, and for more than twenty years she taught in Bangor High School, continuing, as best as she was able, her self-education.

Throughout her life, Susan was an avid seeker of knowledge and, wanting to improve her education, traveled to Europe. Although universities on the continent were closed to women, Susan was the first woman to be admitted to the botanical lectures and laboratories of the University of Berlin, Germany. She would not have been granted a degree, but she was able to persuade the authorities that she should be allowed to attend lectures.

Her insatiable appetite for knowledge led her to work in the Boston laboratories of Asa and Jane Gray (see 4.11) and Louis Agassizo. The founder of Wellesley College, Massachusetts, Henry Durant became familiar with Hallowell's work in the Gray and Agassizo laboratories. Impressed by her knowledge, dedication, and determination, he appointed her chair of natural history at the college in 1875. Susan immediately saw that this remit was too big for one department, so she proposed dividing it into two: zoology and botany. This was accepted, and she was given the choice of which to oversee. She chose botany and formed the original botany department, becoming the first chair and professor of botany at Wellesley College in 1877.

Susan Hallowell. Photographer: Partridge. *Photo supplied by and reproduced by permission of Wellesley College Archive Department*

In her time there, Susan contributed impressively to the availability and quality of higher education for women. She was determined to build the new department's strength in botanical science, and under her guidance and auspices the botany department began cultivating a number of prominent botanists, including "disciple" Margaret Clay Ferguson (see 4.32) from the class of 1891. Susan was a true lover of nature, and her knowledge, organizational abilities, and enthusiasm inspired and enriched the lives of her pupils and associates. In 1893 she gave Margaret Clay Ferguson a position as instructor before appointing her head of botany in 1894. Clara Eaton Cummings (see 4.20) was another of Susan's protégées.

Susan maintained her department for more than twenty-five years. The foundations she laid and the several courses she instigated were so carefully and fully organized that, except where needed because of developments in botany, only small changes in her arrangement and distribution of the courses and work have been necessary over the passing years.

She developed the herbaria and organized and built up a botanical library that was second to that of no other college in the country. Even today her herbaria is surpassed only by the botanical libraries of very few of North America's greatest universities.

Susan was an enthusiastic and leading member of the Torrey Botanical Society, which began informally in the 1860s, inspired by Columbia College professor John Torrey. It is thought to be the oldest botanical society in America and was instrumental in founding the New York Botanical Garden.

In 1902, when Susan finally retired from her position as professor when she was sixty-seven years old, she was then appointed emeritus professor of botany at Wellesley in recognition of her unceasing efforts to establish the department as one of the very best in the USA.

4.13 ANNIE LINDA JACK (1839–1912)

Canada's first professional female horticultural writer, Annie authored the popular manual of the day, ***The Canadian Garden: A Pocket Help for the Amateur.*** *She was also a widely published poet, columnist, and social commentator.*

Born Annie Linda Hayr in Northamptonshire, England, in 1839, Annie moved to Troy, New York, in 1852, where she attended Troy Female Seminary. She married Scottish-born fruit farmer Robert Jack and settled on his 240-acre farm Hillside in Chateauguay Basin, Quebec.

Already a keen gardener, in her marriage agreement Annie stipulated that 1 acre of the farm's land should be devoted to any department of horticulture that she chose, with any profits made on the land to be her own.

Once married, she cultivated this acre into an extensive garden of flowers, fruits, and vegetables and used it for experimentation. The results would be described almost twenty years later in the *Rural New Yorker*, a periodical in which she had articles regularly published.

For the next fifty years, not only did she develop and maintain her garden at Hillside and contribute to various newspapers and magazines, but she also raised eleven children.

Under her supervision, numerous fruit-bearing trees, bushes, and vines were planted around Hillside, and a greenhouse was erected. Over the years Annie and her husband gained reputations as industrious and prosperous fruit growers and market gardeners. In 1876 they added more than 1,000 apple trees to their orchard; a few years later they started shipping apples to England. By the 1890s, as a plant nursery, they sold many varieties of fruit trees, shrubs, and plants.

Annie Linda Jack. Photograph by William Notman, Montreal, Canada. Henry J[ames] Morgan (1842–1913), *Types of Canadian Women and of Women Who Are or Have Been Connected with Canada (Volume I, Toronto 1903).*

Annie's garden at Hillside became a popular destination for fellow horticulturalists to visit. Here they could not only admire Annie's achievements, but buy plants, study techniques, and get advice (Annie was happy to share her tips). In 1915 Liberty Hyde Bailey (1858–1954), cofounder of the American Society for Horticultural Science, included a biography of Annie in his *The Standard Cyclopedia of Horticulture*.

Along with her work for the *Rural New Yorker*, where Annie wrote articles about her experiences under the title "*A Woman's Acre*," she also found time to write regularly between 1877 and 1890 for *Reports of the Montreal Horticultural Society* and *Fruit Growers' Association of the Province of Quebec* (at its shows and exhibitions Annie was a frequent prize winner).

As with all her work, Annie's clearly written articles were based on her own observations, her extensive experiments, and her experiences. She also read horticultural books and pamphlets and corresponded with other horticulturists to further her knowledge. Annie was also the author of a column on flowers and fruit titled "*Garden Talks*" published in the *Montreal Daily Witness*. The piece usually opened with a paragraph on a social or moral topic, then discussed various aspects of gardening and answered readers' questions. It was the success of this column that led to the publication (1903) of her book *The Canadian Garden: A Pocket Help for the Amateur*. It was the first Canadian book on gardening and remained the only such book available until after WWI. Inside, Annie offers practical advice, advising readers that *in every garden the rose is queen ... for it is the flower of our desires and yet so often the flower of our failures*. She instructed readers to make a rose bed: *five feet wide if it is to hold three rows, and let the distance between the roses be twenty-four to twenty-six inches*. A second edition would appear in 1910.

The Canadian Garden is still regarded as an important work in the history of gardening and one of the few Canadian books available at the time. According to historian Edwinna von Baeyer, it also *influenced gardeners all over eastern Canada*. The book combined helpful advice with almost lyrical passages that reflected the author's belief in the morally uplifting values of gardening, as well as the practical advantages.

During her life, Annie also contributed to the *Canadian Horticulturist*, *Canadian Horticultural Magazine*, and *Harper's Young People* with stories and poems. She also published five books: *The Little Organist of St Jerome and Other Stories of Work and Experience* (1902), *Rhyme-Thoughts for a Canadian Year* (1904), *Maple Lore* (1910), *Belated Violets*, and *The Christmas Hearth*.

By the time of her death in 1912 at age seventy-three, Annie Linda Jack—mother, homemaker, author, and horticulturist—had become a national treasure in her adopted country of Canada. She had been Canada's first professional woman garden writer and is remembered best for her popular manual *The Canadian Garden: A Pocket Help for the Amateur*.

4.14 BUFFALO BIRD WOMAN (CA. 1839–1932)

Passed on the traditional ways of her culture and oral tradition through interviews with anthropologist Gilbert L. Wilson

Buffalo Bird Woman was from the Hidatsa tribe of Native Americans who lived on the Fort Berthold Reservation in North Dakota. Her Hidatsa name was Maaxiiriwia (also transcribed as Maxidiwiac and Waheenee). She was known for maintaining the traditional Hidatsa skills of *gardening, the preparation of food, weaving and many others*. Maaxiiriwia's father was Small Ankle, and her mother, Want-to-Be-a-Woman. She had one child, Edward Goodbird (Tsaka'kasaḳic), born about November 1869. Her stepmothers were Red Blossom and Strikes-Many-Women. She had a brother, Henry Wolf Chief, and her grandmother was Otter. She was born in one of the villages at Knife River two years after the *smallpox year* (about 1839).

Tradition says that the tribe came from Miniwakan, or Devils Lake, in what is now North Dakota, and that migrating west they met the Mandans at the mouth of the Heart River. The two tribes formed an alliance and attempted to live together as one people. Later they were moved to the Fort Berthold Reservation.

Because writing was not part of Native American culture, we have very few records of their daily lives and few references to individuals. However, we are fortunate in

Buffalo Bird Woman from *The American Indian* by Clark Wissler, 1917. Originally published as *Agriculture of the Hidatsa Indians: An Indian Interpretation*. Edited by Gilbert Livingstone Wilson, 1868–1930. *University of Minnesota (Studies in the Social Sciences 9)*

having the detailed notes of anthropologist Gilbert L. Wilson. He first visited the reservation in 1906, at which time he began to observe and examine the remnants of the Hidatsa tribe. He returned in 1908, sponsored by the American Museum of Natural History, and for every summer of the next ten years he worked among the Hidatsas, studying the tribe's agricultural techniques and making copious notes of all he saw.

Unlike nomadic tribes who came to rely heavily on bison and the men who hunted them as their economic mainstay, corn and other vegetables were central to the economies of the village tribes. It was the women who worked the gardens, cultivating them with their sisters and daughters. An incredible amount of hard work was involved in the preparation, planting, cultivating, and harvesting of food from the garden. The women's work played a crucial role in the village tribes' economics. The women owned the products of their labors. Those who also farmed dressed skins, built houses, and produced clothing that made themselves and their families rich. Because men did not engage in these types of activities, they needed industrious, hardworking wives to be considered affluent. The women produced the clothing to be worn, as well as the food and gifts to be distributed at the men's ceremonies. The profit the tribes realized from the trading of corn created the economic surplus that allowed tribes to hold their ceremonies. Consequently, a hardworking woman was a source of wealth and prestige.

Buffalo Bird Woman tilling the soil. *The University of Minnesota (Studies in the Social Sciences, #9)*

One of Wilson's chief informants and guide was Buffalo Bird Woman. She passed on the traditional ways of her culture and oral tradition through interviews with him, in which she described her own experience and the lives and work of Hidatsa women. These were transcribed into a book that provides an excellent insight into a Native American woman's life, *Native American Gardening: Buffalo-Bird-Woman's Guide to Traditional Methods* (ISBN-13: 978-0-486-44021-7). It was published by Dover in 2005. It is a republication of a work originally issued under the title *Agriculture of the Hidatsa Indians: An Indian Interpretation*, published by the *Bulletin of the University of Minnesota*.

Two other books use these interviews as the basis for the text: *Buffalo Bird Woman's Garden: Agriculture of the Hidatsa Indians* (Minnesota Historical Society Press, 1987) and *Waheenee, an Indian Girl's Story* (Lincoln: University of Nebraska Press, 1991).

Buffalo Bird Woman's son, Edward Goodbird, acted as interpreter for Wilson, and Wilson writes about him: *Goodbird was one of the first of the reservation children to be sent to the mission school. He is now native pastor of the Congregational Ael at Independence. He speaks the Hidatsa, Mandan, Dakota, and English languages. Goodbird is a natural student; and he has the rarer gift of being an artist. His sketches—and they are many—are crude but they are drawn in true perspective and do not lack spirit.*

Of Goodbird's mother, Wilson writes: *She is a conservative and sighs for the good old times, yet is aware that the younger generation of Indians must adopt civilized ways. Ignorant of English, she has a quick intelligence and a memory that is marvelous. In the sweltering heat of an August day she has continued dictation for nine-hours, when too weary to sit longer in a chair, lying down but never flagging in her account.* Goodbird's testimony states that his mother *knows more about old ways of raising corn and squashes than anyone else on this reservation.* In her own words, Buffalo Bird Woman described her life growing vegetables to feed her family and the tribe.

Buffalo Bird Woman states that her day was long and hard with physical work. She said:

> *We Hidatsa women were early risers in the planting season; it was my habit to be up before sunrise, while the air was cool, for we thought this the best time for garden work.*
> *Having arrived at the field I would begin one hill, preparing it, as I have said, with my hoe; and so for 10 rows each as long as from this spot to yonder fence - about 30 yards; the rows were about four feet apart, and the hills stood about the same distance apart in the row.*
> *The hills all prepared, I went back and planted them, patting down each with my palms, as described. Planting corn thus by hand was slow work; but by 10 o'clock the morning's work was done, and I was tired and ready to go home for my breakfast and rest; we did not eat before going into the field. The 10 rows making the morning's planting contained about 225 hills. I usually went to the field every morning in the planting season, if the weather was fine. Sometimes I went out again a little before sunset and planted, but this was not usual.*

Telling Wilson about the role of men in gardening, she said:

> *Did young men work in the fields? [laughing heartily] Certainly not! The young men should be off hunting, or on a war party; and youths not yet young men should be out guarding the horses. Their duties were elsewhere. Also, they spent a great deal of time dressing up to be seen by the village maidens; they should not be working in the fields! But old men, too old*

to go to war, went out into the fields and helped their wives. It was theirs to plant the corn while the women made the hills; and they also helped pull up weeds.

By passing on her knowledge of the old ways of village tribes, Buffalo Bird Woman has both preserved knowledge and taught new generations about the farming traditions of her grandmothers. She tells how in the variable and often-extreme environmental conditions of the Northern Plains, the women produced enough corn and vegetables to feed their own, as well as a substantial surplus to offer as trade goods. The family diet was a combination of food grown in the extensive gardens and from the bison, elk, antelope, and fish of the prairies and rivers. Beans, squash, and sunflowers supplemented the corn harvest. The size and quality of the harvest would vary from year to year. Native gardeners had to contend with hail, high winds, grasshoppers, early and late frosts, droughts, and animals. They also had to deal with raiding enemy tribes and concealed their produce in underground cache pits. Buffalo Bird Woman said:

I am an old woman now. The buffaloes and black-tail deer are gone, and our Indian ways are almost gone. Sometimes I find it hard to believe I ever lived them. Sometimes, at evening, I sit, looking out on the big Missouri. The sun sets, and dusk steals over the water. In the shadows I seem again to see our Indian village, with smoke curling upward from the earth lodges; and in the river's roar I hear the yells of the warriors, the laughter of little children as of old.

Wilson, writing of his book, says, *Agriculture of the Hidatsa Indians is not, then, an account merely of Indian agriculture. It is an Indian woman's interpretation of economics; the thoughts she gave to her fields; the philosophy of her labors. May the Indian woman's story of her toil be a plea for our better appreciation of her race.*

Buffalo Bird Woman died in 1932, but her voice, as recorded by Wilson, brings to life the villages of the Hidatsa people—men, women, and children. Her invaluable insight left behind the knowledge that it was the women who worked the soil, preparing, planting, cultivating, and harvesting the food. The women's work played a crucial role in the village tribes' economics. Her reminiscences are a vital record of the life of late-nineteenth- and early-twentieth-century Native American women.

4.15 EMMA HOMAN THAYER (1842–1908)

Botanical artist and author of books about native wildflowers

Emma Homan was born in New York City in 1842, the daughter of George Wand and Emma Homan. Her father was a businessman and the first person to operate omnibuses on Broadway in New York City. He moved the family to Omaha, Nebraska, when she was around fifteen. In 1860 she married George A Graves, a native of western New York, who went on to work for the war department in Washington, DC.

Emma was widowed after only four years of marriage, at which point she decided to pursue higher education. She attended Rutgers Female College for a time and then enrolled at the National Academy of Design, where she studied painting to fulfill a desire to become an accomplished artist. Many of her figure paintings have been exhibited in the National Academy of Fine Arts. One life-size piece titled *Only Five Cents!* won her two gold medals.

In 1877 she married again, to Elmer A. Thayer of Massachusetts, who was a manager for hotels on the Denver and Rio Grande lines. They moved to Chicago, Illinois, where she continued her career as a painter. In 1882 his business interests required them to move to Salida, Colorado, now in Chaffee County, where they lived in a beautiful home in the very heart of the Rocky Mountains. There Emma found nature offered a new and inexhaustible field for her art. She moved from figure painting to botanical art, focusing on wildflowers native to America depicted in natural settings. She began to paint the wildflowers of the region, and her first book, *Wild Flowers of Colorado*, was published in New York by Cassell & Co. in 1883.

Illustrated with twenty-four chromolithographs of her watercolors, these paintings were accompanied by descriptions of her travels throughout the state, and it sold well. The list of flower plates included anemone or wind flower, yucca or soap plant, columbine mariposa, lily, primrose, iris or fleur-de-lis, primula argemone Mexicana or prickly-poppy ipomoea or man-of-the-Earth, asters, tree cactus, dwarf or cup cactus, cactus knight's plume, gilia gentian golden, spider aster, epilobium or butterfly flower thimble plant, castelia or painter's brush, linum or fairy lily, mallow, oenothera or evening primrose, cleome, and wild geranium leaves.

After the success of her first book, two years later *Wild Flowers of the Pacific Coast* was published (1885, also by Cassell & Co.) and proved even more beautiful than its predecessor. Some of the areas she includes are Monterey, Santa Rosa, Napa, San José, Pasadina [*sic*], and Yosemite.

One of the best examples of Emma's artistic talent is a memorial stained glass window that she designed for the Church of the Ascension in Salida, Colorado. It is dedicated to the memory of her father, who died in 1886. Emma was not only a gifted artist, but also a versatile and talented writer of fiction, as demonstrated in her novel *An English-American*, published in 1890.

The flowers in both books are painted in a lively, impressionistic style, and according to one critic *without great attention to scientific detail*. In addition to detailing the wildflowers, both books also described, in a first person, narrative style, Emma's travels and adventures while out on camping trips in rugged, often unexplored wild terrain. These excursions could last up to thirty days. In 1889 a new edition of *Wild Flowers of Colorado* was published under the title *Wild Flowers of the Rocky Mountains*. The only changes were to the cover and title page. Emma Homan Thayer died in Denver, Colorado, in 1908. She was one of North America's best botanic artists, illustrating several bestselling books.

4.16 THEODOSIA BURR SHEPHERD (1845–1906)

Leader in floral horticulture and of the seed and bulb industry

Born in Keosauqua, Iowa, Theodosia was the daughter of lawyer Augustus Hall, who later became chief justice of Nebraska. She married W. E. Shepherd in 1866, and they moved to Ventura, California, for her health in 1873.

One year later, Theodosia started a California flower seed business, starting off by swapping seeds through a ladies' magazine. After a few years she expanded her property and began growing her own flowers for their seeds. In 1881 she sent a package of seeds to Peter Henderson of New York, one of the nation's leading nurserymen, who, impressed, encouraged her to grow more seeds and flowers in the Ventura climate. She named her company the Mrs. Theodosia B. Shepherd's, which annually issued a retail catalog and two wholesale lists. Accolades and encouragement were also received from W. Atlee Burpee, founder of the Burpee seed company, as well as other well-known horticulturists.

Eventually Theodosia was known throughout the United States as the *Flower Wizard of California who put Ventura on the map*. Theodosia was the first woman in America to hybridize flowers. She sent her seeds and bulbs all over America, as well as to England, Europe, and even as far as Australia and Algiers.

Theodosia's hope was that her daughters, and other women, would find an alternative to the drudgery of housework by becoming involved in growing flowers and selling seeds. With daughter Myrtle Shepherd Francis, Theodosia created many multicolor, double, and ruffled petunias. She campaigned for this and wrote and lectured on plant life, her hybridization work, and her success as a woman in the seed industry. Her Ventura gardens were full of her exotic creations and attracted many notable visitors, among them suffragettes Julia Ward Howe and Susan B.

Anthony. In 1896 Susan B Anthony said, *Theodosia Burr Shepherd has blazed a trail for other women to follow*.

She became known for her many successful experiments with petunias, poppies, and morning glories, and she was an authority on cactus before it was fashionable. Theodosia introduced many new flowers, including new varieties of chrysanthemums, nasturtiums, poppies, geraniums, cosmos, calla lilies, cannas, dahlias, pansies, petunias, zinnias, fuchsias, azaleas, heliotrope, and the golden oriole rose, including her hybrid morning glory *Ipomoea Heavenly Blue*, which she described in 1892 as a cross of *Ipomoea learii* and *Mina lobate*.

The title page of Theodosia's *Descriptive Catalogue*, 1900. *National Agricultural Library, Agricultural Research Service, US Department of Agriculture*

She also takes credit for the then-popular California poppy cultivar *Eschscholzia Californica Golden West*.

A 1905 *Pittsburg Dispatch* includes a quote from Theodosia:

> *I sometimes think that we do not always choose our work, but are chosen, or called to it. It has always seemed to me that I was called into the field of flowers with a special mission for them: to grow and disseminate them, where they are loved; to write about them; to talk about them, and, most of all, to create new varieties.*

In addition to spreading her enthusiasm and love for plants and her mission to tell of opportunities for women in gardening through her lectures, she also wrote more broadly about horticulture and women's place in it. A typescript titled *The Woman in Floral Culture* makes it very clear that she encouraged outdoor recreation for women, and she championed dress reform in gardening, because long skirts got in the way of real gardening work.

Theodosia stated that the field of horticultural hybridizing was wide open to women, and she encouraged them to cultivate hardy flowers whose seeds could be sold to novelty-hungry gardeners on the East Coast. In her writing she *bolstered her readers'* confidence in their existing botanical knowledge, and she advised that they could learn more through hands-on experimentation.

The community gardens on the corner of Chestnut and Poli Streets in Ventura are the original site of the home and farm where Theodosia founded California's seed industry with her world-renowned seed and bulb business. The gardens are now a Ventura Historic Landmark and are currently maintained by the nonprofit Community Organized for Liberty Opportunity and Respect.

Theodosia's biography, *Theodosia: The Flower Wizard of California*, was written by her daughter Myrtle and published in 1946. It was then reissued in 2014 by Mystic Ink Publishing. Theodosia Burr Shepherd died in Ventura on September 6, 1906. She was sixty-one years old.

She is remembered for being the first woman in North America to hybridize flowers and introduced many new varieties. She was also known for her campaigning for women's rights, as well as writing and lecturing on plant life, her hybridization work, and her success as a woman in the seed industry. In the 1800s horticulturist Peter Henderson wrote of her: *The intelligent and energetic Theodosia occupies the proud position of the pioneer of floral horticulture and of the seed and bulb business.*

4.17 FRANCES "FANNIE" GRISCOM PARSONS (1850–1923)

Initiator of the School Gardening movement who introduced countless children to the joys of growing their own food

Frances's father, John Hopkins Griscom (1809–1874), was a physician and one of the founding members of the New York City Board of Health. He was one of the first people to see a link between negative environmental conditions in slum neighborhoods (overcrowded tenements, poor sanitation, lack of recreational facilities) to the high mortality rates, unemployment, and low morale found there. He campaigned vigorously for public health reform to address these issues.

His daughter, known as Fannie, had no professional experience in gardening or landscape design, but she was influenced by her father's crusade and the demand for reform. Her work was influenced by this and by her personal experience as a mother of seven children, whom she raised in Brooklyn, New York. She believed that sharing the experience of getting to know plants, growing vegetables, and gardening contributed to the wholesome development of a child. It was what led her to later move to the country in upstate New York, where her children could gambol and play outside in the garden and experience nature.

In the nineteenth century, the neighborhood on the west side of Midtown Manhattan in New York City was a cauldron of mostly poor and working-class Irish Americans. The neighborhood was so notorious for squalor, disease, and vice that it earned the name Hell's Kitchen. In 1902, determined that the children living there should experience the outdoors through gardening, Fannie set out to find a solution.

She saw a plot of land there that had been intended as public parkland, but the lack of funds for its development meant it was unimproved and had become derelict. Surrounding this patch of land were warehouses, factories, slaughterhouses, tenements, and congested streets—one nicknamed Death Avenue. It was on this unlikely site that she created her Children's School Farm, leading the Children's Garden movement.

A WWI poster encouraging the planting and raising of vegetables. *US National Archives, US Food Administration Educational Division, Advertising Section*

Helping to counteract the dreadful slum conditions in Hell's Kitchen, the garden provided an open space and an experience of nature that was so obviously absent from the neighborhood. Children ages nine to twelve years old were given individual plots to grow vegetables and flowers.

When Fannie began working in Hell's Kitchen, she declared *I simply went out to live with the thousands, as I had lived with my own seven, believing that the thousands had the same traits and are amenable to the same influences.*

Fannie let it be known that she did not start the farm *simply to grow a few vegetables and flowers*, and that she believed gardening would teach children values and skills that would be applicable to their lives in the city. Specifically *brotherhood, cooperation, self-respect, and the dignity of labor.* By playing the part of little farmers, as she described it, she hoped children would become urban citizens—particularly essential, since many of them were children of immigrants or were recent immigrants themselves. Vegetables grown included corn, beets, beans, peas, turnips, lettuce, spinach, cabbage, celery, and radishes. Little emphasis was given to what happened to the vegetables that were produced; it was the effect that participation had on the children's welfare that was the focus.

An 11-by-18-foot farmhouse was constructed in the second year of the garden's existence, in which girls were taught household chores and boys learned outdoor tasks. Skills taught also included showing the children how to cook their harvest. Frances ensured that girls were taught how to farm right alongside boys—a fundamental part of a school garden. Both boys and girls kept diaries and noted the progress of their vegetables throughout the growing season.

For Frances the social benefits followed. *So, in the first place the children are taught the economy of space,* she explained. *Economy of other things follows. We teach them honesty in their work, neatness and order, justice as well as kindness to their neighbors. I assure you that all the virtues can be taught from a little patch of ground not 8 ft square.*

For three years Frances thought of the farm as a temporary experiment, given that it had been created with private funding on land borrowed from the Department of Parks. Frances instigated a campaign to make it a permanent facility. She convinced Parks Commissioner William R. Willcox and Mayor Seth Low, both reform-minded officials, to encourage and support the project. Commissioner Willcox appreciated the way the garden helped change children's behavior. He noted in 1903: *Older persons who live thereabouts declare they can see a decided difference in the courtesy and general conduct of the youngsters since the plan was first adopted.*

The Department of Parks reviewed Frances's farm and saw it as a great success. In 1905 they initiated De Witt Clinton Park, a 5.8-acre New York City public park in the Hell's Kitchen neighborhood of Manhattan, New York City, between West 52nd and 54th Streets and 11th Avenue. They incorporated a permanent farm there and hired Frances to manage it.

This park was designed by Samuel Parsons Jr. (no relation). His work at De Witt Clinton and other small parks was assisted by Frances and represented a new era in park design. A defining feature included integrating innovative facilities such as playgrounds, bathhouses, and school farms within each park's landscaped, open space.

Early in the program, Frances claimed there was a waiting list of several hundred children. She noted in 1905: *Such work as this for the children of our city is the truest reform work, I know of. The contact with Nature, the learning to use her ways for himself is a wonderful educator for the street boy, whose knowledge is limited to stone pavements and one small room in a tenement house.*

Building on this success, Frances, who had always been an enthusiastic promoter of her work, began working harder to spread the school garden concept to other areas, especially any urban environments with deprived neighborhoods. She gave numerous lectures and created exhibitions to show the benefits of the farms, and she personally trained teachers. As she emerged as a leading advocate, the De Witt Clinton Park Children's School Farm became nationally recognized as a model for others.

The Department of Parks appointed Frances the director of the newly created Bureau of School Farms, making her the first woman to hold a high-level position in the department. In this capacity Frances created new farms, including a 2-acre farm garden at Thomas Jefferson Park in East Harlem—built in 1911—and providing more than 1,000 plots that went through two growing cycles each summer.

Another park, a ¾-acre garden at Corlears Hook, on Manhattan's Lower East Side, opened in 1913. In Brooklyn, sites included McCarren Park (1914) and Betsy Head Park (1915). In each garden 715 plots served 1,430 children.

The 1915 *Annual Report* of the Children's School Farm noted that the average yield was *400 radishes, 2 quarts of beans, 5 ears of corn, 40 beets, 1 peck of beet greens, 60 carrots, 15 heads of lettuce and 20 turnips*—quite a result, and a profitable one.

By 1918 an astonishing 3,565 children were participating in a school farm scheme. The Children's School Farm was a product of the country's shift from an agrarian to an urban society, and evidence of the important role that women and children played in shaping public spaces, particularly neighborhood parks throughout the USA.

Thanks to Frances the Children's Garden movement grew to be a nationwide initiative, unfolding in cities across the country, including Boston, Dayton, Philadelphia, and Chicago. In 1906 there were more than 75,000 of these school gardens across the country, not only in parks but also in vacant lots, backyards, and (primarily) urban schoolyards. In the mid-1910s, with the federal government providing financial support to create gardens in cities nationwide, its focus moved to address the crisis of WWI. The government began promoting gardening as a way to supplement local food production and inspire patriotism. Naturally Frances became involved in this new phase of the movement.

Frances died in 1923, but many she had trained, including her son, continued her work in New York City parks, where many of the gardens existed well into the 1950s. Today Fannie's legacy lives on with neighborhood-based initiatives such as Red Hook Farms in Brooklyn, New York, and the Obamas planting a vegetable garden on the South Lawn of the White House in 2009. During World War II,

Eleanor Roosevelt had her own *victory garden* there as part of the movement to increase the national food supply.

Many children's gardens are again being created to help promote healthful nutrition and environmental stewardship and provide a more interactive educational environment. They reflect widespread concerns about children's health, particularly the growth of childhood obesity and of the effects of society's growing disassociation with the natural world.

With roots in Frances's work, chef, author, and activist Alice Water started an Edible Schoolyard project to provide *an edible education* in 1995. Alice's organization, inspired by Frances Parsons, has since partnered with more than 5,600 schools around the world.

4.18 MARIANA GRISWOLD VAN RENSSELAER (1851–1934)

One of the nation's earliest perceptive writers on architecture, art, and landscape design. Mariana was also the first to introduce the term "landscape gardening" in magazine-of-the-day Garden and Forest.

Mariana Griswold was born in New York City in 1851, one of seven children who grew up with tutors and governesses in a prestigious house on 5th Avenue. The family fortune came from the China porcelain trade. For this reason, in 1868 she moved with her family to Dresden, Germany, where she remained for five years, becoming fluent in French and German.

Mariana also began to develop her scientific knowledge via fortunate connections with eminent academics of the time, including Charles Darwin,

German natural historian Alexander von Humboldt, botanist Asa Gray, geologist Nathaniel Southgate Shaler, and naturalists Henry David Thoreau and John Burroughs. This led to a lifelong interest in botany and geology sciences, which she would put to effective use in later life.

In 1873 she married mining engineer Schuyler Van Rensselaer, and they moved to New Brunswick, New Jersey. He was often away from home for work, leaving Mariana with their young son. With time on her hands, she began to write and within a few years was contributing to the most-influential periodicals of the era.

Over the years she had work published in *The Atlantic*, *American Art Review*, and *American Architect & Building News*, to name a few. Sometimes her articles were unattributed, as was the case with her articles for *Garden and Forest*. More than 330 previously unattributed editorials and unsigned articles have now been identified as having been authored by Mariana in *Garden and Forest*. She remained the sole female editorial voice for this influential journal.

After turning down an offer to edit the *American Art Review* in 1881, she began writing regularly for magazine *The Century*. By the time her father and her husband died in 1884, writing had become an economic necessity.

Although she also wrote fiction, children's stories, and history books (perhaps the best known is her *History of the City of New York in the Seventeenth Century*), Mariana's passion was art and landscapes. In 1887 she began ten years of focused writing on landscape architecture, courageously insisting that she be paid the same rate as men for her work.

The first woman architectural critic, Mariana became one of the premier figures in landscape writing and design at the turn of the twentieth century—a time when the increasingly professionalized landscape design field was being recognized. Playing a pivotal role in the history of landscape architecture, Mariana was one of the new breed of American art and architecture critics who closely examined the nature of the profession.

Fortunately, Mariana's cosmopolitan education and high social status gave her access to the homes and gardens of the upper classes; this allowed her to mingle with—and learn from—authors, artists, and affluent patrons of the arts. Consequently, she was able to write with confidence about her chosen field.

In 1893 Mariana published *Art Out-of-Doors: Hints on Good Taste in Gardening*, which included several of her unsigned *Garden and Forest* editorials.

One of Mariana's most valuable contributions was a seven-part series that outlined the artistic principles of landscape architecture, which she defined as such: *The (fine) art whose purpose it is to create beautiful compositions upon the surface of the ground*. She contributed another series of twenty-one historical essays to *Garden and Forest* on the art of gardening, which looked at gardening *as an individual and independent manifestation of the artistic instinct, yet one which has . . . a vital relation to the general course of human development*. Among the many garden traditions and styles examined in the book were Japanese, Egyptian, Persian, Greek, Roman, and Moorish.

In 1925, Mariana had a new edition of her *Art Out-of-Doors* published. This time it featured a chapter on the changes that had taken place within the sphere of landscape architecture since the publication of the first book. She believed the field had become more ambitious and versatile.

One development of particular interest to her was the invention of the automobile. She stated that this now permitted *everybody and his wife and child to go a-wheel*, to leave the city on extended tours. Mariana saw the need for landscape architects to deal with the automobile's effect on recreation and on city and rural planning.

Mariana's view on architecture was that it should *harmonize with the ideas of cultivated men and women who are heirs of all the ages, living in a state of superior enlightenment, rather than indulging the regrettable popular taste for the new and marvelous*. She was critical of gardeners too: *Today the art of gardening is practised much more often than any other, in ignorant, impulsive ways, by people who never stop to think that it is an art at all*.

Many of the women featured in this book were passionate advocates and supporters of the equality of women. Interestingly, Mariana was not one of them. When Colorado women were granted the vote while she was there in winter 1893–94, she voted because it was her civic responsibility. However, she openly opposed the suffrage movement. *Women*, she wrote, *are much weaker than men ... their bodies fitted especially for motherhood*. She believed that *although women needed more intellectual liberty than they then enjoyed, men were still the executives*. Because men had the whole economic responsibility, they should have the whole decision-making responsibility that voting exemplified. She accepted that women were sometimes forced to take the leading role in their own families, but this was *a misfortune, not an opportunity*.

She was awarded an honorary membership to the American Institute of Architects, and in 1920 to the American Society of Landscape Architects. In 1910, she received a doctor of letters degree from Columbia University—an extraordinary achievement for a woman at that time, and in 1923 Mariana was awarded an American Academy of Arts and Letters Gold Medal.

Mariana Griswold Van Rensselaer died in New York City in 1934. She was buried next to her husband and only child at Green-Wood Cemetery in Brooklyn, New York. She was eighty-three years old. She had played a vital role in the history of landscape architecture as the first woman architectural critic.

4.19 ALICE MORSE EARLE (1851–1911)

American historian and gardening author

Her father, Edwin Morse, was from Andover, Vermont, and he came to Worcester, central Massachusetts, in 1846 with his family. He became one of the city's leading citizens, serving as alderman, director of the First National Bank, president of the Mechanics Association, and trustee of the Worcester County Horticultural Society. Both Edwin Morse and his wife were enthusiastic gardeners, and they passed this passion on to Alice. Fortunately, the ¾-acre garden of their Worcester home was built on the site of a previous commercial nursery, and the rich soil in the family garden yielded prizewinning fruit and flowers for three-quarters of a century.

Alice's childhood was mentioned in her book *Old Time Gardens* (1901), and it sounds idyllic. Gardens became a dominant feature in her youth—the family's own large city garden, but also those of their relations and the many lush gardens that lined neighboring streets in Worcester.

One of the most descriptive chapters in Alice Earle's book on gardening is called *"Childhood in a Garden."* Alice stated of herself that *for nothing is she more happy than to have been given a flower-loving mother and father*. The garden was the center of her childhood world. In winter it was the setting for snow forts, snowmen, and skating

Alice Morse in 1873

at the bottom of the property, while in summer she wrote, *the old fashioned garden was paradise for a child*.

Alice graduated from Worcester Classical and English High School at a time when very few Americans were high school graduates. She also attended the Gannett Institute for Young Ladies in Boston. Founder Dr. George Gannett was progressive and, unusually for his time, refused to be limited in his views of education that women should receive. He believed that female students should be taught with *the same freedom and thoroughness which was then enjoyed in our principal American colleges*.

After Alice's 1874 marriage to Henry Earle of New York and their move to Brooklyn, Alice took the library course at nearby Pratt Institute, so she was considerably better educated than most of her contemporaries. Her writing career began in 1890, when, at the suggestion of her father, she wrote an article on old Sabbath customs at her forebears' church in Chester, Vermont, and submitted it to the *Youth's Companion*. The next year an expanded version of this article was published by the *Atlantic Monthly*, and later, in 1891, she published her first book, *The Sabbath in Puritan New England*, which sold well, establishing her as an author.

Her research and her style of writing emphasized the homely details of everyday life, and her explanations of her findings and her memories helped spark a renewal of public interest in the American past. She wrote eighteen books between 1890 and 1904 on gardening and colonial life, as well as one biography.

Home Life in Colonial Days was published in 1893. Some scholars of her day dismissed Alice's work, criticizing her as a woman too focused on the details of everyday life, decrying it as *pots and pans history*. Today she is regarded as an important source of material about everyday life in the colonial era and an invaluable source of material for modern social historians.

Alice's enthusiasm for historic garden designs was rooted in her strong sense of the garden as a place to live in and to interact with nature, family, and friends. For her, the significance of gardens lay not just in their design and plants, but also in their association with the people who cultivated and used them. She constantly sought to educate her children with garden values because she believed that gardens were an expression of culture and connections with the past. In 1895 she wrote the article *"Flower-Lore of New England Children"* for the *Atlantic Monthly*.

Old Time Gardens was published by the Macmillan Company in 1901 and was one of the most popular and influential garden books of the early twentieth century—and one of the first to be extensively illustrated with photographs. The book appealed to many devotees of different types of gardens—perennial gardens, country gardens, cottage gardens, old-fashioned gardens—and it was a useful work of reference for a landscape historian, or designers interested in early American gardens, colonial revival gardens, the arts-and-crafts garden, the Italian garden phenomenon, or the plants to design and build elements in Americans' landscape history.

A new edition, featuring an introduction by landscape historian Virginia Lopez Begg, was published by University Press of New England in 2005. Garden ornaments and furnishings such as arbors, summer houses, and especially sundials receive close attention. *Old Time Gardens* has more than 200 vintage photographs illustrating American gardens in the 1900s. It is among the few books in its era to feature middle-class gardens, providing an invaluable record.

In her book, Alice further increased the value of the photographs by identifying the locations of many gardens, as well as the names of plants, gardens, owners, and a cross section of highly regarded amateur and professional photographers. In her garden books, Alice was able to portray the wide variety of perennials found in the gardens in watercolors. A portfolio of her watercolors, probably painted in her teens, were drawn with such accuracy that professional horticulturists were able to identify each specimen in the collection. It is recorded that her books were read in Europe—for example, her reference to ambrosia (*Chenopodium botrys*) brought *many letters from English flower lovers telling me they know it not: had the pleasure of sending the seeds to several old English and Scots gardens*. Her topics include plants of the colonial era, such as herbs and lilacs, and others long forgotten, such as honeywort. Alice's niece, Alice Earle Hyde, was responsible for the *Hyde Chart of Wild Flowers*, which first appeared in *Webster's Unabridged Dictionary* and was later reprinted by the Garden Club of America in 1960.

Alice was also one of the earliest writers about American history to look seriously at women's roles in the evolution of the nation. She advocated the expansion of women's place in American life, and several of her books refer to women's history, making frequent references to their lives, their work, and material culture.

In addition to her books, Alice produced numerous articles, pamphlets, and speeches about the life, manners, customs, and culture of colonial New England. These, and her books, were written in a style calculated to appeal to a wide readership. There are two wonderful quotations by Alice Morse Earle worth recording:

> *Every day may not be good . . . but there's something good in every day.*
> *The clock is running. Make the most of today. Time waits for no man.*

> *Yesterday is history. Tomorrow is a mystery. Today is a gift. That's why it is called the present.*

Her books were well illustrated and recorded the intimate details of what she described as colonial *home life*, including the role of women in growing crops and vegetables in colonial New England. They reflected her belief that women had played a key historical role, helping to nurture communities by building households that served and shaped their families. Among the books she wrote concerning gardens and life in colonial America were

Customs and Fashions in Old New England (1893);
Costume of Colonial Times (1894);
Colonial Dames and Goodwives (1895);
Colonial Days in Old New York (1896);
In Old Narragansett: Romances and Realities (1898);
Child Life in Colonial Days (1899);
Old Time Gardens (1901);
Sun Dials and Roses of Yesterday (1902); and
Two Centuries of Costume in America, 1620–1820 (2 vols, 1903).

In 1909 Alice was a passenger aboard the RMS *Republic* off the coast of Nantucket when, in a dense fog, the ship collided with the SS *Florida*. During the transfer of passengers, Alice was twice submerged in the icy Atlantic water and had to be rescued by a sailor's grappling hook. Her near drowning weakened her health, and she never really recovered. She died two years later, in 1911, in Hempstead, Long Island.

4.20 CLARA EATON CUMMINGS (1855–1906)

American cryptogamic botanist and Hunnewell Professor of Cryptogamic Botany at Wellesley College in Massachusetts

Clara was born in Plymouth, New Hampshire, on July 13, 1855. In 1876 she enrolled at the Women's Liberal Arts College in Wellesley, Massachusetts, only one year after it had opened. Clara was taught by Susan Hallowell, professor of botany at Wellesley College (see 4.12). After studying as an undergraduate, she showed such talent in the field of botany that she was retained as an employee at the college's museum. Clara mostly studied cryptogamous plants, which are spore reproducing, such as mosses and lichens. A cryptogam (scientific name Cryptogamae) is a plant that reproduces by spores, without flowers or seeds. The best-known groups of cryptogams are algae, lichens, mosses, and ferns, but it also includes nonphotosynthetic organisms traditionally classified as plants, such as fungi, slime molds, and bacteria.

Clara was a curator at the Botanical Museum at Wellesley from 1878 to 1879 and became an associate professor of cryptogamic botany at Wellesey in 1879. In 1886 and 1887 she traveled to Europe and studied under Dr. Arnold Dodel at the University of Zurich, Switzerland. There she did private work and prepared charts to accompany illustrations for the *Crytogamic Botany* journal. While in Europe she visited various botanical gardens, especially interested, of course, in the mosses and lichens on display.

A lot of her research work appeared in the books of other botanists, although she did publish a catalog of liverworts and mosses of North America titled *Catalogue* [*sic*] *of Musci and Hepaticae of North America, North of Mexico*, published by Howard and Stiles in 1885.

Clara Eaton Cummings. Photographer unknown. *The Bryologist* 10, no. 3 (May 1907).

In 1904 she published a catalog of 217 species of Alaskan lichens collected during the Harriman Expedition, which was conducted with the cooperation of the Washington Academy of Sciences. It was published in 1904 by Doubleday, Page & Co., and included seventy-six species of lichens new to Alaska, and at least two species new to science.

In February and March 1905, Clara took a trip to Jamaica, where she sought and collected lichens. Later that year she was named Hunnewell Professor of Botany at Wellesley and took temporary charge over the botany department. Clara became an associate editor of *Plant World* and was named a fellow of the American Association of the Society of Plant Morphology and Physiology in 1904. She was a member of the American Association for the Advancement of Science and the Boston Society of Natural History.

Clara characterized hundreds of lichen specimens but was *very conservative* on declaring new species. Her meticulous research and her dedication to her work resulted in an important contribution to horticultural knowledge at the highest level. After her death in 1906, her collection was donated to the New York Botanical Garden. Clara Eaton Cummings is a good example of a woman who, with a keen interest in her chosen subject and the benefit of a good scientific education to study it, was able to rise to the top of her field in a domain then dominated by men.

4.21 KATHERINE OLIVIA "KATE" SESSIONS (1857–1940)

Environmentalist, conservationist, botanist, horticulturalist, and landscape architect

Katherine Sessions

Kate grew up among the massive pines and redwoods of Northern California. In 1881 she was the first woman to graduate from the University of California, Berkeley, with a degree in science. Her graduation essay was titled *"The Natural Sciences as a Field for Women's Labor."* While attending a San Francisco business school, at the request of a friend she moved to San Diego in 1883 to work as an eighth-grade teacher and vice principal at Russ School (now San Diego High School). It was here that Kate developed her real interest, the cultivation of plants.

In 1885 she purchased a nursery, and within a few years she was also the owner of a flower shop as well as growing fields and nurseries in Coronado, Pacific Beach, and Mission Hills. The Mission Hills Nursery, which she founded in 1910, was eventually sold to her employees, the Antonicelli brothers, in 1926, and is still operating today.

In 1892 Kate negotiated a deal with the City of San Diego to lease 30 acres of land in Balboa Park (then City Park) as growing fields. In return she agreed to plant 100 trees a year in the mostly barren park, as well as 300 trees a year in other parts of San Diego. This arrangement resulted in the park displaying a range of trees including cypress, pine, oak, pepper trees, and eucalyptus—all grown in her nurseries from seeds imported from around the world. Virtually all of the older trees seen in the park today were planted by Kate.

The jacaranda is now a very familiar sight in the city, and Kate is credited with importing and popularizing it, among many other plant introductions. She also collected, propagated, and introduced many California native plants through her nurseries to the horticulture trade and into private gardens.

Kate Sessions at the Old Cactus Garden, Balboa Park, 1932. *San Diego City Clerk Archives*

She published numerous articles. Together with Alfred D. Robinson she cofounded the San Diego Floral Association in 1907. This is the oldest garden club in Southern California. The garden club was influential in teaching San Diegans how to grow ornamental and edible plants at a time when most San Diego landscaping consisted of dirt and sagebrush.

Kate was appointed supervisor and teacher of agriculture and landscapes for city schools in 1915. Kate's experiments with plant introductions won her the 1939 Frank N. Meyer Medal from the American Genetic Association—the first woman to receive this prestigious award.

At the California Pacific International Exposition, the date September 22, 1935, was dedicated to Kate, where she was named the Mother of Balboa Park. In 1998 a bronze statue of Kate was erected in the park. It is situated in a prominent location in the southwest corner of Sefton Plaza, near the 6th Avenue entrance to Balboa Park.

Kate was one of California's first environmentalists and conservationists, long before these terms became popular. Her work with plant introductions, as well as her extensive writing on the subject, won her international recognition.

When she embarked on a seven-month trip to Europe, she collected several plant varieties that she eventually helped plant in Balboa Park. She worked with architect Hazel Wood Waterman on the landscaping and garden design for a group of houses built by San Diego socialite Alice Lee near Balboa Park. George Marston, speaking at a 1935 garden dedication in her honor, said this of her: *Botanically speaking, I would call Miss Sessions a perennial, evergreen and ever blooming.*

Katherine Olivia "Kate" Sessions never married. She died in 1940 after a lifetime dedicated, in particular, to the San Diego region. There the Kate Sessions Elementary School in Pacific Beach bears her name, as does Kate O. Sessions Memorial Park on Mount Soledad, less than a mile from the school. In 2006 the Women's Museum of California inducted Kate into the San Diego County Women's Hall of Fame under the title of trailblazer.

A 2013 children's picture book by H. Joseph Hopkins, *The Tree Lady: The True Story of How One Tree-Loving Woman Changed a City Forever*, commemorates Kate's life, education, and contribution to San Diego's environment and life.

4.22 ELIZABETH GERTRUDE BRITTON (1858–1934)

Botanist and bryologist (the study of mosses), she was a campaigner for the preservation of native North American wildflowers.

Elizabeth Britton at work, 1886. Photographer unknown. *Simco Ontario*

Elizabeth was born in 1858 in New York City. Her family operated a furniture factory and sugar plantation in the vicinity of Matanzas, Cuba, and she spent much of her childhood there. In later childhood she attended a private school in New York; she then attended Normal College (later renamed Hunter College) and graduated from there in 1875 at the early age of seventeen. After graduation, Elizabeth joined the staff of Normal College as a teacher.

Her interest in plants already piqued, Elizabeth joined the Torrey Botanical Club in 1879. The society, which began informally in the 1860s under the aegis and inspiration of Columbia College professor John Torrey, is thought to be the oldest botanical society in America. In 1881 she published her first scientific paper in that organization's bulletin, reporting her observations of unexpected white flowers in two species of plants. In 1883 she was named a tutor in natural science at Normal College. In the same year her first paper concerning mosses was published.

In 1885 she married Nathaniel Lord Britton, an assistant in geology at Columbia College who shared her interest in botany. After her marriage, Elizabeth resigned her teaching position at Normal College and took charge of the moss collections at Columbia in an unofficial, unpaid capacity. She served as editor of the *Bulletin of the Torrey Botanical Club* from 1886 to 1888. In 1889 she published the first of an eleven-part series of papers titled *Contributions to American Bryology* in that journal. Her catalog of the mosses of West Virginia appeared in 1892, and the first of eight articles, titled "How to Study the Mosses," for a popular magazine was published in 1894.

In the 1880s her research led toward an organized study of the mosses of the eastern United States, and she also wrote papers on moss systematics for the project known as the North American Flora. Elizabeth, along with her husband, was one of the Torrey Botanical Club members who pioneered the establishment of the New York Botanical Garden. The couple had traveled to England in 1888, where Nathaniel was performing research at the Royal Botanic Gardens, Kew, and Elizabeth worked on mosses at the Linnaean Society of London. Inspired by the quality and quantity of Kew's herbarium, library, and gardens, the couple set about organizing an institution of comparable stature for New York. A meeting was held in October 1888; rich and prominent citizens were recruited as incorporators and Elizabeth was a prime mover in the raising of funds for the organization. The New York Botanical Garden (NYBG) was established by act of the state legislature in 1891.

Nathaniel became the first director in chief of the Botanical Garden in 1896; Elizabeth joined him in a volunteer capacity. In recognition of her service, Elizabeth was named honorary curator of the mosses in 1912, a post that she held until her death in 1934.

Elizabeth traveled to various locations in the United States to collect botanical specimens, including the Great Dismal Swamp, the Adirondack Mountains, and the mountains of North Carolina. She accompanied Nathaniel on twenty-three of the twenty-five trips he made to the islands of the Caribbean and West Indies. Under her own name she published her findings in the *Bulletin of the Torrey Botanical Club* between 1913 and 1915. Elizabeth wrote the chapters concerning mosses for Nathaniel's *Flora of Bermuda* and *The Bahama Flora*. She worked with organizations to promote the study of mosses, especially by women scientists. She chaired the division of bryophyta for the National Women's Science Club in 1897. She joined the Sullivant Moss Society (renamed, after 1949, as the American Bryological and Lichenological Society) and served as its president from 1916 to 1919.

Elizabeth on one of her expeditions. Unknown photographer. *New York Botanical Gardens / LuEsther T. Mertz Library Vertical Files*

Elizabeth wrote descriptions of six families of mosses for the New York Botanical Garden's *Flora of America*, but she continued to study plants other than mosses. She published *A Revision of the North American Species of Ophioglossum* (adder's-tongue ferns) in 1897.

In the late 1890s Elizabeth began to devote energy to the conservation of wildflowers. A gift of $3,000 to the NYBG spurred the creation of the Wild Flower Preservation Society of America. The first meeting was held on April 23, 1902, and Elizabeth was elected to the board of managers and served as secretary and treasurer of the organization. She vigorously promoted the cause of preserving wildflowers and their habitats for nearly thirty-five years. She focused on publishing, lecturing, and correspondence; her efforts led to adoption of legislation in various states, as well as local conservation activities in garden clubs and schools. She published fourteen articles in the NYBG's *Journal* under the series title Wild Plants Needing Protection. From 1881 to 1930, Elizabeth published 346 papers. About half of them were on mosses, and the rest on the preservation of ferns and wildflowers.

Marshall Avery Howe (1867–1936) was a botanist, taxonomist, and morphologist. He was curator and the third director of the New York Botanical Garden. He described Elizabeth as such: *A woman of extraordinary physical and mental energy—the possessor of a remarkably quick and brilliant intellect. She has left an enduring record in the literature of science, and her well-directed activities have had an outstanding influence in the conservation of the native flora of the United States.*

In 1893 Elizabeth was the only woman among twenty-five scientists nominated for charter membership in the Botanical Society of America. In 1905 she was one of three bryologists appointed to the nomenclature committee that would report to the 1910 meeting of the International Botanical Congress in Brussels, Belgium. In 1906 she was one of only nineteen women out of the 1,000 scientists featured in the first edition of *American Men of Science*. Her entry was marked with an asterisk: this *starred* listing was limited to the top 1,000 scientists in the book as determined by the editors.

Elizabeth Gertrude Britton died at her home in the Bronx on February 25, 1934. At a time when professional opportunities for women were rigidly limited, Elizabeth was all the more outstanding through her leadership, influence, determination, and strong personality.

The moss genus *Bryobrittonia* is named for Elizabeth, as are fifteen species of plants and one animal.

4.23 HELENA RUTHERFURD ELY (1858–1920)

One of the most influential garden writers of the early twentieth century. Her book ***A Woman's Hardy Garden*** *(1903) is widely acknowledged by gardeners and scholars as the most influential practical garden book written by an American woman at that time.*

Helena Rutherfurd Ely before 1920, likely in a book published 1903–1911. *meadowburnfarm.com*

Helena was born on September 28, 1858. In 1881 her mother, having been widowed, gave her a farm, Meadowburn, in Vernon Township in northwestern New Jersey, as a wedding present when she married Alfred Ely, a young lawyer practicing in New York. At that time it was 350 acres of farmland. She set to work on the garden, she said, *with a trowel in hand and joy in my heart*.

Meadowburn Farm in Vernon Township, northwestern New Jersey. *meadowburnfarm.com*

Helena had gardened since she was a child, and, following the fashion of the day, she began to make geometric beds with bright red annuals such as geraniums and salvia. She quickly found this unappealing and began filling plots with the perennial plants that she already knew would do well in her area. She focused on planning her gardens around planting *hardy perennial plants found in the agricultural landscape*. She would stop during rides through the countryside to beg—from complete strangers as well as local friends—cuttings or divisions to grow in her garden.

Her usual gardening outfit consisted of a tweed skirt, old leather gloves, and a leghorn straw hat. She was said to have spent hours on her knees in the mixed borders, which often featured her favorites: phlox, nigella, petunias, and nicotiana. She designed her evergreen garden to include a reflecting pool surrounded by conifers. The 150-foot dahlia border—filled with heirloom varieties—is there today and still explodes with color in the later summer months.

Helena wrote: *I would make the strongest plea in favor of a garden to all those who are so fortunate to possess any land at all. The relaxation from care and toil and the benefit to health are great, beyond belief*. She added, with some spite: *If the rich and fashionable women of this country took more interest and spent more time in their gardens, and less in frivolity, fewer would suffer from the nervous prostration, and necessity for the multitude of sanitariums would be avoided*. Among her other amusing quotations are *I always think of my sins when I weed. They grow apace in the same way and are harder still to get rid of*, and *the watering of a garden requires as much judgement as the seasoning of a soup*.

Her first book, *A Woman's Hardy Garden*, was published by the Macmillan Company in 1903 and sold more than 40,000 copies—an impressive achievement for a garden book, even today. It was reprinted sixteen times before eventually going out of print in 1930. Unlike most gardening books of the time, it offered detailed, practical advice in a manner that was accessible and not intimidating for the beginning woman gardener. It drew on her personal gardening experiences, and it filled a need for practical, easy-to-follow gardening advice that had not been featured in earlier books. Unusually for the time, it was specifically targeted at women, and it assumed that the reader had limited or no experience of gardening techniques. It encouraged the use of hardy plant material with long blooming periods at a time when that concept was unfamiliar in American home gardens. It included plans for possible garden designs and details of suggested plantings. Helena's preface reads: *This little book is only meant to tell briefly of a few shrubs, hardy perennials, biennials and annuals of simple culture. I send it forth, hoping that my readers may find within its pages some help to plant and make their gardens grow.*

Helena followed her first success with *Another Hardy Garden Book*, published in 1905, and *The Practical Flower Garden*, published in 1911 and reissued in 2008. All three of her books encouraged a generation of women gardeners to abandon the Victorian practice of *bedding out* garish-colored tender annuals in geometric beds. Instead, she urged her followers toward a more informal and sensual style. What started as a matter of personal taste became a revolutionary movement and made Helena and her garden early stars of American horticulture.

Helena saw gardening as a common language that all women could turn to in order to improve their own lives and society as a whole, and she set an example for women gardeners throughout America. She was one of the founding members of the Garden Club of America, and she joined like-minded friends in founding the Garden Club of Orange and Dutchess County, an original affiliate of the Garden Club of America. Helena's garden at Meadowburn was a model for thousands of American home gardens. Her 5-acre garden on the New Jersey–New York border became a mecca for her followers, and she was inundated with fan mail.

Helena Rutherfurd Ely died in 1920. For nearly forty years she had welcomed visitors, offered them practical advice, and shared cuttings, bulbs, and plant material. She had been one of the most influential garden writers of the early twentieth century.

At her Meadowburn home, letters were still arriving more than twenty years after her death. On August 9, 1993, Meadowburn Farm was placed on the National Register of Historic Places to recognize Helena Rutherfurd Ely's contributions to gardening.

4.24 MABEL OSGOOD WRIGHT (1859–1934)

Author, ornithologist, and dedicated campaigner for promoting the love of gardening and nature for children

Mabel was born to Samuel and Ellen Haswell Osgood in New York City in 1859. She was educated at home and in private schools in the city, but her father discouraged her from her wish to attend Cornell Medical School because he did not believe that women belonged in the medical profession. Fortunately he did believe that young women should be educated and exposed to ideas, so he introduced her to artists and writers and allowed her to engage in intellectual discussions with prominent thinkers. He built Mosswood, the family's country home, in Fairfield, Connecticut, on a large piece of land and saw to the creation of a beautiful garden. It was here that Mabel learned to appreciate the outdoors and developed her keen observation skills that helped her with her future writing.

In 1884 she married James Osborne Wright, an Englishman, and after an extended visit to England the couple moved to Fairfield so she could be with her family. She was elected the first president of the Fairfield Garden Club. The aims of this were written: *That it might be for the pleasure and profit of amateur gardeners, where ideas could be exchanged, and interest stimulated in the proper care of flowers and vegetable gardens.*

Sometimes Mabel could be found behind a camera, taking beautiful photographs of the natural world. She was an enthusiastic and prolific photographer, and her own photographs often appeared as illustrations in her books. She spent most of her time writing books for children and adults, focusing on helping them form a better appreciation of the beauty of the outdoors. She found inspiration while gardening in her own backyard.

Mabel photographed by her husband, James Osborne Wright.
Library of Congress's Prints and Photographs division

Mabel dedicated her life to the preservation and promotion of natural beauty. Like Frances *"Fannie"* Griscom Parsons (see 4.17), she believed that educating young people to recognize the value of nature and preservation was the key to conservation. Frances Parsons had devoted her life to creating school farms to introduce young people to the joys of gardening and nature, whereas Mabel wrote many stories for children and sought to encourage them to love and appreciate the outdoors through her books and articles in newspapers and magazines. Her ambition was that her stories would bring a greater appreciation of nature to a new generation being raised in a more urban environment.

Mabel's first printed work was the essay *"A New England May Day,"* which appeared in the *New York Evening Post* in 1893. This work was collected with other pieces into her first book, *The Friendship of Nature*, published by Macmillan in 1894.

Apart from gardening and her passion for campaigning for promoting the love of gardening and nature for children, Mabel's other abiding passion was for birds. In 1895 she released the first of many books on birds, *Birdcraft: A Field Book of Two Hundred Song, Game and Water Birds*, published by Macmillan in 1895.

This was a modern field guide to birds for a popular audience. It featured color reproductions from John James Audubon and other artists to illustrate bird species commonly encountered in America. She helped organize the Connecticut Audubon Society, becoming its first president in 1898 and serving for many years. From 1905 to 1928 she was a director of the National Association of Audubon Societies (now the National Audubon Society). She became an associate member of the American Ornithologists' Union in 1895 and was one of the first three women raised to elective membership in 1901.

Mabel pioneered bird protection by establishing Birdcraft Sanctuary in 1914 near her home in Fairfield. The refuge is the oldest private songbird sanctuary in the United States. Within ten years of its opening in 1914, Birdcraft Sanctuary received more than 10,000 visitors and was home to thirty-two different nesting bird species. By the 1940s the sanctuary was home to more than 150 species, and a museum and education center had been added. The site continues to be visited by ever-increasing numbers of school groups as Mabel had envisioned. The Birdcraft Museum and Sanctuary was officially designated a national historic landmark in 1993 and is now a site on the Connecticut Women's Heritage Trail.

In addition to her books on birds Mabel's gardening books include

Flowers and Ferns in Their Haunts (New York: Macmillan, Wright, 1901);
The Garden of a Commuter's Wife, Recorded by the Gardener (New York: Macmillan, 1901);

The Garden, You, and I (New York: Macmillan, 1906) (she published under the pseudonym "Barbara"); and
The Heart of Nature (New York: Macmillan, 1906).

Her gardening books promoted the concept of educating children on the love of nature and the joys of plants and gardening. She was convinced that a respect for, and enjoyment of, nature would improve the character of a growing child. For her gardening books she found inspiration in the large garden at her home in Fairfield. Although Mabel is best known for her nature writing, she also tackled fiction, and some aspects of her work are notable, especially her thoughts on changing social patterns, such as the spread of suburbs and increasing urbanization. Her views on the growth of feminism are interesting—she notes the changing role of women with sympathy on the one hand and attacks careerism on the other. Her inquisitive mind and her appreciation of nature's diversity is typified by one of her quotations: *There is so much to see, so much to learn, and so little time between the first consciousness of the eye and its closing.*

On July 16, 1934, Mabel Osgood Wright succumbed to hypertensive myocardial disease with angina and died in Fairfield. She is buried in Oaklawn Cemetery in that town. She is remembered for her belief that educating young people to recognize the value of nature and preservation was the key to conservation. As such, she had devoted her life to writing many books targeted at children, seeking to encourage them to love and appreciate the outdoors.

4.25 ALICE EASTWOOD (1859–1953)

Self-taught botanist, conservationist, and plant collector; through her 310 articles, Alice promoted a better understanding of plants from the more remote regions of North America.

Alice Eastwood. Unknown photographer. *California Academy of Sciences*

Alice was born in 1859 in Toronto, Canada. The family moved to Denver, Colorado, in 1873. In 1879 she graduated from Shawa Convent Catholic High School in that city. For the next ten years she taught there. Alice became a well-regarded high school teacher and used her teaching salary to explore and identify botanical specimens in the Rockies during her summer vacations. She was a self-taught botanist, obtaining her knowledge from published botany manuals, including Asa Grey's *Manual of Botany* and his *The Flora of Colorado*.

She was a member of the Colorado Biological Association and became known for her botanical trips, her dedication, and her hardiness. Astute and profitable real estate investments in Denver meant that she was self-sufficient, and this allowed her to resign her teaching job and concentrate full time on her real passion: botany.

She had made a name for herself in the botany community, and the California Academy of Sciences invited Alice to write articles for their botany journal *Zoe*. In 1891, after reviewing Alice's impressive specimen collection in Denver, Mary Katharine Brandegee, curator of the botany department at the California Academy of Sciences in San Francisco, hired Alice to work in the academy's herbarium. In 1892 she began the task of organizing the herbarium and oversaw tremendous growth of the number of specimens held there. Alice was soon promoted to a position as joint curator of the academy, sharing the post with Mary Brandegee. By 1894, with the retirement of Mary Brandegee, Alice became procurator and head of the department of botany, a position she held until her retirement in 1949.

In her early botanical work, Alice's expeditions had concentrated on Colorado and the Four Corners region and to the edge of the Big Sur region in western California, comprising a 100-mile-long ruggedly beautiful stretch of seacoast alongside the Pacific Ocean. At the end of the nineteenth century this was a virtual frontier, since no roads penetrated the central coast beyond the Carmel Highlands.

On these expeditions, amazingly, Alice slept rough in abandoned sheds. She got to know all the stagecoach routes by heart and was reputed to average 4 miles per hour on foot. She discovered several unknown plants, including *Salix eastwoodiae*, a shrub growing up to 13 feet tall. This was later named Eastwood's willow for her discovery.

In Alice's day these regions of the West were dangerous and difficult to explore, often uncharted, and made passage through the wild terrain difficult in restrictive, long skirts. Alice solved this problem by designing and making a skirt that could be buttoned in the center to make pants. In one incident she was robbed, and another time she became lost near Colorado's border with Utah and was forced to spend the night on a narrow, precarious canyon ledge.

The herbarium at the California Academy of Sciences in San Francisco had progressed well by 1906 due to Alice's diligent work. Departing from the usual, established curatorial conventions of her day, she segregated the type specimens from the main collection. In the earthquake of 1906 she bravely entered the burning building, and her accurate classification system allowed her to find and rescue 1,497 different specimens. The building had to be demolished, and the academy began construction of a new building. Alice took this opportunity to travel to Europe to study herbaria, including at the British Museum and the Royal Botanic Gardens at Kew, London. She also spent time visiting herbaria in North American regions, including the Gray Herbarium at Harvard University and the New York Botanical Garden.

In 1912 the new academy facilities at Golden Gate Park, San Francisco, were opened, and Alice returned to the position of curator of the herbarium. She set about replacing and reconstructing the lost parts of the collection. She went on numerous collecting expeditions in the western United States, including Alaska and, in 1914, Arizona, Utah, and Idaho. Her method was to keep the first set of each collection for the academy and exchange duplicates with other institutions. Alice contributed thousands of sheets to the academy's herbarium, personally accounting for its growth in size and its representation of western flora. Between 1912 and 1949 she added an impressive 340,000 specimens to the herbarium.

As well as the many articles she published during her career, Alice served as assistant editor for *Erythea*, a journal of botany published by the University of California, Berkeley, between 1893 and 1922. Her main botanical interests were western American Liliaceae and the genera *Lupinus*, *Arctostaphylos*, and *Castilleja*.

Alice was director of the San Francisco Botanical Club for several years throughout the 1890s. In 1929 she helped form the American Fuchsia Society, and in 1949, in recognition of her achievements, they awarded her with its medal of achievement. Among Alice's many campaigns, she succeeded in getting most of Mount Tamalpais in Marin County, California, declared a state park, where a campground is named in honor of her conservation efforts.

She was a prime mover in saving a grove of redwood trees in Humboldt County, which was later named Alice Eastwood Memorial Grove. She was worried about the loss of plant diversity and was an advocate that we should be good stewards and preservers of nature, especially flora, and most particularly if humans were the cause of any loss.

In 1892 Alice was elected a member of the California Academy of Sciences, and later, in 1942, she was unanimously elected an honorary member of the academy. In 1903 she was one of only two women listed in *American Men of Science*. She was denoted, by a star, as being considered to be among the top 25 percent of professionals in their discipline.

The genera *Eastwoodia* and *Aliciella* are named for her; there are currently seventeen recognized species named for Alice, including

Agoseris apargioides var. eastwoodiae (woolly goat chicory),
Eastwood's seaside agoseris (beach dandelion),
Amsinckia eastwoodiae (Eastwood's fiddleneck),
Delphinium parryi ssp. eastwoodiae (Eastwood's larkspur),
Fritillaria eastwoodiae (Butte County fritillary),
Salix eastwoodiae (Eastwood's willow),
Aliciella latifolia,
Erigeron aliceae, and
Eastwoodia elegans.

Alice gave a lecture at the Santa Barbara Museum of Natural History in 1929. As reported in that institution's *April Leaflet* of that year: *Miss Eastwood is not only an admirable scientist, but a rare human being as well. A simple, kindly woman stood before her audience and told with utter lack of self-consciousness of experiences which not one woman in a thousand would care to undergo.*

Alice worked until the age of ninety, then curator emeritus. She never married and was heard to state that a romantic attachment might interfere with her true love—botany. Alice Eastwood died in San Francisco on October 30, 1953.

A skilled and tenacious botanist, conservationist, and plant collector, she has left a rich legacy. She wrote more than 310 articles on flora and encouraged a better understanding of plants from more remote regions of North America. She was a tireless campaigner of better appreciation of rare species—and of their conservation. In 1959 the California Academy of Sciences opened the Eastwood Hall of Botany in her honor.

4.26 MARY VAUX WALCOTT (1860–1940)

Botanical watercolor artist and photographer

Mary Morris Vaux was born in Philadelphia, Pennsylvania, to a wealthy Quaker family. She was given a set of watercolor paints as a present when she was eight years old, and she began experimenting with painting flowers. After graduating from the Friends Select School in Philadelphia in 1879, when not working on the family farm she began painting illustrations of wildflowers. After her mother's death when Mary was only nineteen, she had to take on the responsibility of looking after her two younger brothers and father. The family used to spend their summers in the Canadian Rockies. After 1887 Mary returned to western Canada almost every summer with her brothers and became an active mountain climber, outdoorswoman, and photographer.

One summer a botanist asked her to paint a rare blooming *Arnica montana*, a moderately toxic flowering plant of the sunflower family noted for its large yellow flower head. The botanist was pleased with the resulting watercolor, and this encouraged Mary to concentrate on botanical illustrations.

For many years after, Mary explored wild, difficult terrain in the Canadian Rockies, looking for flowering species to paint. On one of these trips she became the first woman to reach the 10,495-foot summit of Mount Stephen, in the Kicking Horse River valley of Yoho National Park, British Columbia, Canada. In 1887, on her first transcontinental trip by rail, she wrote a travel journal of the family's four-month trek through the American West and the Canadian Rockies.

In 1913 Mary met Charles Doolittle Walcott, then secretary of the Smithsonian Institution, when he was conducting geological research. Her love of nature was expressed in a letter to Charles: *Sometimes I feel that I can hardly wait till the time comes*

Mary Vaux Walcott at Great Falls on the Potomac River on April 30, 1914. *Smithsonian Institute Archives*

to escape from city life, to the free air of the everlasting hills. They married a year later, when she was fifty-four, and she played an active part in her husband's research projects. From 1915 onward, the couple spent three to four months every year in the Canadian Rockies, where Dr. Walcott worked on his geological and paleontological studies. During these summers Mary painted hundreds of watercolor studies of flowers native to the region. Her work is regarded as extremely skillful, accurately depicting every detail.

In addition to her paintings, Mary took hundreds of photographs, capturing her travels through the Rockies. Many of her photographs are kept in the collections of the Whyte Museum of the Canadian Rockies in Banff, Alberta. Her paintings, photographs, and writings provide an early record of the unspoiled mountains.

In 1925, the Smithsonian Institute published some 400 of her illustrations, accompanied by brief descriptions, in a five-volume work titled *North American Wild Flowers*. It was published in an edition limited to 500 sets, and each portfolio contained eighty loose lithographs of floral specimens with descriptive text. The reproduction of her paintings was instrumental in the development of a new technique for printing, which came to be known as the Smithsonian Process. Later, in 1935, the Smithsonian would again publish a volume of her work; *Illustrations of North American Pitcherplants* included fifteen of Mary's paintings.

From 1927 to 1932 Mary served on the Federal Board of Indian Commissioners, and she traveled extensively throughout the American West, diligently visiting and reporting on Native American reservations. In 1933 Mary was elected president of the Society of Woman Geographers.

Mary wrote her thoughts on field photography in an article titled "Camping in the Canadian Rockies," published in the *Canadian Alpine Journal*. She wrote:

> *A camera is a very delightful adjunct, for it is pleasant to have some tangible results to show, on your return home. A Kodak, if no larger instrument can be managed, yields most satisfactory results, although the better records from a larger-sized camera are an increased delight, when one has the patience and skill to obtain them.*

Following the death of her husband in 1927, Mary established the Charles Doolittle Walcott Medal in his honor. It was awarded for scientific work on pre-Cambrian and Cambrian life and history. Mary Vaux Walcott died in St. Andrews, New Brunswick, in 1940. A mountain in Jasper National Park, Alberta, Canada, carries the name Mount Mary Vaux in her honor.

4.27 FRANCES THEODORA PARSONS (1861–1952)

A naturalist and author who wrote a number of books, including a very popular guide to American wildflowers

Frances was born in New York in 1861 to Denton Smith, a tea merchant, and Harriet Shelton Smith. Her sister, Alice Josephine (1859–1909), became an artist and later illustrated some of her books. Frances was educated privately at Miss Comstock's School. During summer vacations she would stay with her grandparents in rural New York State, and it was here that she found a love of botany.

She married a naval officer, William Starr Dana, in 1884, but he died in an 1890 flu epidemic. Six years later she married James Russell Parsons, a politician in the state of New York. He died in 1902 in an automobile accident in Mexico City. Following James's death, Frances moved to New York City, where she was an active supporter of the Republican Party, as well as the Progressive Party. She served in various official capacities on party committees, and she managed Fiorello H. La Guardia's successful campaign to become president of New York's Board of Aldermen. She was also a keen supporter of women's suffrage.

During this time she became friends with Marion Satterlee, a botanical illustrator. Their walks and chats together inspired Frances to sit down and write her first book, *How to Know the Wild Flowers: A Guide to the Names, Haunts, and Habits of Our Common Wild Flowers*.

The book was published under the pen name Mrs. William Starr Dana, from her first husband. *How to Know the Wild Flowers* was the first field guide to North American wildflowers and was very successful, with the first printing selling out in

Photograph of Frances Theodora Parsons as the frontispiece in the *Fern Bulletin* 10, no. 1 (Jan. 1902). Charles Scribner's Sons (her publisher) provided the photo to Willard N. Clute (*Fern Bulletin* editor), photographer not listed. *Guttenberg.org*

five days. It received critical acclaim, including favorable remarks from Theodore Roosevelt and Rudyard Kipling.

The beginnings of the conservation movement took place in the 1890s, and this book was the first of many such books published between 1890 and the early years of the twentieth century. Arranged by flower colors, *How to Know the Wild Flowers* describes each plant, as well as giving botanical data and a guide as to where to find it. Several editions of the work were published in Frances's lifetime, and the book remained in print well into the twentieth century, including one published by Houghton Mifflin Harcourt in 1989.

Frances's second book, *According to Season*, was published in 1894—this time under her own name. The book was a compendium of nature articles that she had previously published in the *New York Tribune*.

Her third book, *Plants and Their Children* (1896), published by the American Book Company, was intended for children and was listed as one of the fifty best children's books of its day. It was again illustrated by Marion Satterlee, and France's sister, Alice, also provided artwork. Frances reverted to her pen name Mrs. William Starr Dana, and the first printing of *Plants and Their Children* was by the Publisher's Syndicate Limited. There were at least seven more printings between 1899 and 1925 by Charles Scribner's Sons and Dover Books, and one in 2005 by Kessinger.

The text is divided into seven parts, six of which examine different facets of plants, including flowers, stems, roots, seeds, leaves, and buds. It provides detailed descriptions unencumbered by scientific jargon. In the final chapter, Frances encourages her child readers to *learn to see* nature by taking time during their summer vacations to look for the minute differences between different plants described in the text. As she explains, *The world is full of things that are beautiful and interesting; things that do not cost money, that can be held for the seeing.*

For Frances's next book she used her own name once more, insisting that Marion Satterlee once again be the illustrator. *How to Know the Ferns* (1899), also by Charles Scribner's Sons, was given the subtitle *A Guide to the Names, Haunts, and Habits of Our Common Ferns*.

Botany was not the only thing in France's life; during her lifetime she worked tirelessly for wounded WWI veterans, New York City public schools, and the protection of Central Park.

It was in 1952, at age ninety, that Frances Theodora Parsons published a memoir, *Perchance Some Day*. Her life's work complete, Frances died that same year. It is as a successful author that she will be best remembered, but in addition to her nature writing, Frances had been very involved in the politics of her era.

4.28 EDITH WHARTON (1862–1937)

Edith was a Pulitzer Prize–winning novelist, as well as a talented house and garden designer.

Edith was born Edith Newbold Jones in 1862 to George Frederick Jones and Lucretia Stevens Rhinelander. Growing up, she lived within the inner circle of New York society. Her father, although not really wealthy, was able to live, as she said, *a life of leisure and amiable hospitality*. When she was four years old the family went abroad in pursuit of culture and to benefit their health, and thus her early impressions were influenced by Rome, Paris, and Madrid, as well as New York, Newport, and Rhode Island in the USA.

She was never sent to school, but, as was the custom of families of her time who could afford the cost, she was taught at home. Edith was born into a tightly controlled society at a time when women were discouraged from achieving anything beyond finding a suitable partner to result in a successful marriage and children. Despite not being encouraged to write by her parents, friends, or siblings, Edith broke through these strictures to become one of America's greatest writers. Her first novel was written when she was just eleven years old, and she began writing short stories in her early teens. Edith's first work was written on brown paper she had rescued from parcel wrapping. Later in her career she looked back on these early days and said, *In the eyes of our provincial society, authorship was still regarded as something between a black art and a form of manual labor*.

Edith got her surname from Edward Wharton, a Boston banker whom she married in 1885. In her private life Edith would keep writing, although precisely

Edith Wharton, taken by E. F. Cooper in Newport, Rhode Island. Cabinet photograph ca. 1889–1890. *Beinecke Rare Book & Manuscript Library, Yale University*

how much is unknown. Eminent author Henry James became Edith's closest friend and her most helpful mentor in pursuing her writing, and over her seventy-five years she was to publish thirty-eight books.

Edith's first success was three poems she sent to an editor with her calling card attached. But Edith's first published book was cowritten with architect Ogden Codman Jr. *The Decoration of Homes* (1897), published by Charles Scribner's Sons, was illustrated with fifty-six plates and is a comprehensive look at the history and character of turn-of-the-twentieth-century interior design, moving from historical traditions to the distinctive styles of contemporary taste. It is considered a seminal work, and its success led to the emergence of professional decorators working in the manner identified by its authors.

The sunken Italian Garden at the Mount uses tones of greens and whites. The centerpiece is a rustic rock pile fountain surrounded by white begonias. *edithwharton.org*

It wasn't until 1899 that she published her first fiction, *The Greater Inclination*, again published by Charles Scribner's Sons, as were many of her future endeavors. However, the volume did not make her an overnight success. In fact, it was not until 1905 that she achieved a large public.

In the interim period she wrote several books, and her love of travel resulted in two volumes on the villas and gardens of Italy. In 1905 she published the first of her bestsellers, *The House of Mirth* (1905), and its popularity established her as a writer.

Other novels came in rapid succession, but none attracted real attention or book sales like *Ethan Frome* (1911), the novel journalist Elmer Davis called *the last great American love story*.

The Age of Innocence (1920) was her next book and, in terms of sales, her most successful. It focused on the social life of New York into which she had been born. It was awarded the Pulitzer Prize in 1921.

Beatrix Farrand (see 4.42) was Edith's niece, and her relationship with Edith was significant in terms of garden design. Beatrix was a towering figure in the world of landscape architecture and one of North America's most influential figures. Edith was especially well connected in the elite social circles of the day and helped further Beatrix's garden design career by introducing her to many people who soon became her clients. She arranged for Beatrix to do some work for some of their cousins and others: Clement B. Newbold in Pennsylvania, Tom Newbold in New York, Mrs. Gordon Bell in Connecticut, and Emily Vanderbilt Sloane.

As a successful writer, Edith was somewhat of an arbiter of good taste in American society during what came to be known as the Gilded Age—an era of rapid economic growth, especially in the North and West. She once wrote the following in a letter to a friend: *The American landscape has no foreground and the American mind no background*. Edith produced many books on architecture, gardens, and interior decorating. Similarly, during this time Edith's country estate, the Mount, in Lenox, Massachusetts, was being finished. The estate and garden were representative of the Country Place era in the United States, which began in the late nineteenth century and had all but ended by the 1920s as the Great Depression approached.

The Mount's situation in the Berkshire Mountains of western Massachusetts provided a picturesque backdrop for Edith's country estate. A panoramic view of the American mountains and surrounding natural wild landscape helped make a real contrast to the geometry of a formal garden.

A view of the Mount Gardens. As Wharton elaborated in *Italian Villas and Their Gardens* (1904), a garden should be architectural compositions, just like houses. She envisioned her gardens as an elegant series of outdoor rooms in harmony with the house and the surrounding natural landscape. *edithwharton.org*

Like other members of the cultural elite, Edith felt it necessary to import European elements into her garden design. While she was aided by Beatrix Farrand in the design and planting of the garden, Edith contributed greatly to the finished landscape. Both architects and landscape architects were much in demand during this era and received large commissions for the designing and building of the gardens for country estates. However, there is no doubt that the garden design of the Mount was greatly influenced by Edith's input. Edith had her gardens at the Mount landscaped and laid out around her thoughts about Italian gardens. However, Beatrix Farrand designed Edith's kitchen garden; there is a design drawing by her dated July 14, 1901.

Edith loved phlox, stocks, lilies, hydrangea, dianthus, delphinium, and dahlias, all of which still feature in the flower beds of the Mount today.

Edith had written in her *Italian Villas and Their Gardens*, published in 1904, that European garden elements could not simply be appropriated into the American landscape, or any landscape. She believed these more formal garden elements and designs had to be fitted correctly into their own existing landscape settings.

The main feature of her gardens at the Mount is a Lime Walk—a gravel path lined with pleached (branches entwined or interlaced) linden trees—which connects the Italian garden to the more formal French flower garden, in which a rectangular pool is surrounded by beds of annuals, perennials, and shrubs. The gardens also include a rock garden complete with molded grass steps cut into a sloping hill—a landscape feature rarely seen in America.

In a letter to Morton Fullerton, Edith confessed how much of herself she had put into the Mount: *I am amazed at the success of my efforts. Decidedly, I'm a better landscape gardener than novelist, and this place, every line of which is my own work, far surpasses the House of Mirth*.

The Whartons sold the Mount in 1911, and they divorced in 1913. When WWI broke out, Edith was in Paris. She immediately volunteered for relief work, opening a room for skilled women who were thrown out of employment by the closing of workrooms. She also fed and housed 600 Belgian refugee orphans. After four years of intense effort, she decided to leave Paris in favor of the peace and quiet of the countryside. She settled 10 miles north of Paris in Saint-Brice-sous-Forêt, buying an eighteenth-century chateau on 7 acres of land that she called Le Pavillon Colombe. She lived in France the rest of her life, spending the colder months in the French Riviera.

Over the years, Edith was increasingly recognized for her contribution to writing. In 1924 she became the first woman to be awarded an honorary doctor of letters degree by Yale University. Then, in 1929, Edith was awarded the gold medal of the National Institute of Arts and Letters, the first woman to be so honored. By 1930 she had been made a member of the National Institute of Arts and Letters, and four years later she was elected to membership in the American Academy of Arts and Letters.

Three years after that, in 1937, Edith had a stroke and died at her beloved French retreat. She was buried in the Cimetière des Gonards in Versailles. She had been a hugely successful author but had also been known and highly regarded as a garden designer. Her feel for combining Italianate design and features with nature and the existing landscape was innovative and had resulted in exceptional gardens in the USA and France. The prime example of her garden design skills remains her home the Mount in Lenox, Massachusetts.

4.29 LOUISA BOYD YEOMANS KING (1863–1948)

A leading advocate of gardening and horticulture and the establishment of garden clubs, she wrote books and articles on all kinds of horticultural topics.

Born in 1863, Louisa's parents were Henry W. and Aurelia Yeomans. They lived at an estate called Wilder Park in Elmhurst, Illinois. Louisa's mother-in-law was a skilled gardener, having cultivated 200 varieties of herbs, flowers, plants, and fruit trees, and her library was well stocked with horticultural books. Under her instruction and encouragement, Louisa developed both an academic interest in the study of plants and a practical enjoyment of hands-on gardening: improving the soil, pruning plants, and controlling pests.

In 1890 she married a wealthy Chicago man, Francis King, and moved near the home of her parents in Elmhurst, Illinois. In 1902, as a result of poor health, Francis moved to a sanatorium in Alma, Michigan. The couple liked the area and built a home called Orchard House there, where Louisa began to design and plant a garden. The garden at Orchard House would later feature in a number of her writings.

Louisa quickly rose to prominence as a lecturer, author, and organizer of garden clubs, and in gardening circles in the early 1900s, few women were as influential. By 1910 she was contributing articles to magazines such as *Garden Magazine*, *Saturday Evening Post*, *Garden Life*, and *Country Life*. For three years, starting in 1922, she wrote a monthly gardening column for *House Beautiful*. She corresponded with notable British and American gardeners of the day, including renowned garden designer Gertrude Jekyll in England. As an advocate of *modern*

Louisa Boyd Yeomans King (ca. 1910) from her biography at the website of Clarke Historical Library. Photographer unknown. *Central Michigan University Library*

gardening, Louisa favored gardens that fit naturally into the landscape, and she promoted solid fields of color, as opposed to the scattered arrangements used by more traditional Victorian era gardeners.

She believed that gardening and garden clubs should not be elitist and could be important forces to promote democracy and peace. She insisted that gardening was fundamental to American democracy. In her writing she often argued that a love of plants could break down differences between different economic groups and neighbors, and she believed that gardening served the human spirit. She said,

Rich or poor, old or free, when we garden we are at the same work; we work in faith that the seasons will still roll for us and for our sowings and plantings. There is no other such meeting-ground, there is no community of interest such as this of gardens.

"The Woman's Land Army of America Training School, University of Virginia—Apply Woman's Land Army, U.S. Employment Service, Richmond, Va.," Herbert Andrew Paus (ca. 1918). *Prints and Photographs Division, Library of Congress, Washington, DC*

The garden clubs in which Louisa was involved were more than simple social organizations; they gave women a means to organize and educate themselves in an era when women's public roles were highly restricted. The clubs provided them access to educational sources, discussion groups, and resources that otherwise would have been denied them.

In 1912 Louisa formed the Gardeners Club of Michigan, serving as its first president. The following year she was one of the cofounders and original vice presidents of the Garden Club of America in Philadelphia, which had a substantial influence on how landscape architecture developed as a profession in subsequent decades. In 1914 the Horticultural Society of Massachusetts, which describes itself as the oldest formally organized horticultural institution in the United States, awarded her its George Robert White Medal, the first female recipient.

After being introduced to the British Women's Farm & Garden organization during a visit to Europe, Louisa returned home, determined to create a similar association in the USA.

In 1914 she helped found the Women's National Agricultural and Horticultural Association, which two years later changed its name to the Woman's National Farm & Garden Association (WNF&GA). Louisa, who served as the first president from 1914 to 1921, saw horticulture and gardening as a means for women to establish themselves in the world; under her guidance the association established scholarships for women to pursue the academic study of agriculture, botany, and landscape architecture. It provided an outlet for many whose access to formal higher education was limited or denied.

During WWI the association helped organize the Woman's Land Army of America: 15,000 so-called *farmerettes* worked in agriculture, replacing men called into military service.

Louisa's first book, *The Well-Considered Garden*, appeared in 1915, published by Charles Scribner's Sons. It was the first of ten books published in a fifteen-year period on topics such as soil management, garden planning, and tool care.

In the years after the end of WWI, gardening in small suburban plots grew in popularity, in part inspired and encouraged by a nine-volume set of books known as The Little Garden series. Louisa edited these and wrote some of them. She strongly believed that gardening broke down barriers between people. Louisa's earlier books had been targeted at the affluent, but her The Little Garden series was directed to a new and broader audience: wives in the rapidly expanding postwar suburbs who could create gardens in their small urban lots. Gardening was no longer a pastime for the rich, who could afford to hire laborers to do the work. She also strongly advocated involving children in gardening. Her descriptive prose was supplemented by plant lists, garden diagrams, photographs, and illustrations.

In writing about gardens, Louisa discussed design, color, planning, and function, with an emphasis on the garden as an entire unit of space. She had little to say about pests or diseases; her interest lay in the garden as a work of art. Design, not pest control, was her crusading interest. She said, *It is the lack of plan that is responsible for most that is ugly in America*. She advocated artistry over practicality, particularly when it came to groupings of plants and color combinations.

The Medal of Honor (also known as the Gold Medal) of the Garden Club of America was awarded to Louisa in 1923. A few years later, in 1927, her husband died unexpectedly, and this forced the sale of Orchard House. Louisa traveled in Europe and then settled in New York. She bought a home in South Hartford, New York, naming it Kingstree, and planned and designed a smaller garden there. She continued to lecture and write, and she served as a gardening advisor to the department store chain Montgomery Ward in 1943.

An avid supporter of the United Nations, Louisa proposed an International Horticultural Society, writing, *Gardeners never fight with each other*. She saw gardening as a democratic force that could bring people together and help women establish themselves in numerous garden-related professions. As an ardent suffragist, she was active in the Michigan campaign for women's suffrage, promoting the advancement of women throughout her career.

Louisa Boyd Yeomans King died on January 16, 1948; her ashes were scattered at Kingstree, in South Hartford.

Louisa was once toasted by the Prince of the Netherlands, tongue in cheek, as the *King of America*, and she had been called the *fairy godmother of gardening in America*, the *Dean of American gardeners*, and *the best-beloved and best-known American woman gardener* of her era. Cultivars of tulip, gladiolus, and daffodil were named for her, and the Dogwood Collection at the National Arboretum in Washington, DC, was created in her honor.

4.30 HARRIETT RISLEY FOOTE (1863–1951)

Pioneer, rosarian, and author

Born in Waterville, New York, in 1863, Harriet was awarded a bachelor's degree from Smith College in 1886, traveled Europe, attended graduate school in Germany, then returned to the USA to teach. In 1891 she married the Rev. Henry Foote, and they lived in Marblehead, Massachusetts. Harriet began experimenting with growing roses in the rectory garden. She did not start out totally ignorant, but she and her husband avidly read everything that they could find in the few books that were available on growing roses. Many of the great advances in rose breeding had not yet occurred when she began her work. She soon recognized the effects that variation in climate and soil had on her plants.

Her name first appears in a list of commendations from Albert Emerson Benson's *History of the Massachusetts Horticultural Society*. In 1910 Harriet's rose garden in Marblehead contained 900 varieties of roses, principally hybrid teas, hybrid perpetuals, noisettes, and bourbons. Because commercial rose growing did

Harriet Foote

not really start in North America until about 1914, Harriet was somewhat ahead of her time. Prior to 1914 the public could buy only prairie queen, Baltimore belle, and a few hybrid perpetuals.

As word of her work spread, she received commissions to design rose gardens, expanding her practice after her husband's death in 1918. In her 4-acre nursery she grew almost 10,000 specimens of roses known for their vigor, height, and their abundant blooms. Many of her varieties were extremely demanding to grow, unlike the tough, disease-resistant varieties of today. There were very few grafted roses—every specimen was *own-root*. She developed her growing techniques through trial and error.

She joined the English National Rose Society, and her first garden contained roses imported from Scotland. These were the first tender roses to be grown outdoors in New England. The Massachusetts Horticultural Society Garden Committee singled her out for special commendation, and its archives tell us that Harriet created rose gardens for other people with one assistant, Miss Emma Schumaker. For instance, it is recorded that she planted 400 bushes for the Spaulding family. Her rose garden at the Cedars, the summer home of architect Henry Sargent Hunnewell, won a Massachusetts Horticultural Society Gold Medal in 1923. In 1927 the society awarded her a Gold Medal for her lifelong achievements.

Harriet noted that there was little available to give amateur gardeners advice on preparing the soil, planting, pruning, feeding, and nurturing roses, which resulted in her writing a book on the subject. In 1948 Charles T. Branford Co. of Boston published *Mrs Foote's Rose Book*, which described her cultivation methods in detail.

Her insistence that enough leaves remain on a rosebush was based on good science. A rose's nutrition comes from the leaves, and if one removes those recklessly, the plant has less energy to produce flowers. Harriet claimed that one reason her hybrid tea roses grew very tall was that she planted them close together, between 12 and 16 in. apart. They tended to give each other a little support, and their tops shaded the soil beneath them.

As Harriet's reputation grew, her work was featured in a number of garden magazines. Her garden designs include the Henry and Clara Ford estate in Michigan; the Arthur and Harriet Curtiss James's estate, sitting atop the tallest hill on Aquidneck Island, Rhode Island; the garden of Mr. and Mrs. Edwin Webster in Quissett, Massachusetts; and the Richard and Florence Crane Castle Hill estate on Argilla Road in Ipswich, Massachusetts.

Mary Frothingham was a client. Her Georgian Revival style mansion known as Wayside in Easton, Massachusetts, was built in 1912. Harriett designed her rose garden, selected the roses, and supervised their planting. In 1924 the American Rose Society honored her rose garden with a visit during their annual meeting.

Harriett Risley Foote, pioneer rosarian and respected garden designer, died in 1951. She is an excellent example of a garden enthusiast who, despite a total lack of any formal training, became a knowledgeable and competent expert in her field through diligent research, experimentation, and sheer hard work.

4.31 HULDA KLAGER (1863–1960)

German-born Hulda became known as the Lilac Lady.

Hulda was born in Germany and arrived in North America in 1865, when she was two years old. The family first lived in Wisconsin. She often spoke of her love for flowers and how, as a little girl in Wisconsin, she would wander through the woods near her home looking for wildflowers. They moved for a short time to Minnesota before settling in Lewis County, Washington, near the town of Woodland, thirty minutes north of Portland. There, when Hulda was thirteen, they purchased farmland and built a home.

Part of Hulda Klager Lilac Gardens in Woodland, Washington. *WoodlandLilacGardens*

Hulda's schooling never went beyond eighth grade. Her interest in horticulture began at home. She studied botany and avidly read gardening books and gardening

Hulda Klager in 1948, after the floods. *columbian.com*

catalogs. In her early teens Hulda married Frank Klager. While she was recovering from an illness in 1903, some of her friends brought her a book, *New Creations in Plant Life* by W. S. Harwood, published by Macmillan in 1905. Here she learned about the work and methods of Luther Burbank, a renowned flower hybridizer of the time. This was a source of inspiration to her, and she was anxious to begin her own experiments with hybridizing plants—initially on apples. She felt it took too long to peel little apples to make pies, and, to save time, she wanted to develop a bigger apple by crossing the mild Wolf River apple with the sour, juicy Bismarck apple. She was delighted with the result, and, encouraged, this led to her hybridizing one of her favorite plants, the lilac.

Lilacs—*Syringa* species and cultivars (a variety of plant that originated and persisted under cultivation)—are native to woodland and scrub regions from southeastern Europe to East Asia. They are a flowering, woody plant in the olive family. They are widely grown in temperate regions and valued for their fragrant blooms in spring. The genus contains more than twenty species and more than a thousand named cultivars. Common lilacs (*Syringa vulgaris)*, often referred to as French hybrids, make up the majority of garden favorites.

Hulda's breeding objectives were to create vigorous, disease-resistant plants through hybridization; to extend the plant's flower color range into clear blue, pink, and rose; and to create variations in flower cluster forms and floret size. In only five years she had created fourteen new cultivars. According to lilac expert Reverend John Fiala, the cornerstones of her crosses—her "magic three"—were *Syringa vulgaris* 'Mme Casimir Périer,' *Syringa vulgaris* 'President Grevy,' and *Syringa vulgaris* 'Andenken an Ludwig Späth.' Reverend Fiala's 1988 book *Lilacs: A Gardener's Encyclopedia* (known worldwide as the "lilac lovers' bible") tells how Hulda introduced more than 100 lilac cultivars and became known as the Lilac Lady.

By 1920 Hulda had developed so many new varieties that she decided to hold an open house each spring, when the lilacs were in full bloom, to share her efforts with other lilac enthusiasts. It was a success and became an annual event eagerly anticipated by lilac enthusiasts, who would travel many miles to see what was new and to purchase plants to take back for their own gardens. Around 1930, neighboring towns began sending delegations during Hulda's Lilac Week to choose one of the new varieties that she had developed to be named for their community. In this manner, lilac varieties such as the 'City of Longview,' 'City of Kalama,' 'City of Gresham,' and 'City of Woodland' were designated.

Following the death of her husband, in 1922 Hulda was depressed and was thinking about abandoning her work with lilacs. She almost threw away a number of hand-pollinated plants that she had taken a special interest in. Fortunately her son Fritz insisted that she continue to nurture them, and from these plants emerged some of her very best lilacs. Spring 1948 brought a major catastrophe when the swollen waters of the Columbia River flooded her property, wiping out her lilac gardens and nearly every other shrub on the site. Only the big trees withstood the flood, but, undaunted even at age eighty-three, Hulda set about rebuilding her garden.

Many people who had purchased her lilacs in the past dug them up and returned them to her so that she could replace her losses. It took two years and a great deal of work, but in 1950 she was able to open her gardens for Lilac Week once again.

Through the years Hulda has been honored by many organizations for her work as a leading hybridizer of lilacs, including the State of Washington, the Arnold Arboretum at Harvard University, the Federation of Garden Clubs in Washington and Oregon, and the city of Portland, Oregon.

After Hulda Klager's death in 1960 at age ninety-six, the Woodland Federated Garden Club heard that the garden was to be bulldozed to make way for an industrial site. They decided to save it and succeeded in having it declared a state and national historic site. The Hulda Klager Lilac Society, a nonprofit organization, was formed in 1976 to administer the estate. Today the Hulda Klager Lilac Gardens contains more than ninety varieties of lilacs, as well as Victorian gardens and a farmhouse. The house was restored and has been turned into a museum to honor the Lilac Lady. Hulda Klager is an excellent example of a woman devoting her whole life to just one species of plant.

4.32 MARGARET CLAY FERGUSON (1863–1951)

Plant physiologist and geneticist, Margaret was the first woman president of the Botanical Society of America.

Margaret Clay Ferguson. Photographer unknown. *Smithsonian Institution Archives*

Margaret was born in Phelps, New York, in 1863. The family operated a farm focused on growing cabbages, wheat, and potatoes. This was the basis for her interest in agriculture and in plant genetics. In 1877, when just fourteen, Margaret was both a student at Genesee Wesleyan Seminary in Lima, New York, and also a teacher in the local public school. She graduated from Genesee in 1885 and was appointed assistant principal in 1887. In 1888 she enrolled in Wellesley College's *teacher special* program. This had been set up for working teachers who wanted to further their careers as educators.

After specializing in botany and chemistry, in 1891 Margaret accepted a position as head of the science department at Harcourt Place Seminary in Gambier, Ohio. In 1893 she returned to Wellesley as a botany instructor. In 1896 she left Wellesley to tour Europe. Returning in 1897, she enrolled at Cornell University, from which she received a BS in 1899 and a PhD in botany in 1901. She was then appointed associate professor of botany at Wellesley in 1904 and, shortly after, was elevated to professor of botany and head of the department, a position she held until her retirement in 1930.

Margaret is credited with opening up the world of botany to women and encouraging and training more women than any person before her. Laboratory work was always the focus of her teaching, and her diligent work resulted in her department being acknowledged as one of the leading institutions in the whole of the USA for the study of plant science.

Margaret worked on a variety of plant systems, including fungi, pines, and petunias, while at Wellesley, and she planned, designed, and raised the money for a new botany building and two greenhouses. The Margaret Clay Ferguson greenhouse complex in Wellesley College Botanic Gardens is named in her honor. It now includes more than a dozen interconnected greenhouses with a permanent collection of plants ranging from desert to rainforest habitats.

She insisted that space was provided in these greenhouses for students to grow plants and conduct their own experiments in plant genetics, horticulture, and physiology.

In the 1890s Margaret's focus moved to genetics. She identified the potential for petunia plants as a tool for studying plant genetics. The principles of Mendelian inheritance were named after Gregor Johann Mendel, a nineteenth-century Austrian monk who formulated his ideas after conducting simple hybridization experiments with pea plants (*Pisum sativum*) that he had planted in the garden of his monastery.

Between 1856 and 1863, Mendel cultivated and tested more than 5,000 pea plants. From these experiments he formed two generalizations, which later became known as Mendel's principles of heredity, or Mendelian inheritance. He conceived the idea of heredity units, which he called *factors*. Mendel discovered that there are alternative forms of factors—now called genes—that account for variations in inherited plant characteristics.

Within her experiments with petunia plants, Margaret found no proof of Mendelian inheritance for flower color or pattern, and she bravely suggested that the long-held accepted facts proposed by Mendel in this context were, in fact, unreliable. This controversial statement was confirmed as correct in later experiments and studies conducted by others in the 1970s. Margaret was also known for her work on the life histories of North American pines.

Margaret was a member of Sigma Xi, California Academy of Science, American Association of University Professors, American Genetic Association, American Society of Naturalists, American Association of University Women, Science League of America, Massachusetts Horticultural Society, Eugenics Society of the United States, American Microscopical Society (vice president 1914), and Botanical Society of America (vice president 1922). Margaret was elected the first woman president of the Botanical Society of America in 1929. Later, in 1932, she was elected a fellow by the American Association for the Advancement of Science.

She retired from Wellesley College in 1930, although she continued her research work until 1938 at age seventy-five. Margaret received an honorary doctorate from Mount Holyoke and remained a highly respected teacher and specialist in botany, having authored twenty-seven scientific papers dealing with problems in plant physiology, genetics, cytology, and comparative morphology. In her later years Margaret Clay Ferguson spent time in Florida before moving to San Diego, California, where she died of a heart attack in 1951.

4.33 FRANCES BENJAMIN JOHNSTON (1864–1952)

Photographer, lecturer, and conservationist

Frances "Fannie" Benjamin Johnston was an early American photographer and photojournalist. She is most known for her images of southern architecture and for recording North American gardens. The only surviving child of wealthy and well-connected parents, she was born in Grafton, West Virginia, and raised in Washington, DC. Frances studied at the Académie Julian in Paris and the Washington Students League. After her graduation in 1883 from Notre Dame of Maryland Collegiate Institute for Young Ladies (now known as Notre Dame of Maryland University), she wrote articles for periodicals before finding her creative outlet through photography.

George Eastman, inventor of the new, lighter Eastman Kodak cameras and a close friend of the family, gave Frances her first camera. She received training in photography and darkroom techniques from Thomas Smillie, director of photography at the Smithsonian Institute.

She took portraits of friends, family, and local figures before working as a freelance photographer and touring Europe in the 1890s. Frances used her connection to Thomas Smillie to visit prominent photographers and gathered items for the museum's collections.

Frances gained further practical experience in photography by working for Kodak in Washington, DC. There she forwarded film for development and advised customers when their cameras needed repairs. In 1894 she opened her own photographic studio in Washington, DC, on V Street between 13th and 14th Streets and was the only woman photographer in the city at the time.

Frances Benjamin Johnston self-portrait (as *New Woman*), 1896, taken in her Washington, DC, studio. *Library of Congress's Prints and Photographs division*

Photograph by Frances Johnston of Millefiori, Albert Barnes Boardman house, Great Plains Road and Coopers Neck Lane, Southampton, New York. Steps to flower garden, 1914. *Library of Congress Collection*

Frances was well connected among elite society and was commissioned by magazines to do celebrity portraits, such as Alice Roosevelt's wedding portrait, Admiral Dewey on the deck of USS *Olympia*, and the Roosevelt children playing with their pet pony at the White House. She was nicknamed *photographer to the American court*. Perhaps her most famous single photograph is her self-portrait taken in 1896, with petticoats showing and beer stein in hand. She named her photograph *Self Portrait (as New Woman)*.

The *new woman* was the description of a new feminist ideal that emerged in the late nineteenth century. It referred to women who pushed the traditional limits of what a woman could do in a male-dominated society. Frances was certainly a woman who forged her own path. She was a constant advocate for the role of women in the new art of photography. She wrote an article in an 1897 issue of *Ladies Home Journal* titled "What a Woman Can Do with a Camera." In this she wrote, *Photography as a profession should appeal particularly to women, and in it there are great opportunities for a good-paying business . . .*

In the 1890s and early 1900s, as one of the first photojournalists, she provided images to the Bain News Service syndicate and wrote illustrated articles for many magazines. She photographed events such as world's fairs and peace treaty signings and took the last portrait of President William McKinley at the Pan-American Exposition of 1901, just before his assassination. Frances turned to garden and estate photography around 1910. With her partner Mattie Edwards Hewitt (see 4.37), another successful freelance home and garden photographer, Frances opened a studio in New York in 1913 and moved in with her mother and aunt. She lectured at New York University on business for women, and together they produced a series of photographic studies of New York architecture in the 1920s. Motivated by a desire to document buildings and gardens that were falling into disrepair, or about to be redeveloped and lost, her focus on architecture grew and she became particularly interested in documenting the architecture of the American South.

Her photographs remain an important resource for modern architects, historians, and conservationists. Publicity about her expertise prompted the University of Virginia to hire her to document its buildings, and the State of North Carolina decided to ask her to record its architectural history. Louisiana hired Frances to document its huge inventory of rapidly deteriorating plantations, and she was given a grant in 1933 by the Carnegie Corporation of New York to document Virginia's early architecture. This led to a series of grants and photographs of eight other southern states, all of which were given to the Library of Congress for public use.

In December 1935, she began a yearlong project to capture the structures of the colonial era in Virginia. This effort was intended to be a one-year project but evolved into an eight-year extensive project in which she traveled more than 50,000 miles, visiting ninety-five counties in Virginia.

Frances was a dedicated advocate of the Garden Beautiful movement. This was inspired by the City Beautiful movement, a reform philosophy of architecture and urban planning that flourished during the 1890s and 1900s, with the intent of introducing beautification and monumental grandeur in cities. It was part of the progressive social reform movement led by the upper middle class, who were concerned with poor living conditions in all major cities. The movement not only promoted beauty for its own sake but also aimed to create moral and civic virtue among the growing urban populations. Supporters believed that beautification could promote a harmonious social order that would in turn increase quality of life.

Frances had 1,134 of her black-and-white photographs reproduced as lantern slides. Frederick Law Olmsted Jr., one of America's most distinguished architects, thought that Frances's fully composed photographs were *the finest existing on the subject of American gardens*. These views on glass, most hand-tinted, illustrated her popular lectures, which she delivered to garden club members, museum audiences, and horticultural societies from 1915 through the 1930s. House and garden historian Sam Watters spent five years cataloging and identifying unmarked slides and jumbles of letters and documents that the Library of Congress acquired in 1953. He researched and tracked down information to identify each garden featured in the slides. The book he wrote, *Gardens for a Beautiful America, 1895–1935*, published by Acanthus Press in 2012, focuses on reproductions of Frances's rare hand-colored glass lantern slides from the Library of Congress collection. Sam Watters said, *Every one of them is a little piece of instruction on how you are going to fix your yard.*

Frances's photographs depict more than 200 sites, mostly private gardens, but also horticultural shows, a public library, museums, and several parks.

Geographically the slides feature the American East, West, and South, with Europe represented by Italy, France, and England. Frances used her slides in various combinations to present garden-themed lectures that included illustrations from books, landscape plans, and close-up views of plants.

Her talk "Our American Gardens" was delivered in the 1910s and 1920s and featured estates from Virginia to Rhode Island. In 1917 she introduced her talk "California Gardens." Other lecture subjects included "Problems of the Small Garden," "Gardens for City and Suburb," "Wild Flower Gardening," and "Garden Lore and Flower Legend." In 1925, with photographs from her nine-month tour of Europe, she created "Old World Gardens." For her final slide set, "Tales Old Houses Tell," Frances turned to photographs she took in the 1930s to promote the study and preservation of southern buildings.

Frances's garden and architecture photographs reflect her ambition to establish an archive that documents America's house and garden heritage, helping to inspire the preservation of historic sites. She worked closely with the Library of Congress from the late 1920s to the 1940s, and the library purchased Johnston's archive from her estate in 1953, including her lantern slides, thought to represent around 70 percent of the slides that Frances used during her lifetime.

Frances was named an honorary member of the American Institute of Architects for her work in documenting and preserving old and endangered buildings. Items from her collections were purchased by institutions such as the Metropolitan Museum of Art, the Virginia Museum of Fine Arts, and the Baltimore Museum of Art.

She bought a home in the French Quarter of New Orleans in 1940, retiring there in 1945. Frances Benjamin Johnston died there in 1952 at age eighty-eight. She had forged her own path and was a constant advocate for the role of women in the new art of photography. Frances will also be remembered for proudly identifying herself as a *new woman* who pushed the traditional limits of what a woman could achieve in the male-dominated world of her time.

4.34 CLARA BRYANT FORD (1866–1950)

Clara helped found the Dearborn Garden Club in 1914, serving as its first president, and served on the boards of more than thirty other local, state, and national garden related groups.

The eldest of twelve born to a farming family, Clara had a lifelong passion for gardening. On April 11, 1888, twenty-four-year-old automobile pioneer Henry Ford married Clara Jane Bryant on her twenty-second birthday at her parent's home in Greenfield Township, Michigan. In 1938, Henry Ford was quoted as saying, *The greatest day of my life was the day I married Mrs Ford*. From their first meeting at a New Year's Eve dance, Clara Bryant Ford was indeed her husband's *great believer*. Clara brought common sense, a charitable spirit, energy, and enthusiasm to Henry's many pursuits, as well as her own extensive activities. As a result of her interest in gardening, she helped found the Dearborn Garden Club in 1914, serving as its first president, and served on the boards of more than thirty other local, state, and national garden related groups.

The magnificent grounds of the Fords' 1,300-acre estate, Fair Lane, featured extensive gardens, including a 5-acre rose garden that boasted 10,000 plants of 350 varieties.

Clara worked closely with prairie-style landscape architect Jens Jensen and other notable horticulturalists to lay out the grounds. Fair Lane was Henry and Clara Ford's home for more than thirty years, and it was the culmination of hopes, dreams, and hard work. With their fame and success soaring, Henry and Clara moved into Fair Lane in Dearborn, Michigan, in 1915, after the booming success of the Model T, the assembly line, and Ford's $5 workday policy. These were ideas that changed the world, and the Fords were people of action and ingenuity. Fair

Clara Bryant Ford, 1915. Unknown photographer. *George Grantham Bain Collection, Library of Congress's Prints and Photographs Division*

The historic rose garden at the Fords' winter estate features antique and heirloom roses of the 1920s era adapted to the southwestern Florida climate. Mrs. Ford's favorites were tea roses in shades of yellow and white. Alongside these, other soft pastel colors of pink and peach have been added as accents. *edisonfordwinterestates.org*

Lane was much more than a simple domestic haven. It was a private laboratory space for Henry's tinkering and discoveries; a canvas for Clara's love of gardens; a retreat to discuss ideas with friends like Thomas Edison, Harvey Firestone, and John Burrows; a hall for favorite pastimes like music and dance; and a place to gather the grandchildren to share their passions and dreams.

Built on 1,300 acres of farmland just miles from Henry and Clara's birthplaces, most of the estate's original structures stand today, including the main residence, the powerhouse that supplied energy to the estate, the greenhouse for Clara's extensive gardens, the boathouse, and the stables. Situated about 10 miles west of downtown Detroit, it is set on rolling land above Michigan's Rouge River.

The home, one of the first historic sites to be designated a national historic landmark, has an eclectic mix of English castle and prairie style, mixing European grandeur and midwestern charm. Fair Lane had more than 350 varieties of roses and 10,000 rose plants in its 5-acre rose garden. Today the site contains more than 1,700 plants representing more than 400 species from six continents. According to Robert E. Grese, director of the Matthaei Botanical Gardens and Nichols Arboretum at the University of Michigan and professor of landscape architecture, Jens Jensen's landscape design for Fair Lane is the earliest and best example of his maturing style of estate design and one of his most complex. However, he and Clara fell out over an argument about plants. He was relieved of his duties as a result of conflicts with Clara over her preferences for exotic plants and his insistence on natives.

A subscriber to *Home Acres*, the magazine of the Woman's National Farm & Garden Association (WNF&GA), Clara was also a devotee of Louisa King's (see 4.29) books and speeches. Following her attendance at a lecture by Louisa in Detroit in 1926, Clara approached her to accept a packet of pink poppy seeds. It was the beginning of a friendship that would lead to Clara becoming the fifth national president of WNF&GA in 1927. This was a seven-year tenure that would set the organization on the path it still follows today.

Clara and Henry hosted many events for WNF&GA, including the 1930 national meeting. Poor health necessitated Clara's resignation as president in 1934, but her remarkable legacy had already been established. Under her leadership there were significant increases in publicizing the association, the growth of the Michigan division and establishment of the Capitol division, the establishing of new scholarships and partnerships, and the reinforcement of the mission to improve women's lives through education and empowerment. After leaving the presidency, Clara later admitted it had taken her some time to fully understand WNF&GA, but said, *Looking back over the years, I may truly say that I care more for this organization than any other for which I have worked.*

Clara Bryant Ford outlived her beloved Henry by about three years, dying in September 1950 at age eighty-four. After her death, the Ford Motor Company acquired the Fair Lane estate from Ford heirs and used it as an archival center and office space. In 1956, the company donated the home and 210 acres of land to the University of Michigan for the development of the Dearborn campus. The home was used for meetings, events, a restaurant, and tours until the university closed it in 2010. In 2013, the estate became an independent not-for-profit organization when the university transferred ownership of the home and 17 acres of land to the newly established Henry Ford Estate Inc.

Clara had worked diligently on creating a much-admired garden for her estate at Fair Lane and had specialized in the design of the rose garden there. She also designed the Rose Garden at the Edison and Ford Winter Estates in Fort Myers, Florida. She is remembered as a leader who inspired others with her passion and drive.

Margaret Armstrong. Unknown photographer. *New York Society Library*

4.35 MARGARET NEILSON ARMSTRONG (1867–1944)

Designer, illustrator, and author best known for her book covers in the art nouveau style, as well as the first comprehensive guide to wildflowers of the American West

Margaret was born in 1867 in New York City, the eldest daughter of an old and artistic family and a descendant of Peter Stuyvesant, the governor of New Amsterdam, on her mother's side. The family, which eventually included seven children, spent considerable time on the Hudson River in a 1750s house known as Danskammer, inherited by her father, and later spent summer vacations at a lake house in North Hatley, Quebec, Canada. When Margaret was a young girl the family lived in Florence, where her father, Maitland Armstrong, a diplomat and stained-glass designer, practiced his craft.

An example of Margaret Armstrong's distinctive cover designs. *The Valley of Vision*, published by Charles Scribner's Sons (New York, 1919). *Library of Congress*

She began her career as a book cover designer in the 1880s, working initially for A. C. McClurg and later for other publishers as well. She designed more than 270 book covers and book bindings, about half of which were for Charles Scribner's Sons. She worked in the art nouveau style and favored plant-related motifs, bold colors, gold stamping, and often slightly asymmetrical designs—an unusual combination that helped distinguish her among her peers.

Around 1913, dust jackets began to come into fashion, and decorative covers were no longer required. Margaret cut back on her book design work and focused on writing her own books. Margaret was always a keen naturalist, and her passion for natural forms reflected her interest in botany and, in particular, wildflowers. Between 1911 and 1914 she traveled and camped throughout the western United States and Canada, becoming one of the first women to reach the floor of the Grand Canyon. She discovered several species of flowers that had not yet been identified by botanists. She detailed these discoveries and many other species in her *Field Book of Western Wild Flowers*, published in 1915 by G. P. Putnam's Sons. With its 550 illustrations (48 of which were in color), her *Field Book* was the first comprehensive handbook to supply detailed information about the plethora of flowers growing in the western United States. It includes detailed information on seventy-five plant families, such as water-plantain, lily, buttercup, poppy, mustard, hydrangea, plum, rose, cactus, wintergreen, figwort, valerian families, and many others.

Margaret included information on key characteristics of each species, including height, leaf and petal features, colors, where each flower can most likely be found, ideal conditions they flourish in, and much more. A 664-page facsimile edition of the book was published in 2008 by Kessinger.

In her sixties and seventies, Margaret wrote three critically praised mystery novels: *Murder in Stained Glass* (1939), *The Man with No Face* (1940), and *The Blue Santo Murder Mystery* (1941). She also wrote two biographies: *Fanny Kemble: A Passionate Victorian* (1938) and *Trelawny: A Man's Life* (1940). Along with this she completed her father's memoirs.

Margaret Neilson Armstrong died in New York City in 1944. She had lived a full life, having started as a book cover designer before moving to plant hunting and botany. She had traveled and camped throughout the western United States and Canada on her expeditions, often in unexplored, rugged terrain, and discovered several new species of flowers. Margaret will also be remembered for her *Field Book of Western Wild Flowers* as the first comprehensive handbook about the wildflowers growing in the western United States. Her work is represented in the Metropolitan Museum of Art's collections and the collections of the New York Botanical Garden.

4.36 JENNIE FOSTER BUTCHART (1868–1950)

A novice gardener who created a spectacular sunken garden

Jennie was born in Toronto, Ontario, to James and Martha Kennedy. She lost both parents by the time she was twelve years old, and she moved to Owen Sound, Ontario, to live with her aunt, Mrs. Robert Paterson. A gifted, bright girl, Jennie attended one of the most prestigious schools in Canada, the Brantford Young Ladies' College. She was offered a scholarship to study art in Paris but never took the opportunity, focusing on getting married and starting a family.

Jennie Kennedy and Robert Butchart were seen as a well-suited match when they married in 1884 in Buffalo, New York. They traveled to England for their honeymoon. Always on the lookout for business opportunities, Robert obtained a cement recipe that would make him one of the first in Canada to produce Portland cement. He would later pioneer advancements in cement and introduced the first sacks of cement, rather than the standard barrels that were common.

In 1902 Robert and Jennie moved to Vancouver Island, British Columbia, where Robert believed the rich limestone deposits necessary for cement production could be found. The West Coast was exploding with development, and cement was in constant demand from San Francisco to Seattle. Two years later the Tod Inlet cement plant was started.

The Butchart estate was some 14 miles north of Vancouver Island's capital, Victoria, at 800 Benvenuto Avenue, Brentwood Bay. It included both the Butchart home and the quarry. The Butcharts named their home Benvenuto, which is Italian for welcome. Over the years their house would grow, adding a bowling alley, indoor swimming pool, billiard room, and Aeolian pipe organ. Back in 1905, when the

Jennie Butchart. *butchartgardens.com*

first sacks of cement sailed out of Vancouver Island, Jenny planted some sweet pea seeds and one single rosebush that she had received as a gift. She said that at that time, she knew *next to nothing about gardening*, little realizing that this was to be the beginning of an extraordinary horticultural venture.

When Robert's cement company eventually exhausted the limestone in the quarry in 1908, it left a massive, ugly 3½-acre hole on the property. In her efforts to make the area more appealing to the eye, Jennie's creativity was sparked, and, always up for a challenge, she began the mammoth task of transforming the hole into a beautiful garden.

Jennie busied herself around the estate by planting flowers and shrubbery in an area between the house and Butchart Cove, the area that is now the Japanese garden. As time passed, Jennie's efforts increased and her husband often supplied workmen from the factory to assist in the ever-growing gardening project. In an attempt to hide the hideous excavation, Jennie planted Lombardy and white poplars along with Persian plums between the pit and the house.

Jennie had huge amounts of topsoil brought to the site by horse cart to form the garden bed in the quarry. The rubble on the floor of the pit was pushed into tall mounds on which terraced flowers were planted. The largest tower in the lower garden supports an observation platform from which most of the original pit can be viewed. Jennie solved the unsightly problem of the grim, gray quarry walls by dangling over their sides in a bosun's chair and tucking ivy into any discernible pocket or crevice in the rock.

In 1921 the project was complete. It had become a garden of immense curiosity to the local community. From the beginning, friends, acquaintances, and even complete strangers were welcomed as they came to admire the horticultural masterpiece. As the garden had grown, so did public interest surrounding it.

A view of the stunning Sunken Garden that Jennie created from an ugly quarry. *butchart-gardens.com*

Robert and Jennie would serve tea to all who came, invited or uninvited. This would continue until the sheer number of people arriving made it impossible. In 1915 alone it was reported that tea was served to 18,000 people. Jennie would, on occasion, serve tea herself in such a manner that she was sometimes not recognized, and on one occasion she received a server's tip from a visitor.

The colorful Italianate Garden at Butchart Gardens. *butchartgardens.com*

Between 1906 and 1929 the Butcharts had created a Japanese garden by the seashore, an Italian garden on their former tennis court, and a beautiful rose garden. By 1930, thousands of people were attracted to Jennie's gardens. In appreciation of her generosity, in 1930 she was named Victoria's Best Citizen.

WWII stripped the area of available manpower, and the garden began to decline. Robert's failing health caused them to move to mainland Victoria. Their two daughters continued on as best as possible until Jennie's son Robert Ian Ross returned from the war. Before they died—Robert in 1943 and Jennie in 1950—they gave the gardens to him as a twenty-first-birthday gift. By then the passage of time and the war years had taken a toll on the gardens, and he set about bringing them back to their former glory. It was an enormous project, but eventually the gardens once more flourished.

Following Ian Ross's death in 1997, ownership of the gardens was passed to his son, Christopher. Christopher's untimely death shortly afterward in 2000 placed ownership and the running of the gardens in the hands of his sister, Robin Clarke.

Jenny Butchart is an inspiring and classic example of a determined woman achieving a really significant result in horticulture, despite having no formal training and relying on her own instincts and perseverance. She had transformed a difficult site from a wasteland to a horticultural masterpiece. The Butchart Gardens was designated a national historic site of Canada in 2004, and approximately one million people visit from all over the world every year.

4.37 MATTIE EDWARDS HEWITT (1859–1956)

Eminent garden photographer

Mattie was born in October 1869 in St. Louis, Missouri, to a middle-class family. After a period of studying art, she married Arthur Hewitt, a photographer. As his assistant she was trained in principles of photography, involving the techniques of processing and printing. She started her career in photography as a small operation in St. Louis, Missouri, where she lived and learned from the camera clubs and photography journals that flourished during the late nineteenth century. Mattie divorced her husband in 1909 and moved to New York to work and live with Frances Benjamin Johnston (see 4.33), a fellow photographer who taught her the finer nuances of photography. After her divorce, she was dependent on photography as a profession for her living and pursued it with dedication. This coincided with substantial innovations and improvements in photographic equipment. She called photography *the most fascinating of arts* and described her photographic career as a *transition from an amateur in the 19th century to 20th-century professional*.

Mattie lived and worked with Frances Johnston from 1909 to 1917. Together they established a firm called the Johnston-Hewitt Studio in New York City in 1913, and they became well known in the field of architectural and landscape photography. They took many pictures of famous buildings and gardens.

After the partnership with Frances Johnston broke up, Mattie ventured out on her own and became famous in her own right as a commercial photographer. She set up her business establishment in photography with specific orientation to taking pictures for designers, architects, and landscape architects, recording interior and exterior views of homes, businesses, houses, and gardens. From her

Frances Benjamin Johnston's photograph of her partner, Mattie Edwards Hewitt, taken between 1890 and 1910. *Library of Congress's Prints and Photographs Division*

office in New York City she became a specialist freelance photographer and executed many assignments, taking pictures of the mansions and gardens of wealthy people on the East Coast.

Photograph by Mattie Hewitt of Grey Gardens in the 1920s, a 4-acre estate in East Hampton, New York designed by Anna Gilman Hill and landscape architect Ruth Bramley Dean. *Credit: Library of Congress Prints and Photographs Division*

Many of these pictures were published in newspapers and magazines, along with accompanying descriptive articles on the mansions, such as the *New York Times*, *Evening Post*, *House Beautiful*, *House & Garden*, and *Garden Magazine*. These brought her aptitude and professional skills to the attention of the public and encouraged further assignments.

On a commission Mattie would carry heavy wooden cameras and wooden tripods herself. She maintained good records of the negatives with names of clients, architects, and locations. In the words of Robin S. Karson, author of the book *Fletcher Steele, Landscape Architect: An Account of the Gardenmaker's Life, 1885–1971*, Mattie was *one of the best known and most lyrical garden photographers of her day*. Mattie's photographs are a remarkable visual record of nearly four decades of architecture, design, and garden landscaping.

Although she worked with an assistant or hired a boy to help with the equipment when her budget permitted, the work was demanding. When landscape and garden assignments were scarce during the winter months, she would occasionally freelance at banquets at the large hotels in New York. At these events she photographed early in the evening, made prints in a hotel room fitted with a makeshift darkroom, and sold them to the banquet guests as they left the party.

Mattie Edwards Hewitt died in Boston in 1956. Her skill, determination, and persistence had carried her through more than thirty years as a professional photographer, mostly preserving on film early American gardens for posterity.

Photographs of late-nineteenth- and twentieth-century gardens are a remarkable and invaluable record of landscaping, garden design, and the development of North American horticulture through the ages. Many earlier gardens, especially those of larger estates, proved too costly to maintain when the cost of gardening staff became prohibitive to all but the very wealthy, and, sadly, many were demolished to make way for housing. Apart from landscape architects' plans and notes, our understanding of these plots would have been lost; the dedication and skill of early photographers such as Mattie, who specialized in preserving the images of these gardens, provides us with an invaluable record of these lost treasures.

4.38 ELLEN BIDDLE SHIPMAN (1869–1950)

Pioneering landscape architect known for her innovative planting designs, with more than 600 commissions in her forty-year career

Ellen was born in Philadelphia; she spent her childhood in Texas and Arizona. Her father, Colonel James Biddle, was a career army officer stationed on the western frontier. When the safety of his family was threatened, he moved them to the McGowan farm in Elizabeth, New Jersey. Ellen's discovery of gardens came when she was sent there to live with her grandparents, who had an old-fashioned rose-filled garden. She attended boarding school in Baltimore, Maryland, where her interests in the arts emerged, and by her twenties she had already started drawing garden designs.

When she entered the Harvard annex, Radcliffe College, Ellen met a young man attending Harvard named Louis Shipman. Louis was a dashing young playwright from New York. They left school after one year, married, and moved to Plainfield, New Hampshire, in the Cornish Art Colony. The colony is said to have been landscaped by artists who were not architects but had artistically trained eyes and an awareness for the aesthetics of repose, which gave rise to a collection of some of the finest gardens in the country. Ellen took strongly to the Cornish style, one

Ellen Biddle Shipman at her NYC home, Beekman Place, ca. 1920. *arnoldia.arboretum.harvard.edu*

that focused on geometric patterns and colonial plantings, and with it created her own style—a style that did not go unnoticed.

By the time the Shipmans divorced in 1910, Ellen was well on her way to establishing herself as a talented garden designer nationwide. She was known for her formal style and lush planting. Ellen was heavily influenced by British garden designer Gertrude Jekyll's brilliant use of borders, as well as memories of her grandparents' farm. She was also influenced by the traditionalism of the Northeast, especially the colonial revival style. Her intent was to provide privacy, familiarity, and comfort, and a place for interaction with the surroundings.

By the early 1920s, Ellen's gardens were receiving editorial coverage and publicity in magazines and books, inspiring many new clients to commission a garden from her. One editor summed up a garden in Philadelphia: *Sheltered and friendly and livable . . . a delightful bit of artistry, so skillful and so finely balanced that one forgets the plan and is conscious only of the pervasive pleasantness of it all.* This was the type of garden that appealed to her clients, largely the wives of prominent industrialists, who sought traditionalism in the form of good taste and also privacy.

Ellen created residential gardens all over the United States, sometimes collaborating with other architects. Noted architect James Greenleaf Warren Manning, with whom she collaborated on many projects, considered her *one of the best, if not the very best, Flower Garden Maker in America*.

Ellen's work was widespread, but clusters of her gardens once proliferated in areas such as Grosse Pointe, Michigan; Greenwich, Connecticut; and Chagrin Falls, Ohio. The 1920s were the busiest for Ellen, but commissions decreased dramatically in the Great Depression years of the later 1920s and 1930s. Her planting plans softened the bones of geometric architecture with planting designs that were muscular enough to speak for themselves. She once described her use of plants as *painting pictures as an artist would*. She also offered this advice: *Remember that the design of your place is its skeleton, upon which you will later plant to make your picture. Keep that skeleton as simple as possible*. Ellen's compositions varied little throughout her career and balanced formality and informality. She wrote, *Working daily in my garden for 15 years taught me to know plants, their habits and their needs*. She specialized in surrounding the garden with an enclosing curtain of trees and always used good quantities of small flowering trees, shrubs, and standards such as roses, lilacs, or wisteria to create structural notes. She said of trees: *Planting, however beautiful, is not a garden. A garden must be enclosed . . . or otherwise it would merely be a cultivated area*. Among her favorite features were designs for rose arbors, pergolas, benches, teahouses, dovecotes, and other structures that were sympathetic to the architectural style of the house in question.

Ellen's gardens often appeared in magazines, including *House Beautiful*. In 1933 *House & Garden* named her the "Dean of Women Landscape Architects." She lectured widely and completed more than 600 projects during her forty-year career. Her archives are at Cornell University.

Longue Vue house and gardens, a historic house museum and associated gardens at 7 Bamboo Road in the Lakewood neighborhood of New Orleans, Louisiana. *museum/longue-vue-house-and-gardens-new-orleans*

Along with Beatrix Farrand (see 4.42) and Marian Cruger Coffin (see 4.46), Ellen dictated the style of the time and strongly influenced landscape design as a member of the first generation to break into the largely male occupation. Commenting about the male-dominated field to the *New York Times* in 1938, she said, *Before women took hold of the profession, landscape architects were doing what I call cemetery work*. Because most of her commissions were for grand estates, which were therefore particularly labor intensive to maintain, unfortunately many eventually disappeared even within her own lifetime. Only a few have survived to the present day.

Ellen's most significant gardens include Duke University's Sarah P. Duke Gardens, often named one of her finest works and cited as one of the most beautiful American college campuses. She also did the Moonlight Garden at the Edison and Ford Winter Estates in Fort Myers, Florida; Stan Hywet Gardens, Akron, Ohio; the Bayou Bend Gardens, Houston, Texas; Longue Vue Gardens in New Orleans; the Graycliff Estate, Buffalo, New York; the Stranahan Estate, Toledo, Ohio; and the Robert M. Hanes House in Winston-Salem, North Carolina.

It is said that throughout the forty years she practiced landscape architecture, Ellen would hire graduates only from Lowthorpe School of Landscape Architecture, Gardening, and Horticulture for Women. Why this was her hiring practice is debated, but it is widely believed that because of the time, women were not being given apprenticeships in male landscape-gardening offices. In later years she taught at the Landscape Institute, Arnold Arboretum of Harvard University.

The Gardens of Ellen Biddle Shipman chronicles Ellen's achievements and, in doing so, describes the mostly neglected subject of women and American landscape architecture. It was published in 1996 by Sagapress. The author, Judith B. Tankard, is a landscape historian, preservation consultant, and author or coauthor of seven other books on landscape history.

Ellen Biddle Shipman died in 1950 and is buried in Plainfield, New Hampshire.

4.39 MARY AGNES CHASE (1869–1963)

A suffragist considered one of the world's outstanding agrostologists of the day and known for her in depth study of grasses

Born Mary Agnes Meara in Iroquois County, Illinois, in 1869, but known as Agnes, she was the daughter of a railroad blacksmith from Tipperary, Ireland, who died when she was just two years old. Because of prejudice against Irish immigrant workers, the family name was changed from Meara to Merrill after her widowed mother moved the family to Chicago. Agnes attended grammar school but was expected to help support the family, so she also worked as a proofreader and typesetter on newspapers. At age nineteen, Agnes married William Chase, editor of the *School Herald*. It was short lived, since he died of tuberculosis less than a year later, leaving her with an unpaid debt. She paid off his creditors by living frugally and working nights on newspapers, while in the daytime still attending extension courses at the Lewis Institute and the University of Chicago.

Agnes's childhood interest in plants was kindled by one of her nephews, Virginius Chase, who later became a botanist in his own right. Their visit to the plant-collecting exhibit at the 1893 Columbian Exposition in Chicago made a deep impression on both of them and inspired her to make a personal study of the flora of northern Illinois. She began her first field book in 1897, and the following year, while collecting in an Illinois swamp, she met Rev. Ellsworth Hill, a retired minister and amateur bryologist—a branch of botany concerned with the scientific study of bryophytes (mosses, liverworts, and hornworts). Hill encouraged her research and became her mentor. Discovering her talent as a botanical artist, he employed her to illustrate his publications and introduced her to Charles

Mary Agnes Chase seated at a desk with herbarium sheets, ca. 1960. Unidentified photographer. *Smithsonian Institution Archives*

Frederick Millspaugh, curator of botany at the Field Museum of Natural History. Millspaugh commissioned her work for his books *Plantae Utowanae* (1900) and *Plantae Yucatanae* (1903–1904).

At Hill's urging, Agnes applied for a position as a botanical artist in the US Department of Agriculture and was hired in 1903 to work in the division of forage plants in Washington, DC. In 1907 she was appointed a scientific assistant botanist and in 1925 associate botanist, all under Albert Spear Hitchcock. Agnes worked with Hitchcock for almost twenty years, collaborating closely with him. In 1910 they coauthored *The North American Species of Panicum*, published by the US Government Print Office, Washington, DC. In 1901 Hitchcock joined the US Department of Agriculture (USDA) and began his worldwide travels to collect grass samples for the National Herbarium in Washington, DC. He increased its collection of grasses to one of the largest and most complete in the world. Using these specimens, in 1905 he began to publish a series of monographs and handbooks on the grasses of many parts of the Americas. His most important work, *Manual of the Grasses of the United States* (1935), remains a standard reference.

Soon after joining the USDA, Agnes started using her spare time to work in the grass herbarium on a study of the Paniceae, a large tribe of the subfamily Panicoideae. It includes roughly 1,500 species in eighty-four genera, primarily found in tropical and subtropical regions of the world. This research resulted in a series of scientific publications starting in 1906. That same year she made the first of her mainly self-financed collecting expeditions for the USDA.

As a female government employee, Agnes realized how difficult it was to nurture her passion for the sciences when she could not convince her superiors to provide her with the money or the resources to travel and complete research. She was forced to finance her own trips to collect samples while struggling on an annual salary of $720.

She collected extensively in the United States, visiting nineteen states in total, and Mexico. In 1913 she spent two months in Puerto Rico, collecting grasses, bamboo, and ferns. Then, in 1924 and 1929 she made trips to Brazil, where she collected more than 20,000 specimens in areas that had been largely ignored by botanists. She got used to traveling by whatever means were available across often hazardous terrain. She called these two trips *the hardest physical feat of my life*. One story has her detained as a suspected lunatic after being seen on her hands and knees pulling up clumps of grass.

In her pursuit of further knowledge, and to aid her research, Agnes also toured Europe's herbarium collections: Vienna, Florence, Pisa, Geneva, Leiden, and Brussels in 1922–1923, and Montpellier, Caen, and Paris in 1935.

Following Hitchcock's death in 1936, Agnes succeeded him to become senior botanist in charge of systematic agrostology and custodian of the Section of Grasses, Division of Plants, at the Smithsonian's United States National Museum (USNM). Agnes retired from the USDA in 1939, although she continued her work as custodian of the USNM grass herbarium. A year later she was invited to Venezuela to advise its ministry of agriculture on the development of a range management program. During her stay she collected more than 400 different types of grasses from a variety of ecozones, including the Andes Mountains, savannah, and cloud forest. On these trips she met many Brazilian and Venezuelan students of botany whom she encouraged to study in the United States, and some she even boarded in her Washington home.

Mary Agnes Chase collecting plants in Brazil in 1929. Unknown photographer. *Credit: Smithsonian Institution Archives*

Many of the species she collected were new to science and were incorporated into Hitchcock's aforementioned book, *Manual of the Grasses of the United States*.

Apart from her dedication to botany, Agnes believed it was essential to address gender discrimination, which was negatively impacting a woman's ability to achieve success. She was forced to disregard the potential damage that her support for women's rights could have on her career as a respected agrostologist to succeed as a legitimate supporter for the cause of women's rights. She experienced discrimination based on her gender in the scientific field; for example, being excluded from expeditions to Panama in 1911 and 1912 because the expedition's benefactors feared that the presence of women researchers would distract men.

In the early 1900s the majority of women interested in the sciences could pursue careers as museum curators only if they wanted access to research opportunities or connections to other scientists. This drove Agnes to redefine the *vision of what constitutes a career in science* in her positions of mentorship. Her support for women's rights continued to increase, both in the sphere of science and in the political world surrounding it. She acted as a mentor for advanced but underprivileged students in the sciences, as well as women wanting to become botanists.

Throughout her career, Agnes was a dedicated pacifist, prohibitionist, and socialist, and an early and active contributor to a number of political organizations: the Fellowship of Reconciliation, the National Association for the Advancement of Colored People, the National Women's Party, and the Women's

International League for Peace and Freedom. As an active suffragist, Agnes took part in a series of demonstrations led by the Silent Sentinels—members of the National Women's Party (NWP) who wanted President Wilson to listen to what women had to say about the vote. These Silent Sentinels attempted to infiltrate the White House in every way possible. On one occasion, 300 delegates were sent to meet with the president to discuss the need for a federal suffrage amendment. Women unfurled a banner reading *Votes for Women* down into the White House gallery while in the attendance of a House of Representatives meeting. Pickets took place at every entrance of the White House gates, with signs and banners reading *What Will You Do for Woman Suffrage?* and *Mr President, How Long Will Women Have to Wait for Liberty?*

She was twice arrested and jailed for agitating in the cause of women's suffrage. The first time was in 1918 for making a speech in Lafayette Square; the second time was in 1919, as one of a group of protesters who had vowed to maintain a continuous fire in front of the White House by burning copies of presidential speeches containing the words *freedom* and *liberty* until women had the right to vote. When it was made public that these women had undergone forced feeding after going on a hunger strike in workhouses, it increased the support of the suffragist cause. This sympathy from the public ultimately released her and the others who were arrested. The persistence shown by the NWP played a major role in influencing the ratification of the Suffrage Amendment in 1919 and the Nineteenth Amendment in 1920. Agnes's awards and honors include

Certificate of merit from the Botanical Society of America (1956)
Honorary doctorate from the University of Illinois (1958)
Honorary fellow from the Smithsonian Institution (1959)
Fellow of the Linnaean Society of London (1961)

Of her seventy publications, Agnes published her last, *Index to Grass Species*, coauthored with CD Niles and others, a year before her death at age ninety-four. It is considered her culminating achievement. Her popular guide to grasses for nonprofessionals, *First Book of Grasses: The Structure of Grasses Explained for Beginners*, was originally published by the Macmillan Company in 1922. Agnes's field books from 1897 to 1959 are archived in the Smithsonian Institution Archives.

Agnes Chase, self-taught doyenne of American agrostology, worked for the USNM in Washington for more than sixty years. She collected and described more than 10,000 grass-type specimens from her travels in the United States and Latin America and was recognized by the Botanical Society of America, the Smithsonian Institution, the Linnaean Society of London, and the government of Brazil for her contributions to botany. She received her first and only degree, an honorary doctorate from the University of Illinois, at age eighty-nine. Agnes continued her work as custodian of the USNM grass herbarium until her death in 1963 at age ninety-four.

She will be remembered for her outspoken and persistent support of a women's right to vote, which led to her being jailed not once, but twice, as well as her achievements as an eminent botanist.

4.40 JOSEPHINE TILDEN (1869–1957)

Algae botanist and supporter of women in botany

Josephine was born in Davenport, Iowa, in 1869, and grew up in Minneapolis. She showed an early interest in plants and had published a paper on local botany before she even began her association with the University of Minnesota (UMN). In 1895 she earned a bachelor's degree, followed by a master's the following year from the university. In 1897 she wrote a paper, "Some New Species of Minnesota Algae Which Live in a Calcareous or Siliceous Matrix," published in the university's *Botanical Gazette*. The subject matter was algal stalactites, a phenomenon she had discovered near a geyser in Yellowstone Park.

She became an instructor at her alma mater, the first woman scientist on the staff. She took a particular interest in algology or phycology, the studies of algae and seaweeds, respectively. Her superiors at the university were concerned, but

Josephine Tilden later in life. *University of Minnesota*

they agreed to fund this interest in return for her promise to commit to the subject for at least five years. In fact, Josephine gave a commitment that would last until she died. She was appointed an assistant professor at UMN in 1903.

Josephine's first trip to the Pacific was a journey to Vancouver Island, Canada. She was the leading force of the establishment of the Minnesota Seaside Station in Canada. She discovered an untouched area of land in British Columbia that had a good environment for observing and collecting algae. The landowner gave her the area for free, and she chose 4 acres that were ideal to create an algae research station. Josephine used her own funds to build this.

In the summers from 1901 to 1907, students and instructors from UMN made their way—some 1,860 miles—by train, by coastal steamship, and on foot over a muddy forest trail to study marine life on the rugged west coast of Vancouver Island.

Despite the extreme logistical challenges of maintaining a small field station on a remote Canadian shore, from a biological standpoint Josephine could not have chosen better—she'd discovered a phycologist's nirvana. The extensive rock shelf of Botanical Beach, as the area is now known, was a perfect outdoor classroom and laboratory with a rich biodiversity of marine life, particularly algae and invertebrates, that was accessible on foot—whether wearing trousers or a long skirt—at midtide to low tide. For seven summers about twenty-five students, faculty, and scientists studied at the Minnesota Seaside Station, working out of three log buildings: the main Lessonia Lodge (named for a species of kelp) and two bunkhouses.

Young women studying at the Minnesota Seaside Station were advised to wear a short skirt, about 12 inches from the ground, for fieldwork. *University of Minnesota*

In total, some 200 people attended the Minnesota Seaside Station; significantly, female students often made up half of each year's participants. The challenges of fieldwork at the seaside station required the women to plunge into tidal pools, teeter along slippery logs in the dark, and slog over muddy trails while carrying heavy luggage. Some of the women even donned men's overalls for long hikes—a freedom that they no doubt loved.

The students studied geology, algology, zoology, taxonomy, and lichenology with world-renowned scientists participating in the lecture series. Though students worked long hours, they also enjoyed themselves on hiking trips, and with evening plays and storytelling—transforming the group of scholars into close-knit colleagues. Letters from student Alice Misz to her mother during summer 1906 make it clear that her six-week stay at the station was the most unforgettable experience of her life.

Most of the women studied botany—then the most readily accessible, and acceptable, science for them due to a long tradition of women excelling as amateur naturalists. From the late eighteenth century, women adept in collecting, classifying, and illustrating specimens became increasingly active in botanical studies. A noteworthy number of talented American, European, and British women—usually without any formal training—wrote influential papers and even books about botany. However, they rarely identified themselves as scientists, even when doing highly original and serious work. Josephine Tilden stood with a new generation of educated and influential female scientists emerging in many disciplines.

Josephine offered the land and the buildings of the Minnesota Seaside Station to her university. To her disappointment and her colleagues', the university chose not to assume management and funding. Its value seemed to elude them, and the last summer session was held in 1907. Despite the entreaties of Professor Conway MacMillan of the University of Minnesota and Josephine, the university refused to take responsibility for land in a different country. MacMillan resigned over this issue.

The Minnesota Seaside Station was replaced by the more local Lake Itasca Forestry and Biological Station in 1909. The following year, and despite not having a doctorate, Josephine was made a full professor of the University of Minnesota. In 1910 she wrote *Minnesota Algae: The Myxophyceae of North America and Adjacent Regions Including Central America, Greenland, Bermuda, the West Indies, and Hawaii* (1910), published by the Board of Regents of the University for the People of Minnesota, Minneapolis.

Josephine traveled widely, especially around the Pacific Ocean, to gather dried plants. She organized a trip around the world for ten students whose sole purpose was to gather algae and other samples. She charged the students to accompany her and obtained loans and grants to fund the travel. She led many research expeditions, taking students, many of them women, to Tahiti, New Zealand, Tasmania, Australia, and Hawaii, breaking down barriers and defying convention wherever she went. Despite disputes with UMN, she spent her entire career there.

She gained international recognition for her pioneering research into marine algae and for her many publications.

In 1935 she published *The Algae and Their Life Relations*, which was the first scientific work by an American scientist to describe the characteristics of marine and freshwater flora. Among other selected books and articles were included the following for the *Botanical Gazette*:

"Some New Species of Minnesota Algae Which Live in a Calcareous or Siliceous Matrix" (1897)
"Observations on Some West American Thermal Algae" (1898)
"Basicladia, a New Genus of Cladophoraceae" (1930)
"A Classification of the Algae Based on Evolutionary Development, with Special Reference to Pigmentatio" (1933)

Josephine Tilden retired in 1937, having gathered an important collection of algae. She died in Florida in 1957. She had been at the forefront of a new generation of educated and influential female scientists emerging in many disciplines, refusing to submit to the prejudices of men against women scientists.

Josephine's work lives on; after her death, the University of Minnesota's Botany Department acquired many of the algae specimens she had been keeping in her Florida home by collaborating with her friend Joseph Wachter. Josephine had left them in safe hands, having given the collection to him in her will.

4.41 MARTHA BROOKES HUTCHESON (1871–1959)

A prominent landscape architect, conservationist, lecturer, and author who was one of the first American women to receive professional training

Martha Brookes Brown Hutcheson. Photographer unknown. *Morris County Park Commission*

Martha Brookes Brown Hutcheson was born in New York City in 1871. She moved to Vermont when she was young, and it was there that she developed a love of gardening. She grew up in a family of avid gardeners, and as an adult she recalled, among her earliest pleasurable experiences, working in the gardens and fields of her great-uncle John Pomeroy's farm, Fern Hill, near Burlington, Vermont, where her family spent every summer. From 1893 to 1895 she attended the New York School of Applied Design for Women. Like many other young people of the day with the means to do so, she augmented her formal education by undertaking the American equivalent of the grand tour, studying and making notes on gardens in England, France, and Italy during the late 1890s.

In 1900 the country's first academic programs in landscape architecture were instituted: first at Harvard, but this was restricted to male applicants only, and second at the Massachusetts Institute of Technology (MIT). Although MIT's official policy did not specifically exclude women, Martha found gaining admission difficult because of the lack of opportunity for her to study the mathematics and sciences that were vital parts of the entrance requirements and the curriculum. Nevertheless, she was able to enroll in 1900 and entered MIT's new landscape architecture program at age twenty-nine. On examining the curriculum, Martha found that MIT's program strongly emphasized the architectural and scientific aspects of landscape design. The courses that composed a major portion of the curriculum were perspective and topographical drawing, geometry, physics, and structural geology. Only in the second term of the fourth and final year was any requirement listed that focused on the social importance of landscape architecture—the discipline that really appealed to her. Although horticulture was offered in each term of the second, third, and fourth years, Martha found MIT's program inadequate and she later wrote, *I saw at once that the curriculum did not give nearly enough time to what must be known of the plant world.*

Accordingly she left MIT in 1902 without taking a degree. Instead, she took the course of lectures offered by Professor Watson at Harvard University's Bussey Institution and made further studies at local commercial nurseries to *note periods of bloom, combinations in color, variety of species in flowers, and the effects of perennials after blooming*. She opened her own office in Boston in 1902, even though she said, *It was considered almost social suicide and distinctly matrimonial suicide, for a woman to enter any profession*.

Martha designed the grounds of several residential estates near Boston, one of the most notable between 1904 and 1906 for Frederick Moseley's large

Newburyport estate (now Maudslay State Park). The estate was created on agricultural fields by Martha, who designed the grounds around the main house, entry drive, and formal gardens. At its peak about forty staff tended the estate's three greenhouses, head house, cold frames, espaliered fruit trees, and winter plant house, and the 2-acre formal vegetable and cutting garden. There was also a 500-foot perennial border, an Italian garden, a rose garden, and plantings of rhododendrons, azaleas, and specimen trees.

Her work, almost without exception, consisted of private domestic gardens for wealthy northeasterners.

Among the many beautiful photographs illustrating Martha's other designs are examples from the Bamboo Brook Conservation Center in Gladstone, New Jersey, and the Longfellow House–Washington's Headquarters National Historic Site. For the latter, Alice Longfellow commissioned not only Martha but Ellen Biddle Shipman (see 4.38) to redesign the formal garden in the colonial revival style. The garden was restored in 2008 by an organization called Friends of the Longfellow House.

Back end of the Longfellow House–Washington's Headquarters National Historic Site, as seen from the garden. *nps.gov/long/contacts*

Martha married William Anderson Hutcheson at Fern Hill, near Burlington, Vermont, on October 12, 1910, when she was thirty-nine years old. The couple had a mutual love of plants, birds, woods, and nature, so in 1911 they bought Merchiston Farm in Morris County, New Jersey, near the village of Gladstone, for $800. This became their home for the rest of their lives.

The open fields of this 100-acre nineteenth-century working farm were transformed by Martha into an outstanding example of natural and classic landscape design. Its overall design was influenced by classical Italian gardens, featuring a pond encircled by native plants, a vegetable garden, flower borders, orchards, allées, and farm buildings. There were 5 acres of formal gardens with arbors, gateways, reflecting pools, and cascading streams.

The site is now owned and maintained by the Morris County Park Commission as the Bamboo Brook Outdoor Education Center for the study of horticulture. It is open year round for self-guided tours.

Her garden at the farm inspired her to write her best-loved book, *The Spirit of the Garden*, published in 1923 by Atlantic Monthly Press. She noted in her foreword that there already existed a proliferation of literature that provided comprehensive and helpful planting charts, color schemes, and lists of valuable varieties of plants. This was information to enable an amateur to create interesting and attractive set pieces of garden art. Martha was confident that her book would find a place on the shelves of many newly prosperous, upwardly mobile Americans who were avidly seeking advice on home building, decorating, and especially gardening and garden design. Her contribution offered something unique: a straightforward explanation of the basic architectural principles of the design of space and their application in the small garden, combined with an enthusiastic and knowledgeable enthusiasm for the use of native plants. *Every garden lover*, advised one contemporary reviewer, *should have it on a most convenient table*.

Evocative before and after images in the book demonstrate the remarkable effect of plantings. Martha reminds her readers that fine design depends on comprehensive planning, rather than horticultural rarities. In her garden designs and in her writings, she championed the use of native plants and was among the first to urge conservation of *our vast natural beauty*. Although she maintained that her book was neither a practical manual of instruction on how to make a garden nor a substitute for employing the services of a professional landscape designer, nevertheless it clearly filled such a need, particularly for the many Americans in the 1920s who were becoming homeowners for the first time as suburban houses were being built in unprecedented numbers outside major conurbations.

The smaller, domestic private gardens in the United States were usually left to the care of women, while the design of large-scale landscape projects was the nearly exclusive domain of men, who created successful careers for themselves as landscape architects, designers, photographers, and writers. Small, private spaces had been marginalized by men because of a perceived lack of social relevance, as well as its association with *women's work*.

The Spirit of the Garden was illustrated with Martha's own photographs and features some of the more than fifty private gardens that she designed and built over the course of her professional life.

In the book she wrote, *The garden is not only the exquisite playground of the home, but a place of inspiration and promise, of tranquility and intense personal calm*. Her design philosophy focused on combining elements of European (especially Italian) design and vistas, and an architectural framework with the richness and variety of native plant material and a freer planting style. In her foreword to *The Spirit of the Garden* she writes, *As individuals, we are slowly becoming conscious of the value of cultivated and aesthetic knowledge in adapting to our home surroundings the good principles in planning which have been handed down to us from the Old World.* She emphasized *the importance of studying historical precedent and reshaping the best of this legacy in contemporary gardens, no matter how small.*

The Spirit of the Garden was reprinted by University of Massachusetts Press in 2001 and includes three of Hutcheson's own site plans of gardens to illustrate how it might be possible to create a system of logical relationships among house, garden, and the surrounding natural landscape. These relationships not only would *tie everything together* but would also provide what she memorably termed the *reasonable complexity of a garden*. Martha believed that variety and interest can result from revealing controlled vistas or glimpses from one part of the garden into another, making the farther *rooms* seem mysterious and inviting. Martha had three guiding principles for her designs:

1. The necessity of a strong relationship between house and garden
2. The idea of the garden as an outdoor room of which hedges, walls, and paths blend the different elements of the garden into a harmonious whole
3. The use of less structured plantings in more-informal areas to blend the garden naturally with the surrounding landscape.

Martha believed that terracing, steps, and pathways are not only tools for getting from one space to another; they also help set the garden apart from both architecture and nature as a distinct space. The separation of the garden from its surroundings, as *a place apart*, was as important to her as the connections with them. What she calls the *green elements* of a garden—trees, shrubs, and hedges—are given their own chapter in the book. Although many of Martha's basic design ideas were derived from Italian and English traditions, Martha's enthusiasm for native scenery and her use of local plant materials made her gardens distinctly American and helped foster an appreciation for what, even in the early twentieth century, was a rapidly vanishing landscape. In her lecturing and writing she was vocal about her belief that landscape architecture could be used for the betterment of society. She actively promoted many landscape related progressive causes and was one of the founders of the Women's Land Army of America, which attempted to alleviate the shortage of farm labor during WWI by employing women to work the land and produce crops, fruits, and vegetables to feed the nation.

Members of the Women's Land Army at Martha's home in 1917 or 1918. Martha is in the center of the group. *Morris County Park Commission*

Martha's active career lasted only a short time: her first documented work dates from 1901, and she seems to have built little after her marriage in 1910. In 1935 she was named a fellow in the American Society of Landscape Architects, only the third woman to receive this distinction.

Martha Brookes Hutcheson died in 1959. She had been a prominent landscape architect, lecturer, and author and was one of the first American women landscape architects to receive professional training. She is remembered for her signature garden design—the use of local plants to give an authentic American feel to a landscape.

4.42 BEATRIX CADWALADER FARRAND (1872–1959)

Considered one of the most talented and prolific landscape architects, man or woman, of the era. Her career included commissions to design about 110 gardens for private residences, estates and country homes, public parks, botanic gardens, college campuses, and the White House.

Beatrix Cadwalader Jones (later Beatrix Cadwalader Jones Farrand, 1872–1959). Watercolor on ivory by artist Emily Heyward Drayton Taylor (American, 1860–1952). *Yale University Art Gallery*

Beatrix Cadwalader Jones was born in New York City in 1872 into a wealthy family, among whom she liked to claim were *five generations of gardeners*. She enjoyed long seasons at the family's summer home, Reef Point Estate in Mount Desert Island, Maine. There she learned to love the outdoors, especially plants and trees. Beatrix's parents' marriage failed and, when she was age ten, her father absented himself from her life.

Beatrix's uncle John Lambert Cadwalader often played the role of fatherly figure for Beatrix. He was a distinguished New York lawyer and a trustee of the Metropolitan Museum of Art. Beatrix traveled extensively with him, often on shooting trips to Scotland. John Cadwalader recognized that he had a talented niece and gave her opportunities to see Europe and all the house and garden design elements that were there. While still a teenager, Beatrix took over the management of the Reef Point garden in Maine.

At age twenty she was introduced to botanist Charles Sprague Sargent, who at Harvard University was a professor of horticulture at the Bussey Institute, as well as the founding director of the Arnold Arboretum in Boston, Massachusetts. He was perhaps the only person at that time who was willing and able to help Beatrix enter the exclusively male world of landscape architecture. At the arboretum, Beatrix studied botany, and Sargent appreciated her knowledge and enthusiasm for plants. He taught Beatrix the basic concepts of landscape design, as well as how to stake out and survey a piece of land. He also told her that a plan should fit the ground and that one should never attempt to change the ground for the plan. Sargent also encouraged Beatrix to travel as much as possible and to study landscape paintings, to analyze natural beauty, and *to learn from all the great arts, as all art is akin*.

Sargent became Beatrix's mentor and was the person that suggested that she study landscape gardening. Shortly after their meeting in 1893, Beatrix went to live at the Sargent's home, Holm Lea, in Brookline, Massachusetts. She studied landscape gardening, for which there was no specialized school at the time, botany, and land planning. She wanted to learn drafting to scale, elevation rendering, surveying, and engineering, so she studied at the Columbia School of Mines. She was influenced in using native plant species from her study of contemporaneous books from the USA and abroad promoting the advantages of native plant colors.

She began practicing landscape architecture in 1895, working from the upper floor of her mother's brownstone house on East 11th Street in New York. Since women were excluded from public projects, her first designs were residential gardens, beginning with some for neighboring residents of Bar Harbor, a town on Mount Desert Island along Maine's Frenchman Bay. With the help of social connections and introductions by her mother and by her aunt, Edith Wharton (see 4.31), she met prominent people, which led to working on a variety of significant projects. Within three years she was so well regarded in her field that she was chosen to be the only woman among the founders of the American Society of Landscape Architects, although she preferred the British term *landscape gardener*.

Among her major projects, Beatrix did the initial site and planting planning for the National Cathedral in Washington, DC, in 1899. In 1912 she designed the walled residential garden Bellefield for Mr. and Mrs. Thomas Newbold in Hyde Park, New York—an exquisite walled garden (now restored). For the White House, the first Mrs. Woodrow Wilson, Ellen Loise Axson Wilson, commissioned Beatrix to design the East Colonial Garden (now redesigned as the Jacqueline Kennedy Garden) and the West Garden (now redesigned as the White House Rose Garden). In 1913 Beatrix received a commission from J. Pierpont Morgan to design the Morgan Library grounds in New York City and continued as a consultant there for thirty years (1913–43).

White House garden designed by Beatrix Farrand. *Library of Congress*

On December 17, 1913, Beatrix married Max Farrand, a historian at Stanford and Yale Universities. This was when Max and Beatrix set up the family's Reef Point Estate in Mount Desert Island, Maine, as an educational institution. Beatrix had hoped to attract women to study there because there was still a reluctance to acknowledge that women could succeed in horticulture; she used the grounds as a laboratory for her plants, studying soils and finding ways to protect tender plants. It attracted few students.

Perhaps her most notable work was at the Dumbarton Oaks estate in the Georgetown district of Washington, DC, for Mildred and Robert Woods Bliss. Her design was inspired by her European ventures, especially by the Italian Renaissance gardens, and consisted of establishing a relationship between the architectural and natural environments, with formal terraced gardens stepping down a steep slope and transitioning to a more naturalistic aesthetic approaching the creek. It features garden rooms influenced by Italian and English garden elements and American Arts and Crafts sensibility. Much of the garden consisted of *formal rooms* with interwoven elements of nature and architecture.

In 1928 her husband accepted the position as the first director of the Huntington Library in San Marino, California. They moved to California, but Beatrix had trouble building a clientele in that state. Her few commissions came via friends, such as the Bliss winter and retirement estate, Casa Dorinda, in Montecito, California, and the patronage of Mildred Bliss's mother, Anna Blakely Bliss, for the nearby Santa Barbara Botanic Garden project. In the Los Angeles area she had several commissions with astronomer George Ellery Hale and architect Myron Hunt. With the latter she worked on projects at Occidental College and the California Institute of Technology (Caltech).

Beatrix commuted cross-country by train from California for her eastern projects, such as the design and supervision of the Chinese-inspired garden at the Eyrie for Abby Aldrich Rockefeller on Mount Desert Island in Seal Harbor, Maine. She also collaborated with her aunt Edith on landscape and garden design for the Mount, Wharton's home in Lenox, Massachusetts. This was representative of the Country Place era in the United States, which began in the late nineteenth century and virtually ended by the 1920s as the Great Depression approached.

Sunken garden at Hill-Stead Museum, Farmington, Connecticut, USA. *hillstead.org*

Henry James, a prominent author and a good friend of Edith, introduced her to Theodate Pope Riddle, who owned the estate Hill-Stead, now preserved as the Hill-Stead Museum in Farmington, Connecticut. In 1942, with Walter Macomber, she designed the gardens at Green Spring, near Alexandria, Virginia. Beatrix also designed the Italian, Oriental, and cutting gardens for Eolia, the Waterford, Connecticut, estate of wealthy philanthropist Edward Harkness. Harkness left Eolia to the State of Connecticut in 1950, and it is now open to the public as Harkness Memorial State Park.

In England, her major project was Dartington Hall for heiress Dorothy Payne Elmhirst in the county of Devon. Beatrix was recognized for her work in designing the Peggy Rockefeller Rose Garden at New York Botanical Garden, a winning site of Built by Women New York City, a competition launched by the Beverly Willis Architecture Foundation during fall 2014 to identify outstanding and diverse sites and spaces designed, engineered, and built by women.

Beatrix's campus designs were based on three concepts: plants that bloomed throughout the academic year, emphasizing architecture as well as hiding flaws, and using upright and climbing plants so that the small spaces between buildings would not seem reduced in scale. Her designs are noted for their practicality, simplicity, and ease of maintenance.

She was the first consulting landscape architect for Princeton University in Princeton, New Jersey (1912–43). She was the consulting landscape architect at Yale University in New Haven, Connecticut, for twenty-three years (1923–45), with projects including the Marsh Botanical Garden. She later went on to improve a dozen other campuses, including the University of Chicago (1929–43), along with South California's Occidental College and the California Institute of Technology. Beatrix completed design work for the Pennsylvania School of Horticulture for Women (1931–32). Later she was also the landscape consultant to the Arnold Arboretum of Harvard University (1946–50).

During the last part of her life, Beatrix devoted herself to creating a landscape study center at Reef Point, Maine. Here she continued developing the extensive garden and preparing the property for a transition to a public study center. By 1955, Max Farrand had died and she could not find an institution willing to undertake the expense of maintaining Reef Point. After a wildfire on the island, and facing a lack of funding to complete and ensure the continued operation of a center, she made the decision in 1955 to discontinue the preparations, dismantle the garden, sell the property, and use the proceeds for her last years. She ordered the house torn down and gave away her plants, keeping some of her favorites. She gave her library of 2,700 books and her herbarium to the University of California at Berkeley.

Beatrix then moved 6 miles down the road to Garland Farm, owned by Lewis Garland, her driver and handyman. She lived at Garland Farm until her death in 1959. Garland Farm had two private owners until 2004, when the Beatrix Farrand Society bought the farm. It is open to visitors on open days and by appointment. The society renovated the barn as an educational center for workshops, lectures, and other programs.

Beatrix Farrand was one of the founding eleven members—and the only woman—of the American Society of Landscape Architects (ASLA). The ASLA was established on January 4, 1899, in New York City. It bestows various awards annually to professionals and students in the field of landscape architecture for designs and projects. Categories range in size, scale, and type from small residential areas to large parks and waterfronts.

Beatrix is one of the most accomplished persons recognized in both the first decades of the landscape architecture profession and in the centuries of landscape design. Even more remarkable is that she did so as a woman in a world dominated by men. In 1959, at age eighty-six, Beatrix Cadwalader Farrand died at Mount Desert Island Hospital, Maine.

To learn more about Beatrix's garden commissions, *Beatrix Farrand's American Landscapes: Her Gardens & Campuses*, by Diana Balmori, Diane Kostial McGuire, and Eleanor M. McPeck (Sagapress, 1985), is a good source of information.

4.43 ROSE STANDISH NICHOLS (1872–1960)

Among the earliest professional garden designers and landscape architects, Rose was also a writer, a suffragist, and a peace activist.

Rose was born in 1872, the daughter of Arthur H. Nichols and Elizabeth Fisher Homer. She lived most of her life at 55 Mt. Vernon Street in the Beacon Hill neighborhood of Boston.

She trained with Charles A. Platt, Inigo Triggs, and Constant-Désiré Despradelle at Massachusetts Institute of Technology (MIT), and with Benjamin Watson at the Bussey Institute, Harvard University. Rose traveled to Europe, visiting parks and gardens, and studied at the École des Beaux-Arts in Paris. The Beaux-Arts style was modeled on classical antiquities, preserving these idealized forms and passing the style on to future generations. Rose was influenced by this, as evidenced in her tranquil and approachable garden designs.

Rose designed approximately seventy gardens across the United States and abroad. While she did work in Georgia, Arizona, and California, most of her commissions were in Lake Forest, Illinois. Although her designs were inspired by English formal gardens and influenced by American colonial revival gardens and Italian and Spanish ideas, her planting style was American in spirit.

Portrait of Rose Standish Nichols by Margarita Pumpelly Smyth (American, 1873–1959), ca. 1892. Oil on canvas. *Nichols House Museum collection*

Rose also wrote articles about gardens for popular magazines such as *House Beautiful* and *House & Garden*. She also published three books about European gardens: *English Pleasure Gardens* (1902), *Spanish and Portuguese Gardens* (1924), and *Italian Pleasure Gardens* (1928).

When *English Pleasure Gardens* was first published by the Macmillan Company, it was acclaimed as a useful source for gardeners, tourists, and history lovers. It chronicles the history of British gardens, covering, among others, examples of England's best monastic gardens, formal Tudor gardens, and Elizabethan flower gardens. In her first two books she illustrated them with her own pen-and-ink drawings, showing details from famous gardens. Her third book also included her own photographs taken on her travels.

Though not known for really innovative garden designs, Rose used features from famous gardens and was able to incorporate these in new gardens without clashing with twentieth-century architecture. In addition to her writing and landscape architecture work, Rose was a suffragist and a peace activist. Ignoring marriage, Rose devoted herself to her busy career and good causes. She traveled to peace conferences in Europe, established a discussion group called the League of Small Nations (precursor to the Foreign Policy Association), and helped establish the Women's International League for Peace and Freedom (WILPF). This last group is a nonprofit, nongovernmental organization working *to bring together women of different political views and philosophical and religious backgrounds determined to study and make known the causes of war and work for a permanent peace* and to unite women worldwide who oppose oppression and exploitation. In 1919, Rose was elected an officer of the Boston Equal Suffrage Association. Around 1921 she served the American Society of Landscape Architects as chairman of the committee on the Garden Club of America. In 1937 she attended an event organized by the New York Society of the Descendants of Signers of the Independence Declaration.

Upon her death in 1960, Rose Standish Nichols left her home and its furnishings to become the Nichols House Museum at 55 Mount Vernon Street on Beacon Hill in Boston, Massachusetts. Rose had lived in the house for seventy-five years between 1885 and 1960. Her home and its original art and furnishings provide a glimpse into life on historic Beacon Hill from the mid-nineteenth to mid-twentieth centuries and preserves the lifestyle of the American upper class during Rose's lifetime.

4.44 GRACE TABOR (1873–1973)

One of the first women to identify herself professionally as a landscape architect, Grace is best known for her writing on landscape design and architecture.

Grace was born around 1873 in Cuba, New York. She studied at the Art Students League in Buffalo and in New York City, and at the New York School of Applied Design for Women. Her horticultural training was acquired at the Arnold Arboretum in Boston. She started her writing career in 1905 for such magazines as the *Garden Magazine* and *Country Life in America*. In 1920 she began a garden column for *Woman's Home Companion* magazine that ran until 1941. She reached a wide audience through this magazine, which was one of the most influential women's publications in the country. She wrote many fine, thoughtful articles, though usually brief and less complex than those she wrote for other magazines. She contrasted the old and new styles of gardening with a graphic rendering of a landscape before and after renovations, labeling the *before* illustration as a *mistake in landscaping*. Writing for *Woman's Home Companion*, Grace was considered the doyenne of several female advice givers on the subject of garden design.

Women's Home Companion magazine began life humbly as a mail order monthly in the 1870s and gradually grew in stature until Gertrude Lane, editor from 1911 to 1941, made it the leading women's magazine of the 1930s, with a circulation of three million. During the 1930s, Eleanor Roosevelt was a regular contributor and wrote an article on gardening for the March 1935 issue. She did not actually have a garden of her own, but she wrote about what she would like to grow if she did have one. She confided that she would like to have shrubs and flowers constantly in bloom, *but looking as casual as much like wild flowers as possible*, and that *no garden would be complete if it did not have some old-fashioned yellow rose bushes*.

From 1914 to 1915, Grace started to practice landscape architecture privately, mostly around New York City. She preferred to design gardens for people of average income, rather than for the wealthy. As a result, her gardens were not recorded in publications as extensively as larger, more extravagant landscapes. Because of her professional background, the National War Garden Commission sent her on a promotional lecture tour during WWI in the interest of food production in war gardens. After WWI she was made chairman of the agricultural section of Miss Anne Morgan's committee for devastated France and served in this capacity during the committee's existence.

Grace authored twelve garden books, most published between 1910 and 1921:

The Landscape Gardening Book: Wherein Are Set Down the Simple Laws of Beauty and Utility Which Should Guide the Development of All Grounds (1911)
The Garden Primer: A Practical Handbook on the Elements of Gardening for Beginners (1911)
Making a Garden to Bloom This Year (1912)
Making the Grounds Attractive with Shrubs (1912)
Making the Grounds Attractive with Shrubbery (1912)
Making a Bulb Garden (1912)
Old-Fashioned Gardening: A History and a Reconstruction (1913)
Suburban Gardens (1913)
Wonderdays and Wonderways through Flowerland: A Summer Adventure of Once Upon a Time (1916)
Come into the Garden (1921)
Herbs in Cooking (1934)
Making a Garden of Perennials (1951)

Grace became an editor of the *National Plant, Flower & Fruit Guild Magazine*. She contributed significantly to the magazine *House & Garden*, writing a monthly garden column and in-depth advanced articles on gardening. In addition to her writing and garden design practice, Grace taught at the University of Illinois in 1922. She became associate editor of the *Garden Magazine* (later the *American Home*) and was assistant to the director at the New York State School of Applied Agriculture on Long Island.

Grace's *The Landscape Gardening Book*, published by McBride, Winston and Company in 1911, was her most popular. It became the most respected and popular gardening book of the time, featuring examples from larger contemporaneous American gardens. In this book, Grace emphasizes that every garden, no matter how small, needs a place for us to rest and sit. The book includes chapters on boundaries, garden furniture, planting, general accessories, and garden care.

Grace's seventh book, *Old-Fashioned Gardening: A History and a Reconstruction* (1913, McBride, Nast), was published for gardeners who wished to create their own old-fashioned gardens. Here she began by cautioning readers that they would find no romanticism, no *lovely ladies nor courtly cavaliers here. Here all is sober reality and no dream; here is the truth about old gardens, not select glimpses of a path*. One of her goals was to pin down just what exactly was meant by *old-fashioned gardens*—a term that she felt most people used far too loosely and casually to refer to anything quaint or charming. For her, an old-fashioned American garden was one created between around 1635 (when the first gardens appeared in the colonies) to around 1815 (so as to include the famous gardens of Mount Vernon and Monticello). Of course there was a good deal of variation over time, and in different regions, and Grace meticulously traced the history of five different gardening traditions in North America: the Spanish in Florida, the English in Virginia, the Dutch in New Amsterdam, the Puritans in New England, and the Quakers in Pennsylvania. Modern-day Americans who wanted *old-fashioned* gardens were advised to choose from among these five styles, according to their personal taste and circumstances. The compact Dutch garden, for example, was well suited to small urban lots, while those with more space could use the plantations of Virginia as their model. Gardeners could simply draw on these garden traditions for inspiration, or, if they were truly committed, they could attempt to reproduce an old-fashioned garden. *There is no reason against reproducing an old design*, Grace wrote, *providing every phase of it receives proper attention and no anachronism is permitted*.

She argued strongly that an old-fashioned garden built around a modern style house was *unpleasant*. Those living in colonial, Georgian, or mission-style houses, on the other hand, were advised that only gardens of old design were really suitable. She provided simple plans and a list of plants known to have been used prior to 1815. She also reminded readers that old gardens were above all useful, providing food, beverages, medicines, and dyes, and that all plans should be made with that goal in mind. Otherwise one risked producing something that was merely *a blank form and lifeless shell*.

While Grace's book was meant to provide practical advice to gardeners, it is clear that she was not immune to the romance of old gardens and that she was very much in sympathy with the colonial revival style. Mrs. Anne Macvicar Grant (1755–1838) was a poet and author best known for her collection of mostly biographical poems, *Memoirs of an American Lady*. Grace quoted a passage by her in which she reminisced about the Dutch gardens of mid-eighteenth-century Albany: *I think I see yet what I have often beheld in both town and country, a respectable mistress of a family going out to her garden in an April morning, with her great calash, her little painted basket of seeds, and her robe over her shoulders, to her garden labors . . . A woman, in very easy circumstances and abundantly gentle in form and manners, would sow and plant and rake incessantly.*

In 1932 Grace proposed planting ten million new trees in America to celebrate the bicentennial of George Washington's birth. She inspired many to take an interest in garden design. She died in 1971. She is a good example of a practicing landscape architect who also wrote books and magazine articles. While many of these contained practical advice on designing a garden, such as the use of shrubs, her book *Old-Fashioned Gardening* remains a valuable resource of information about North America's earlier gardens in the period 1635–1815.

Grace hoped that women could recapture some of the virtues of their foremothers by creating gardens that were both beautiful and useful and by passing garden lore on to their children.

4.45 NELLIE BEATRICE OSBORN ALLEN (1874–1961)

Landscape architect best known for her knot gardens

Nellie was born in Cameron, Missouri, in 1874. Prior to 1900 she married Sidney P. Allen, founder of the Louisiana Land and Exploration Company. By 1916 she

Nellie Beatrice Osborn Allen. *Staline Rosario*

had raised a daughter, divorced her husband, and decided to enter the field of landscape architecture. Under the name Beatrice Osborn Allen, she enrolled at the Lowthorpe School of Landscape Architecture for Women in Groton, Massachusetts, in 1916. Founded in 1901 under its original name, Lowthorpe School of Landscape Architecture, Gardening, and Horticulture for Women, it was one of the first in the world to open the profession to females.

Nellie remained there for three years, where her thesis project included a knot garden, which was to become a specialty of hers.

After graduating from Lowthorpe in 1919, Nellie traveled in Europe, to which she would return periodically throughout her life. She set up her own practice in New York City in 1921, using Nellie B. Allen as her professional name and specializing in residential landscape design until the 1940s. Due partly to her late start in her field, her practice remained regional, almost entirely in New York and New England. Commissions included Dellwood, the John Henry Hammond estate in Mount Kisco; the Isabel Dodge Sloane estate on Long Island; Three Waters estate in Gloucester, Massachusetts; Thornedale in Millbrook, New York; and the Anne Morgan estate in Mount Kisco, Millbrook, New York.

Nellie's landscape designs were influenced by the work of famed English garden designer Gertrude Jekyll, whom she met in 1921 on her European travels. She featured perennials in her plantings, creating English-style perennial borders and designs featuring topiary work. Nellie became best known for geometric gardens as well as knot gardens, the designs for which were influenced by those that she had seen during her European travels. She created knot gardens for the 1939 New York World's Fair, the Bishop's Garden at Washington Cathedral, and several private residences.

Nellie's knot gardens were very formal in design, inspired by those that were popular in England and France in the seventeenth century. She sometimes incorporated herbs between the low-clipped shrubs such as boxwood, which formed the framework. These were meticulously clipped and planted to look as if they were intertwined, and kept low so that the pattern was easily seen from the pathways. Often, colored gravel, paths, and other objects, such as statues or birdbaths, were included in the pattern.

Apart from garden design, Nellie gave public lectures on garden design and New England history and occasionally wrote articles for gardening magazines. She was a member-at-large of the Garden Club of America and occasionally wrote articles for the club's bulletin. Nellie Beatrice Allen died in 1961. Her specialty had been knot gardens, and she created some of the best known examples of these in North America, many of which were featured in *House Beautiful*, *Landscape Architecture*, and *Country Life in America*.

4.46 MARIAN CRUGER COFFIN (1876–1957)

One of the country's preeminent landscape designers specializing in large private estates, Marian can take credit for more than fifty significant estate gardens in the northeastern USA.

Marian was born in 1876 into a wealthy upper-class family in Scarborough, New York, but grew up almost penniless due to the death of her father, Julian Ravenel Coffin, when she was seven. During her childhood years, Marian and her mother, Alice, lived with relatives in Geneva, New York. She found the beautiful scenery of the Finger Lakes of upper New York State an inspiration, later writing, *Even as a small girl, I loved the country, not so much gardens and growing things, for I had no experience with these . . . but simply the great outdoor world.*

Although the Coffins had little money, their life with Alice's upper-class relatives gave Marian an almost aristocratic upbringing that introduced her to high society on the East Coast and enabled her to make social connections that were to be extremely valuable in later life. She received almost no formal education, a deficiency that caused significant problems for her in her college years. She was tutored at home, where she also enjoyed the benefits of exposure to fine art and music and became an accomplished horse rider. As a relatively impoverished member of the upper class, Marian had no independent income and faced a choice

Marian Cruger Coffin, 1904. Unknown photographer. *Winterthur Archives*

between finding a rich husband or taking up a professional career. She chose the latter, despite the fact that, as noted by fellow landscape architect Martha Brookes Hutcheson (see 4.41), *it was considered almost social suicide and distinctly matrimonial suicide, for a woman to enter any profession*.

Perhaps fulfilling Martha Brookes Hutcheson's prediction that having a career would be *matrimonial suicide* for a woman of her class, Marian never married.

An architect friend suggested that she might like to try *landscape gardening*, which was the term used at the time for landscape architecture. Women at the time were looking beyond the traditional female careers of school teacher, nurse, and office clerk, but relatively few educational institutions admitted them to study in male-dominated fields such as architecture or horticulture. One of the exceptions was the Massachusetts Institute of Technology (MIT), which had begun admitting women in 1870, only nine years after its establishment. Marian applied there but was initially refused entry, since she was not qualified to meet the admission requirements. However, several of the key faculty members were sympathetic and encouraged her to persevere. She undertook intensive tuition in mathematics and enrolled at MIT in 1901 as a special student, one of four women enrolled in the architecture course and one of only two studying landscape architecture. The four women on the course were the only female members of a 500-strong student body.

Marian took the full range of architectural courses, including studying engineering, physics, math, mechanical drafting, and freehand drawing, in addition to architectural and landscape design. She also studied botany and horticulture under Charles Sprague Sargent at the Arnold Arboretum in Boston, Massachusetts. During her course she spent a summer abroad studying landscape design in France and Italy, as well as going on field trips to study estates in the Boston area. She particularly excelled at botany and became friends with a fellow student, Henry Francis DuPont, who was studying horticulture at Harvard. She later collaborated with him to design the gardens of Winterthur, Delaware.

The Reflecting Pool at Winterthur in Delaware is one of many charms of the elegant gardens of the former du Pont estate. *Harvey Barrison*

Marian's college years were nonetheless a *long grind*, as she described it, with a seemingly unrelenting *long routine of hard work* relieved only by summers spent abroad. She and the other three women in the program maintained a friendly competition with the male students, which, she said, *put us on our mettle to prove that we, too, were serious students and competitors. This association with many types of boys and men I found very helpful as we had a fine spirit of camaraderies in the drafting room and many a helping hand was given me at a critical moment, though one had to steel oneself to hear many a severe criticism, which was perhaps even more valuable.*

Marian found that the strongly male-dominated architectural firms were unwilling to employ a woman. She wrote: *One expected the world to welcome newly fledged landscape artists, but alas, few people seemed to know what it was all about . . . while the idea of taking a woman into an office was unheard of. 'My dear young lady, what will you do about supervising the work on the ground?'* [meaning the laborers] *became such a constant and discouraging query that the only thing seemed to be for me to hang out my own shingle and see what I would do about it.*

She moved to New York City with her mother and took rooms in the National Arts Club in Gramercy Park, Manhattan.

Around 1905, Marian set up her own office at the National Arts Club and began taking commissions, using her family connections to find work. It was a fortuitous time to start her new venture; it was the height of the Country Place era, when wealthy East Coast Americans were eager to develop elaborate European-style gardens for their estates. Marian was well connected in such circles, was widely traveled, came from a good family, was professionally trained, and was known for her good taste. She achieved professional recognition in 1906, when she was accepted as a junior member of the American Society of Landscape Architects (ASLA), which had only two other female members at the time. Then, in 1918, she was made a fellow of the ASLA.

Marian's first jobs were to design small flower gardens, such as the suburban garden she designed for Edward Sprague in 1906 in Flushing, Queens. Noted for its original design, it was situated on a modest lot measuring 150 × 300 feet, typical of the new suburban developments being built on Long Island at the time. Marian argued that a *moderately well-to-do homeowner* could create and maintain a substantial and elaborate garden for a modest expenditure, comparable to that of the cost of a midrange car.

She promoted the idea that even the most featureless lot could be beautified through good design: *We certainly cannot create a magnificent view, but we can plan and plant beautiful screens and backgrounds that will be interesting at all seasons of the year. We may not easily be able to construct a picturesque diversity at ground level, but we can plant so as to have much height and variety in our flower and shrub groups.*

Marian was particularly keen on promoting the importance of trees in gardening, since flower beds typically got most of the glory. She wrote dozens of articles for magazines and published *Trees and Shrubs for Landscape Effects* (1940), Charles Scribner's Sons, in which she discusses the critical role of trees as design elements. She had a very firm grasp on the nature of trees, how they would grow, and how they would affect the bones of her gardens over time. In *Trees and Shrubs* she reminds the reader that trees *screen unsightly objects, they camouflage the service quarters and form the background to garden and lawn. They are planted to frame in far views, to give the effect of distance and to create vistas*.

Paying close attention to trees also meant that she was not just designing formal flower gardens close to the house but was instead laying out the whole property, from entry gate to driveway to more-distant forested areas on-site. She shaped the entire landscape and was brilliant in her ability to plan for the evolution of shrubs, beds, and treelines through the years.

As her fame grew, Marian gained the opportunity to put her design principles in to practice on a larger scale. She was recognized for her refined and elegant designs, both formal and naturalistic. She concerned herself with every detail of the landscape, from drives, paths, woodlands, walkways, and formal gardens to creating vistas and backgrounds. She also concerned herself with her client, stating in one article that she first established what the client wanted in a landscape, then designed it to be in scale with the house and grounds, yet still within the means and tastes of the owner. Her practice had grown large enough for her to need an assistant by 1911, and by 1918 she had moved her office to larger premises at 830 Lexington Avenue, New York City. Marian insisted on being paid the same fees as a male architect and to be treated equally in contracts; this was a novelty for the time. She also liked to employ women to work with her on commissions, giving them the chance to undertake apprenticeships that male prejudice had denied her when she first started her career.

Marian's clientele included some of the wealthiest and most famous families in the country, including the Fricks, the Vanderbilts, and the Huttons. During her career she worked on more than 130 commissions, including dozens of major estate gardens. Among her significant commissions during this period was the design of a garden for William Marshall Bullitt's Oxmoor estate in Glenview, Kentucky, in 1909 (probably due to a recommendation from Henry du Pont). The Bullitt commission led to two similar commissions nearby in 1911. In 1910–11 she also designed gardens for Alfred Boardman in Southampton, New York, and for her friend Elizabeth E. Farnum in Norfolk, Connecticut. A relative of the du Ponts, Hugh

Rodney Sharp, gave her what was to become one of her best-known commissions in 1916, the creation of the gardens of the Gibraltar estate in Wilmington, Delaware.

A view of part of the house and gardens of Gibraltar (Wilmington, Delaware). *John 2009*

She designed Gibraltar in an Italianate Beaux-Arts style as a series of *rooms* to parallel the layout of the mansion. It has a strongly geometric layout, profusely planted in a style reminiscent of an informal English garden. Numerous architectural and decorative elements such as fountains, statues, urns, and hand-forged iron gates provide additional ornamentation.

Her success was recognized by her being elected a fellow of the American Society of Landscape Architects in 1918, and by the 1920s she was one of the most sought-after East Coast landscape architects. Her work was widely featured in popular magazines and professional journals at Marian's own instigation as part of an overt marketing strategy.

She sought to reach the wealthy and powerful women who made up an important part of the readership of publications such as the *Bulletin of the Garden Club of America*. Marian commissioned some of America's leading landscape photographers to take photographs of her creations and promoted her work through slide lectures. Her marketing was highly successful and led to a steady stream of commissions. Most of her commissions were carried out during the twelve years or so between the end of WWI and the start of the Great Depression. She took on several major projects, including designing the landscape of the University of Delaware campus in 1919. Other major projects included gardens for the Bayberryland estate in Shinnecock Hills on Long Island; the Marjorie Merriweather Post estate known as Hillwood, in nearby Brookville; and the huge Caumsett estate (now Caumsett State Historic Park) on behalf of Marshall Field III.

Two projects were carried out in the late 1920s for Edgar W. Bassick in Bridgeport, Connecticut, and Joseph Morgan Wing in Millbrook, New York.

In 1926 Marian fell ill with a serious hip infection that forced her to curtail much of her physical activity and required a lengthy stay in hospital. She moved to a newly acquired house in New Haven, Connecticut, although she continued to maintain her office in New York and commuted there daily. In 1930 Marian was awarded the Gold Medal of Honor by the Architectural League of New York. At the height of her career, she had designed more than fifty significant estate gardens in the northeastern US.

Marian's designs were distinguished by her use of *dramatic contrasts in color, inclusion of wild flowers and woodland plantings, and site unity through effective transition spaces*. She was especially noted for her ability to effectively incorporate functional areas such as tennis courts and putting greens with ornamental areas such as allées (a walkway or drive bordered by trees or bushes). Her willingness to innovate made her a particularly sought-after designer, as clients came to value a more adventurous approach to landscape architecture. Many of Marian's theories and principles can be seen in practice in her most famous creation, the aforementioned Winterthur estate. Her work on du Pont's gardens began in 1929 and became the biggest commission of her career. It was very fortuitously timed for her, since the Wall Street crash of 1929 wiped out the fortunes of many of her clients and brought to an end the era of commissioning elaborate gardens for large country estates. Marian had somewhat better luck with her own investments, and the enormous fortune of the du Ponts insulated that family from the worst of the Great Depression, permitting work on Winterthur to continue throughout the downturn.

With the money from her investments and the fees from the du Ponts for the Winterthur commission, Marian was able to maintain two homes, a maid, and a chauffeur, despite the general economic decline. The Depression meant that large commissions became few and far between. For the rest of her career, Marian had to make do with smaller and less well-compensated commissions for suburban gardens and royalties from her books. She wrote the book *The Seeing Eye*, which was completed but never published, and the manuscript was lost after she died.

After WWI she carried out several more commissions and continued working on Winterthur until the 1950s. She designed layouts for the New York Botanical Garden in the Bronx and traveled extensively in Europe and South America into the late 1940s and early 1950s.

She was awarded an honorary doctorate of letters from Hobart and William Smith Colleges in Geneva, New York, in 1946. A few years later, in 1957, Marian Cruger Coffin died at her home in New Haven. She was eighty-one years old.

4.47 LOUISE BEEBE WILDER (1878–1938)

Garden designer considered one of North America's greatest garden writers; her books are now considered classics of their era.

Louise Beebe Wilder was born to a well-to-do family in Baltimore, Maryland, in 1878. Her passion for gardening began in early childhood. At six years old, Louise planted her first garden, a 6-by-12-foot plot marked out by clothespins and conch shells. She was educated in private schools and spent her Fridays giving flowers to the *sick, sad, and disgruntled*.

In 1902 she married architect Walter Robb Wilder, and the couple moved to Pomona, New York, which was then a fairly rural area. In 1925 the couple moved a bit farther south to the village of Bronxville, where Louise transformed a weedy 1-acre property into a diverse Eden with a long grape arbor and stone pillars. Here she transformed the country property known as Balderbrae by adding pathways, a pair of half-moon fountains, a grape arbor, terraces, flowering trees, a walled garden, and an herb bed.

The cover of the April 1909 issue of *American Homes and Gardens* pictures the Bronxville home of Louise Beebe Wilder, painted by Beverly Towles. Published by Munn & Company. *Smithsonian Libraries, Biodiversity Heritage Library*

One of her first commissions was aiding the design of Station Plaza in Bronxville.

She then began to design residential gardens across the county, where her philosophy was to create something *formal in design but most informal in execution*. Her gardens were inspired by British garden designer Gertrude Jekyll and the British tradition of abundance and color, with no place for

Louise Beebe Wilder

austerity and uniformity. Alongside this work, Louise was very active in gardening club circles. She served as vice president of the Federated Garden Clubs of New York State and acted as editor of *New York Gardens*, its journal. She founded a local Working Gardeners Club too, whose early members were poets, painters, and business people. The club went on to start a botanical lending library and contributed money to the planting of a large victory garden during WWII at the New York Botanical Garden. Louise was also a director and member of the advisory council there.

Between 1916 and 1937, Louise wrote ten gardening books and many articles for magazines and newspapers, often mentioning her own gardens in her work. Her books detailed her experiences as a gardener, and they were popular for offering clear, explicit advice, rather than verbose, pompous horticultural writing. Louise was also candid about her failures and what she had learned through experimentation.

Her first book, *My Garden* (Doubleday, Page, 1916), covered many topics and gave general advice. In the foreword she pointed out the suitability of gardening and the manual labor involved in it as a pastime for women. She wrote, *Many a crude and unsightly object is brought into harmony with its surroundings through the kindly tact of some gracious climbing plant. No need to emphasize the charm of vine clad arbors and porches, of green-draped walls and gateways, which do so much toward giving to our gardens the appearance of permanence and livableness so much desired. But perhaps it is a little needful to speak of the fact that the chief factor in this charm is luxuriance.* A paperback reprint was issued in 2010 by Kessinger.

Colour in My Garden (Doubleday, Page, 1918) focused on the use of color in plantings and garden design. In this she wrote, *We are haunted by visions of exquisite colors in perfect harmony . . . the prettiest blue border I ever saw was one wherein a few nasturtium seeds had been accidentally dropped, and between the elegantly aspiring stalks of larkspur and anchusa one got little sparkles of flame and saffron and buff that endowed the blue flowers with a shimmering spirit that would certainly not have been theirs without those unbidden companions.*

Louise's *socio-botanical commentaries*, as author Michael Pollan termed them, captured the spirit of a moment in America when suburban gardening and suitable forms of landscape design for it were on the rise, and the older, more formal style of large estate gardens was in decline. He points out that the enjoyment gardeners get from their gardens is what is most important.

Rock gardening was one of Louise's special interests, dealing with this in her general books as well as specifically in *Adventures in My Garden and Rock Garden* (Doubleday Page, 1923) and *Pleasures and Problems of a Rock Garden* (Doubleday, Doran).

The Fragrant Path (Macmillan, 1932) is a charming book about the scents of a garden. Of the many books on this subject, this is one of the most comprehensive. Of the plant rosemary, for instance, she wrote that this *makes a charming pot plant, neat, svelte, with its dark, felt-lined leaves held sleek against its sides. The smell . . . is keen and heady, resinous, yet sweet, with a hint of nutmeg*. In the chapter "Pleasures of the Nose," Louise wrote, *A garden full of sweet odors is a garden full of charm. . . . It is born of sensitive and very personal preferences yet its appeal is almost universal*. There are chapters on fragrant mushrooms, as well as those on more common herbs and roses.

Adventures with Hardy Bulbs (Macmillan, 1936) is a classic work on its subject. It is illustrated with photographs and line drawings by Louise's son. In the foreword, Louise explains her frequent use of the word *adventures* in her titles: *Adventure is of the mind—a mental attitude toward everyday events wherever experienced. One does not have to sit through the long night of an Antarctic winter with an Admiral Byrd to know this, or to explore uncharted airways. Adventure may be met with any day, any hour, on one's own doorstep, just around the corner; it may lurk in the subway, on a bus stop, in the garden*.

Louise's gardening books are written with humor and grace. Behind her words lie a lifetime of real gardening experience and reading and diligent research. Her gardening books may be out of print, but they are seldom out of date. Her other books were *Adventures in a Suburban Garden* (1931), *What Happens in My Garden* (1935), and *The Garden in Color* (1937).

In 1937 the Garden Club of America honored Louise with the distinguished medal for horticultural achievement. By that time, Louise's writings had made it to the *New York Times*, *Horticulture*, and the English *Journal of the Royal Horticultural Society*. *House & Garden* published more than 141 Wilder bylines. Eden Ross Lipson, former editor at the *New York Times Book Review*, saw Louise as *a great Romantic enthusiast, with a strong vein of scientific curiosity that she exercised on a domestic scale*.

Louise served on the board of the New York Botanical Garden. At the turn of the twentieth century, when suffragists were demanding financial freedom, Louise pioneered this trailblazing sisterhood of determined, autonomous women, becoming one of the first to professionalize a domestic domain that had been previously dominated by men. When Louise Beebe Wilder died on April 20, 1938, she left behind a lasting legacy of lush gardens influenced by her passion and skill. A *New York Times* obituary named her the master behind residential gardens across the country, but it was her books that really make her one of the greatest of the women pioneers of North American gardening. Many of the gardening books that were available during her lifetime had been written in a somewhat scholarly, pompous style and often assumed that the reader was familiar with the basics. Louise changed that with her down-to-earth, practical advice based on her own garden and the trials, tribulations, and experiments that she had experienced in it.

4.48 LESTER *"NELLIE"* GERTRUDE ELLEN ROWNTREE (1879–1979)

A renowned field botanist, horticulturist, and a pioneer in the study, propagation, and conservation of California native plants

Born Gertrude Ellen Lester to a Quaker family in Penrith, England, she spent the first ten years of her life in the picturesque landscape of the Lake District, developing a deep appreciation of nature and living an outdoor life. Throughout her life she was known as Nellie.

In 1889 her family moved to the United States, to a homestead in Galena, Kansas. The family had been promised a developed Quaker community with roads, schools, libraries, and colleges, but, far from settled comfort, the reality was that there were no amenities, and many families were still living in dugouts. Two of her siblings died because of a contaminated water supply.

After a disastrous two years in Kansas, the Lester family relocated to a Quaker community near Los Angeles; Nellie was ten years old, and it was here that she first became acquainted with the California wildflowers that became her life's passion.

Nellie was sent to finish her schooling in a Quaker boarding school in Westtown, Pennsylvania, and graduated in 1902 at age twenty-three. She had to give up a scholarship she was awarded to the Pennsylvania School of Horticulture for Women to nurse her ailing mother. She had no regrets about this and said, reminiscing in

Lester Rowntree with a plant press and the car converted for camping. *California Academy of Sciences*

her 100th year, that to go to horticultural college would have spoiled everything because *all the originality would be gone. It would be all what you learned—put on, veneer, pretense. I don't like pretense.* She settled in Oradell, New Jersey, after her marriage to Bernard Rowntree in 1908. They would have a son together, Cedric.

Nellie designed her first garden featuring two rowan trees at the gates to commemorate the name Rowntree. Oradell featured a fine lawn, a rock garden, a herbaceous perennial border, a separate vegetable garden, and a chicken yard. Meanwhile, Nellie pursued her botanical interests as actively as she could, doing some seed testing for governmental inspection bureaus. She also corresponded with horticulturalists around the world, exchanging seeds and observations.

The Rowntrees relocated back to Southern California in 1920. Their final move was to the Carmel Highlands, a few miles south of Carmel, in 1925. There, on property overlooking the Pacific, Nellie began her career with native plants. By 1930 she owned a business, Lester Rowntree & Company in Carmel, which sold California wildflower seeds to gardeners across the country. She never gathered seeds in the wild to sell directly but took just enough wild seeds to propagate seed stock in her garden. Her packets of seeds cost $.05 postage paid, and 400 different seeds were offered.

In 1931, Nellie and Bernard divorced and Nellie moved up the hill above the coastal pine forest, where she built a small wooden house and nursery on several acres that became her garden and home base until her death. She really started as an independent naturalist only in her fifties.

A self-proclaimed *lady-gypsy*, Nellie spent most of each year doing fieldwork in California and the West while living outdoors, believing that the only way to know native plants was to live with them for weeks at a time in their natural surroundings. Because of her reputation as a field botanist, Nellie has been compared with David Douglas, the nineteenth-century British botanist who first documented western North American flora. Garden writer Joan Parry Dutton writes, *There are striking similarities between Lester Rowntree and David Douglas. In fact, Lester could be Douglas' plant-wise and spiritual descendant* [for] *Lester's knowledge of California wild flowers is unrivaled; it is safe she knows more about them than Douglas ever knew.*

Nellie was a talented and prolific writer, authoring two well-received books on native plants and shrubs, four children's books, and more than 700 magazine, newspaper, and journal articles. She shared her extensive knowledge of wildflowers and shrubs in numerous journal and magazine articles, books, and public lectures, all the time arguing tirelessly for their protection. Her most popular book was *Hardy Californians: A Woman's Life with Native Plants*, first published in 1936 by Macmillan and republished in 2006 by University of California Press.

Flowering Shrubs of California was her second book, published in 1939 by Stanford University Press. A second print was published in 1948 by Stanford University Press. In this, she explains her methods: *I have approached the plants from the gardener's, not the scientist's standpoint, hoping that my account will bridge the too-wide-gap between botanical manuals and books on gardening. . . . In compiling it I have followed the invariable rule of writing only from my own notes, taken on the spot, of the things the plants have told me in personal interviews.*

In her article "The Lone Hunter," published in June 1939, she said, *I inhabit my hillside only from November to February, while the winter storms are blowing and the winter rains pouring. In March and April I have long shining days on the desert, in May happy weeks in the foothills, where a chorus of robins wakes me and my morning bath is in a rushing stream of just-melted snow. In June I am in the northern counties scented with new-mown hay and wild strawberries. In July in the higher mountains, and in August and September up in the alpine zone with mule or burro.*

She would return to Carmel for the winter, spending her time reading, writing, listening to music, and sorting and packaging seed, which she sold under her own label. Her major publishing outlet at this time was the *Santa Barbara Gardener*, to which she contributed thirty-five articles between 1925 and 1942.

Nellie usually traveled alone in a car that she converted into an efficient camping wagon by removing the back seat and outfitting the space with supplies. Leaving the car, she would reach remote places on foot and, when necessary, with a pack animal. Every region of California—desert to redwood forest, sea coast to mountain peak—was explored and recorded in notes, photographs, collected specimens, and seeds.

Nellie's hillside garden in the Carmel Highlands became famous. Only California natives or, as she put it, plants that behaved like natives were allowed. Plants that behaved like natives were those that came from areas with climates similar to that of California, did not take over the garden, and did not require a lot of extra care. She stocked the garden with plants she collected, bought, or exchanged with other horticulturists and occasionally stole for the purpose of conservation. Horticulturist James Roof once asked her how she had acquired a specimen of Laurel Hill Cemetery manzanita. She answered, *I garnered it ghoulishly in a gunnysack.*

The Lester Rowntree manzanita (*Arctostaphylos lester rowntree*) was named in her honor. It grows into a medium to large shrub with a mounding habit, 8–10 feet tall and 10–15 feet wide. It has attractive, colorful pink flowers and new foliage growth with reddish tips during the winter; mature leaves are slate gray green. Large clusters of red-blushed fruit mature in early spring and are among the most attractive of the manzanitas.

During her lifetime, Nellie also did some work as a landscape architect, despite having no formal training. She advertised her specialties as *intimate gardens, rock gardens, wild flower gardens*. She also described herself as a maker of gardens that express the owner's personal tastes and as one who carries them out with beautiful and unusual plants, exotic or native. She designed a rock garden for the Santa Maria Inn, a fashionable resting place of the time for motorists traveling between San Francisco and Los Angeles. Financially on her own from 1932 onward, Nellie recalled sometimes living for ten cents a day on chicken feed boiled and eaten like oatmeal. She did publish more than 100 articles during this period and was probably not as poor as she made herself out to be. Gathering materials for her writing, she took long trips not only in California and most of the rest of the United States, but also in parts of Canada and Mexico. However, it was the above-timberline Sierra peaks that were her favorite places.

Alternating between the wilderness life and the comforts of Carmel, Nellie struck her own balance, proving that she could enjoy both wilderness experiences and domestic comforts.

Writing in *Hardy Californians*, she said, *I wish there was a word one could use instead of the acquisitive-sounding "collecting," which has such a vampirish and predatory ring. Intelligent collecting is a conservation measure; indeed the work is legitimate only when done with knowledge and forethought and when the motive is the preservation of the plants themselves.*

Writer and horticulturalist Judith Larner Lowry said of Nellie's legacy: *Today, it would be hard to find a professional in the field of native plant horticulture who was not, at some point, inspired by Lester Rowntree. The model of her double focus, wildland exploration and landscape use of plants, is followed by numerous California native plant horticulturists, from arboretum directors to landscapers to nursery professionals, who make regular trips into the wild for the pleasure of observing plants in their homes, and to collect seeds and cuttings for propagation.*

Nellie's thoughts on conservation were summarized in *Plant Collecting: An Aid to Conservation* (Garden Club of California, 1938). She said, *Conservation must not stop simply at preventing a plant from being destroyed in situ. . . . Conservation in its broadest sense means also seeing to it that the desirable species exposed to extermination are perpetuated, or at least being given a chance to carry on in another place.*

Her formal honors in the worlds of horticulture and conservation included election as honorary secretary of the British Alpine Garden Society, honorary life president of the California Native Plant Society, and president-at-large of the American Herb Society. She received a national award from the American Horticultural Society, which cited Nellie for the *conservation and propagation of California's flora, famous as author, photographer, and lecturer and children's author. A truly great personality of horticulture*.

Nellie turned eighty in 1959 and continued her active life of fieldwork, travel, lecturing, and writing. She was a cofounder of the California Native Plant Society in 1965 and served as its honorary president until her passing. She lost her driver's license in 1968, a year before her ninetieth birthday. This was a devastating blow to her independent life because she could no longer travel as she pleased. She had to depend on others to do her shopping in town or drive her to field sites. Lester "Nellie" Rowntree died in 1979, just five days after her 100th birthday.

The Lester Rowntree Native Plant Garden was created to display native plants, shrubs, and trees suitable for cultivated gardens and landscaping in coastal California. It is adjacent to the Flanders Mansion in Mission Trail Nature Preserve, on the National Register of Historic Places at 25800 Hatton Road, Carmel, California. The garden was created in 1980 by her son, Cedric, and his wife, Harriette, with funds and volunteer help from the local chapter of the California Native Plant Society.

4.49 ISABELLA PRESTON (1881–1965)

Hailed as the Queen of Ornamental Horticulture, Isabella is widely known for her achievements in plant hybridization and her extensive work in ornamental plant breeding.

Isabella Preston. *Public Archives of Canada and the National Library Building, 395 Wellington Street, Ottawa, Ontario. C-023727. Date: ca. 1956, Reference: Box number: RV90,Item ID number: 3199364*

Isabella Preston was born in 1881 in Lancaster, England, where her father worked as a silversmith. As a child she attended boarding school in Liverpool and later studied at the University of London. She gardened from an early age, helping her father on the family farm. Her only formal education in horticulture was obtained through a course at Swanley Horticulture College in Kent, England, which she completed before immigrating to Canada in 1912 at age thirty-one. She enrolled in the Ontario Agricultural College (OAC) the same year to study plant breeding and was one of the few women pursuing the subject at the time. Within her first year, Isabella transitioned from class-based study to hands-on work under the supervision of J. W. Crow, head of the department of horticulture. Isabella would go on to become the first professional woman hybridist in Canada. From her enrollment in the OAC until 1920, she contributed to the successful breeding of various vegetables, fruits, and ornamental plants, including garden lilies. In 1920 she relocated to Ottawa, Ontario, and worked as a day laborer for the federal government at the Central Experimental Farm (CEF). Her work was noticed by Dominion horticulturist W. T. Macoun, and she was soon offered the position of specialist in ornamental horticulture. She was the first person to focus solely on breeding ornamental plants.

During her twenty-six-year career, Isabella produced nearly 200 new hardy hybrids of lily, lilac, crab apple, iris, and rose for Canada's cold climate. While female plant breeders were rather rare in her day, she quietly challenged gender bias and set the stage for new generations of breeding programs at the CEF and elsewhere. She gained international recognition by introducing the acclaimed 'George C. Creelman' lily. In 1939, Howard L. Hutt, emeritus professor of horticulture at the OAC, recalled his feelings when he first saw the new lilies growing there: *I can well remember seeing their first bloom, four and five immense white flowers on sturdy stems about 3 ft tall. And I thought, well here is a worthwhile new lily. But when I happened to be at the college a week later and saw two or three of the original plants at least 5 ft high and bearing 15 blooms I felt like taking off my hat, even if I did not throw it up in the air.*

The object of Hutt's joy was the new variety of lily developed at the OAC by Isabella Preston. Hutt was hardly the last one enthused by the new flower. The Creelman lily, named after the OAC president, became an international star.

Over the course of her career, Isabella gained international recognition. She developed many of the 125 different strains in the CEF lilac collection. Her lilac and crab apple hybrids can still be seen flowering at the CEF each spring, along with two of her roses. Isabella's achievements include the following:

Preston lilacs: Many of the fifty-two hardy and late-blooming varieties are named for Shakespearean characters. The varieties of lilac that were commonly seen in Europe bloomed too early in the Canadian climate, and the buds or blooms were frequently nipped by late spring frosts, so Isabella worked on hybridizing them to flourish in the Canadian climate. Most of these can be seen in the CEF's lilac collection today. Eighty of Isabella's late-blooming cultivars are recorded in the International Lilac Register, although only about one-half of these were distributed to other institutions or nurseries. Cultivars 'Audrey,' 'Elinor,' and 'Isabella' received awards of merit from the Royal Horticultural Society, London, England, in 1939, 1951, and 1941, respectively; 'Bellicent' was awarded a first-class certificate in 1946.

Stenographer lilies: Named after the seven stenographers working at the CEF at the time, these lilies have dark-red or orange flowers that face outward and upward, which was a unique characteristic of this type of plant. Five of the Stenographer-series lilies won awards of merit from horticulture societies in London and Boston and were widely distributed commercially.

Fighter Aircraft lilies: Named for WWII Allied planes

Canadian Lake crab apples (or rosyblooms): The fifteen hardy crab apple trees with colored leaves and pretty flowers are named after Canadian lakes. Some of these rosyblooms, planted as early as 1928, can still be found in the arboretum and ornamental gardens at the CEF.

Siberian irises: Named after Canadian rivers

Preston roses: At least twenty hardy varieties, many of which were named after Canadian native tribes (Agassiz, Algonquin, Antenor, Ardelia, Caribou, Carmenetta, Chippewa, Conestoga, Cree, Erie, Huron, Iroquois, Langford, Micmac, Millicent, Mohawk, Nascapee, Orinda, Patricia Macoun, Ojibway, Poliarchus, Regina, Rosania, Sylvander, and Valeria). While her roses never won her awards, they provided an excellent stage for the work of Dr. Felicitas Svejda, who worked at the CEF from 1956 to 1986 and became known as Canada's rose expert.

Isabella was hailed as the Queen of Ornamental Horticulture, and a new hybrid species of lilacs, *Syringa prestoniae*, was named in her honor. This was the result of a cross between wild species from China; it put Canada on the lilac map.

Isabella was co-organizer of the North American Lily Society. The Isabella Preston trophy was established by the North American Lily Society in recognition of her work. She received awards from many Canadian and international horticultural societies, including lifetime memberships from the Massachusetts Horticultural Society and the Canadian Iris Society. Notable awards include the Veitch Memorial Medal in Gold (Royal Horticultural Society, London, 1938), Jackson Dawson Medal (Massachusetts Horticultural Society, 1946), Lytell Cup (Lily Committee, Royal Horticultural Society, 1950), and the E. H. Wilson Memorial Award (North American Lily Society, 1961).

In 2005 the CEF created the Preston Heritage Collection. In February 2007 the *Canada Post* released two new stamps featuring a lilac variety developed by Isabella.

Isabella wrote numerous articles on various horticultural subjects and in 1929 published a successful book. *Garden Lilies*, published by Orange Judd, was the first book about lily cultivation in Canada. The book had chapters such as "Where to Plant," "Hybridisation," "Lilies in Pots," and "List of Varieties with Descriptive Notes." In 2013 Coss Press published a reprint under the title *Lilies For Every Garden*.

Isabella Preston retired in 1946 and settled in Georgetown, Ontario, where she remained a fixture in the horticultural scene until her death in 1965. Following her death, 139 of her gardening and plant books, along with her personal archives, were donated to the Royal Botanical Gardens Library in Hamilton, Ontario. She had an international reputation as the first person to focus solely on breeding ornamental plants, authoring two books. While female plant breeders were rather rare in her day, she challenged gender bias and set the stage for new generations of breeding programs, inspiring women to focus on this horticultural area.

4.50 MARIAN "DAISY" HUBBARD FAIRCHILD (1880–1962)

Devoted traveling companion and assistant to botanist husband David, who was responsible for the introduction of more than 80,000 exotic plants and varieties of established crops into the United States

Marian Hubbard "Daisy" Bell Fairchild was born in 1880 in Washington, DC, the daughter of Mabel Hubbard Bell and Alexander Graham Bell. In 1903 her husband-to-be, David Fairchild, became acquainted with the famous inventor Alexander Graham Bell and his family. Two years later he married Bell's daughter, Marian "*Daisy*," and the couple settled in Chevy Chase, outside Washington, DC.

From 1904 to 1928, David served as chairman of the USDA's Office of Foreign Seed and Plant Introduction. In 1917 the Fairchilds began wintering in Coconut Grove, Florida, where they purchased a property at 4013 Douglas Road, naming it the Kampong (which means "a cluster of houses" in Malay).

David worked in the US Agriculture Department but rarely worked at the department. He was sent to Java, Europe, Australia, and the South Pacific in search of plants of potential use to the American people. Daisy accompanied him on most of these expeditions, often to dangerous, unexplored, and rugged locations.

David and Daisy visited every continent in the world (except Antarctica), and their expeditions brought back hundreds of important plants into cultivation in the United States, including varieties of mangoes, alfalfa, nectarines, rice, pistachios, dates, cotton, horseradish, soybeans, bamboos, and flowering cherries—varieties particularly well known for decorating the streets of Washington, DC. Daisy was an important member of the team and the hunting forays. She coauthored several books

Marian Hubbard (Daisy) Fairchild. Photographer Harris & Ewing, Inc., 1937. *Library of Congress's Prints and Photographs division*

with her husband, including an early work on the macrophotography of insects titled *Book of Monsters* (National Geographic Society, 1914).

In 1897 and 1898, David Fairchild helped fellow plant explorer Walter T. Swingle organize the US Department of Agriculture's Office of Foreign Seed and Plant Introduction. The facility moved to South Dade County in 1921, after the War Department offered abandoned Aman Field to the USDA. On April 26, 1923, the first trees were planted at the new USDA Plant Introduction Garden at Aman Field.

The period of great plant explorations continued unabated through the 1930s, with Daisy and David, and other intrepid plant hunters, bringing thousands of new plant specimens into the station for investigation and propagation.

The Fairchild Tropical Botanic Garden, named in their honor, is an 83-acre botanic garden with extensive collections of rare tropical plants, including palms, cycads, and flowering trees and vines, in Coral Gables, Florida.

A view of part of the Fairchild Tropical Botanic Garden, 10901 Old Cutler Road, Coral Gables, Florida, 33156. *publicgardens[S2].org*

It manages one of the largest and most dynamic plant conservation programs of any North American botanic garden. The Fairchild Tropical Botanic Garden, along with Miami-Dade Natural Areas Management, is conserving more than eighty-five species of threatened plant species. There are more than 3,700 palms planted at Fairchild, with 193 genera and more than 550 species represented. Fairchild's cycad collection includes representations of most of the world's 200-plus species. It is the largest North American collection, with more than 700 living plants, and is an important resource for research, as well as a safeguard against extinction of certain plants.

With the help and encouragement of Daisy, David wrote four books that describe their extensive world travels and activities in introducing new plant species to the United States. In addition to sharing some of his legendary tropical botanical expertise, they provide graphic accounts of their travels and of long-gone native cultures that they were able to see before being modernized. David was an accomplished photographer and illustrated these books himself. Those books include

Exploring for Plants (Macmillan, 1930)
The World Was My Garden: Travels of a Plant Explorer (Charles Scribner's Sons, 1938)
Garden Islands of the Great East: Collecting Seeds from the Philippines and Netherlands India in the Junk Chêng Ho (Charles Scribner's Sons, 1943)
The World Grows Round My Door: The Story of The Kampong, a Home on the Edge of the Tropics (Charles Scribner's Sons, 1947)

David, again with the help and support of Daisy, also wrote many monographs about plants, plant exploring, and the transportation and cultivation of new plants in the United States. Even in retirement, David continued leading expeditions to distant corners of the globe, including their last expedition to Central America when he was seventy-five years old. David died in 1954. Daisy continued to live and work in their beloved Kampong and died twelve years later, in 1964.

David and Daisy had been responsible for the introduction of more than 80,000 exotic plants and varieties of established crops into the United States. They visited every continent in the world apart from Antarctica, and their expeditions brought back hundreds of important plants into cultivation. Daisy coauthored several books with her husband, and her legacy also includes helping to create one of North America's most important botanical gardens, the Fairchild Tropical Botanic Garden. It remains an important safeguard against extinction of plants and is a valuable and perhaps irreplaceable resource for research.

Another view of part of the Fairchild Tropical Gardens. *Alex*

4.51 ANNE BETHEL SPENCER (1882–1975)

Poet, civil rights activist, teacher, and librarian who was inspired by her garden

Anne was born in 1882 on a farm in Henry County, Virginia. Her father was Joel Cephus Bannister, born a slave, and her mother was Sarah Louise Scales, whose own mother had been a slave. Her parents moved to Martinsville soon after Anne was born, and her father became the proprietor of a saloon. Anne's parents separated a few years later, so she went with her mother to Bramwell, West Virginia. Anne was later fostered to a prominent, well-to-do Black couple, William Dixie and his wife. In 1893, when Anne was eleven, her mother, determined that she would have a formal education, enrolled her in the Virginia Theological Seminary and College (now Virginia University of Lynchburg). A fellow student at school, Edward Alexander Spencer of Lynchburg, tutored Anne in math and sciences, and she helped him with languages. The couple married in 1901. Edward had some experience and talent in construction and in business, and he designed and built their home on Pierce Street in Lynchburg, today the site of the Anne Spencer Museum.

Anne was a very enthusiastic, keen, and successful gardener. According to the Anne Spencer Museum: *The original garden, with its young shrubs and trees, was an open, sunny garden with masses of flowers and grass paths*. It was recorded that among the garden's plants and features were roses, lilacs, bulbs, perennials, a grape arbor, a pond, and a pergola. The garden itself, as well as its preservation and renovation, has been featured in several gardening publications, both nationally and internationally, and is the subject of a book, *Lessons Learned from a Poet's*

Anne Spencer in her garden.
Anne Spencer House and Garden Museum, Inc.

Garden (2011), by Jane Baber White. To this day, many of Anne's own shrubs, bulbs, and flowers, including her roses, still bloom on the property. She treasured her home garden and the cottage her husband built for her in it, which she named Edankraal (from the couple's names, Edward and Anne, and *kraal*, the Afrikaans word for enclosure or corral). She would draw inspiration there, often reading and writing late into the night in her beloved, peaceful cottage retreat, surrounded by her beloved garden.

Ann had a lifelong determination to improve conditions for African Americans in her community, and it was through her civil rights work that she was inspired to begin her career as a poet. With her husband she often hosted African American travelers in their home, since because of segregation they were barred from staying at local inns and hotels. As a result, their home became a salon and meeting place for prominent individuals. In 1918 Anne helped found the Lynchburg chapter of the National Association for the Advancement of Colored People (NAACP).

She had experimented with writing poetry since she was a child, and some of her poems were included in an anthology, *The Book of American Negro Poetry*, published in 1922. Although she wrote prolifically, only about thirty in total were published in her lifetime. Much later, two dozen more were published in her biography by J. Lee Greene, *Time's Unfading Garden: Anne Spencer's Life and Poetry* (published in 1977). Despite this limitation of published work in her lifetime, the quality of her work established her as a significant poet of the twentieth century. She was the first African American woman poet published in the *Norton Anthology of Modern Poetry* (1973).

Anne worked at the all-white Jones Memorial Library in Lynchburg and was also the librarian for the all-Black Dunbar High School for twenty years. She dedicated her free time to serving on local committees that worked to broaden the social, economic, and legal stature of Black Americans. She absolutely, resolutely refused to ride segregated buses and street cars. Spencer's son said of her: *My mother was full of fire.*

Anne died from cancer at age ninety-three in 1975. She is buried alongside her husband, who died in 1964, at Forest Hills Cemetery in Lynchburg. Inspired by her garden, she created significant poetry and was a pioneer for the advancement of people of color.

4.52 HELEN MORGENTHAU FOX (1884–1974)

Helen published widely, specializing on the topic of gardening with herbs. She lectured extensively on gardening around the world. She was well known during most of her long life as a writer and scholar, particularly on horticultural subjects.

Helen graduated from Vassar in the first decade of the twentieth century, a time when the vast majority of American women had no college education. She married Mortimer J. Fox in 1906, and they went on to have three children: Henry, Mortimer Jr., and Therese. She was a prolific and successful author of gardening books during her long, productive life. She did much to popularize visiting gardens, the growing of and use of herbs in cooking, and growing vegetables for the kitchen. Helen's best-known book was *Gardening for Good Eating* (Macmillan, 1943).

In this book she gives excellent introductory instructions as to soil preparation, she intersperses her text with enticing recipes and suggestions for varied uses, she has a section on pests and diseases, and she gives one section over to instruction—important today—on storage, including the preparation of storage bins, pits, and containers, outdoors or in. Helen also gives essential information on kinds of vegetables and fruits to be stored and when, where, and how. Helen's other books include

Gardens and Gardening: A Selected List of Books (1927)
Garden Cinderellas: How to Grow Lilies in the Garden (1928)
Patio Gardens (1929)

Helen (*center, wearing a black hat*) with Agnes J. Quirk (*left*) and Florence Hedges (*right*). Science Service, Records, 1920s–1970s. Quirk was assistant to the senior plant pathologist, United States Department of Agriculture (USDA), 1901–1927, and served as head of the laboratory, 1928–1948. Hedges worked as a botanist at the USDA for much of her career. *Smithsonian Institution Archives*

What Spain Can Teach Us about Gardening (1929)
Jean C. N. Forestier (1931)
Gardens to See in Travels Abroad (1931)
More Gardens to See When Traveling Abroad (1931)
Gardens in Hawaii (1931)
Gardening with Herbs for Flavor and Fragrance (1933)
Low Growing Native American Flowering Trees (1944)
The Aging Garden (1948)
Abbe David's Diary (1949)
A Visit to California Gardens and Gardeners (1957)
André Le Nôtre: Garden Architect to Kings (1962)
Adventure in My Garden (1965)
Gardening with Herbs (1970)
The Years in My Herb Garden (1973)

Helen Morgenthau Fox died on January 14, 1974, in Mount Kisco, New York. She was eighty-nine years old. She is remembered today as a writer and scholar, having done much to popularize visiting gardens, the growing of and use of herbs in cooking, and growing vegetables for the kitchen.

4.53 MARY GIBSON HENRY (1884–1967)

American botanist and plant collector

Mary was born near Jenkintown, Pennsylvania, to Susan Worrell Pepper and John Howard Gibson in 1884. Her mother's family were Quakers who had arrived

Mary Gibson Henry (*center*) on one of her many exploratory expeditions. *henrybotanicgarden.org*

with William Penn and helped found Philadelphia. The family was known for their horticultural activities, and it is recorded that in 1828, her great-grandfather George Pepper was a member of the first council of the Pennsylvania Horticulture Society, still regarded today as one of America's most prestigious garden societies.

Her father was keen on hunting and camping, and on camping forays with him, she soon discovered the joys of nature, particularly of America's abundant wild plants. Exploring around their camp in Moosehead Lake in Maine, she came across many treasures. A flower (*Linnaea borealis*, a dwarf evergreen shrub) particularly fascinated her and produced, she said, *not only a love for and appreciation of the absolute perfection of the flower itself, but also for the dark, silent forest that shelters such treasures*. Her passion for plants was born.

Her formal education ended in 1902, when she graduated from the Agnes Irwin School in Philadelphia at age eighteen. University education was not considered suitable or appropriate for women of that time, so the dutiful daughter married John Norman Henry, a physician, in 1909. By 1915 she and her husband had bought a large farm in Maryland. While her husband was overseas during WWI, Mary gardened and read horticulture books widely. She found inspiration in the writing of William Bartram, a botanist and explorer who had traveled through the Southeast between 1773 and 1777. (See 4.4, Elizabeth Lamboll, who had a close horticultural association with William and his father, John Bartram.)

Mary spent countless hours poring over horticultural catalogs. She developed long-term relationships by mail with the US Department of Agriculture's Office of Foreign Plant Introductions and the Royal Botanic Garden, Edinburgh, Scotland. From these studies and communications, she built a solid foundation of knowledge about plants. One of her early mentors was Francis Pennell, curator of botany at the Academy of Natural Sciences in Philadelphia, from whom she sought help with identification. When she expressed an interest in collecting wild plants for her garden, he urged her to collect herbarium specimens along with the plants and taught her how to store and document her finds and turn them into dried herbarium specimens suitable for botanical study.

Mary established a large vegetable garden at her home, grew some ornamental plants and native rock plants, and also tended orchids in her greenhouse. An article she wrote on growing orchids was published in *Garden Magazine* in 1924.

In 1926, with her husband, she bought Gladwyne, a run-down farm of 90 acres about 12 miles from the center of Philadelphia. She immediately began building a large greenhouse attached to the house and began a program of cultivating and planting the grounds on an ambitious scale. By 1931 she listed 850 different trees and shrubs on the grounds. Her interest in diversity within a single species was later reflected in her passion for collecting and hybridizing and in her enthusiastic pursuit of particular colors and dimensions. Her plants at Gladwyne included some collected in Asia by famous names associated with the Arnold Arboretum at Harvard, including Ernest Wilson, Joseph Rock, and Englishman Reginald Farrer.

Starting in 1929, Mary undertook biannual collecting trips, focused on searching for interesting specimens that she could not find in commercial or botanical gardens. Over the next forty years she undertook more than 200 botanical expeditions. She was lucky that her wealthy husband was keen to support her work, so when she decided to go plant collecting, she did it in some style. Her husband bought her a luxury Lincoln Continental car and equipped it for collecting, including a ventilated plant chamber, storage spaces, and a desk and bookcase. The rear compartment was insulated and ventilated so that newly collected plants could travel comfortably. Three plant presses and numerous buckets, forks, and spades were part of her tools and equipment. She traveled to remote areas of the American coastal plain, the Piedmont and Appalachian Mountains, and in later adventures to the Ozarks, then the Rocky Mountains from New Mexico to British Columbia in Canada. Her chauffeur on these trips, Ernest Perks, remained with her for sixty-five years.

She collected live plants, especially rhododendrons, one of her favorite groups of plants. On these trips she noted the beginnings of environmental destruction and began campaigns to save threatened areas that were already having rare habitats destroyed. She donated specimens of rare plants to several botanical institutions so her work was scientifically valuable, adding to horticultural knowledge and much more than just a personal, private passion.

Her most ambitious expedition took place in summer 1931 in British Columbia, Canada. Beginning at Pouce Coupé, she explored a remote and uncharted region. On this expedition she had a mapmaker. Seeing the potential for invaluable survey and mapping work, he was provided by the Canadian government. For almost three months, with fifty-eight horses, a doctor, and nine men, Mary trekked through the region, collecting and mapping as they went. The result of this expedition was a valuable trove of specimens, seeds, and botanical data. Her later 1935 expedition in British Columbia formed the foundation for the planning of the Alcan Highway. To commemorate Mary's excellent work throughout British Columbia, the Department of Lands named a mountain, Mount Mary Henry, in her honor.

For the next eighty days they traveled 15 to 20 miles a day on horseback, with stops to collect plants, seeds, and herbarium specimens. Many of the plants collected survived the journey back to Philadelphia, including *Opuntia fngida*, *Monarda molhs* var. *menthaefolia*, *Artemesia frigida*, *Amelanchier florida*, and *Cornus stolonifera*.

Mary gave some idea of the hardships she suffered in her notes: *Collecting plants while riding with a pack is not always a simple matter. A trowel goes in a leather sheath on one side of my belt and a knife on the other side. A strong pair of saddle bags is fastened to the pommel on my saddle, in which each morning are placed several empty jam cans. Each evening all full cans are aired and watered, and in the morning are all carefully packed in wooden packing cases on the horses. Quite frequently the cans were frozen solid to the ground and I had to use my ax to chop them loose.*

Experience quickly taught her that *rare and beautiful plants can be found in places that are difficult of access. . . . Often one has to shove one's self through or wriggle under briars, with awkward results to clothing. . . . Wading usually bare legged through countless rattlesnake infested swamps adds immensely to the interest of the day's work. . . . On several occasions I have been so deeply mired I had to be pulled out.*

From 1931 to 1935, Mary wrote her account of her expeditions in six parts. Titled "Collecting Plants beyond the Frontier," it was published by *National Horticulture Magazine*; two final segments appeared in the same journal in 1949. During this period she also wrote twenty-three other articles, most of them published in *Horticulture* or in *National Horticulture Magazine*. Her topics included uncommon oaks and rare rhododendrons, little known violets and unusual honeysuckles, hybrid jasmines, and Indian begonias. On the basis of her own personal experience, she evaluated plants for cold hardiness and recommended soil mixtures, transplanting methods, and greenhouse techniques for growing them successfully. Mary had established herself as a prominent botanist and plant collector. Her fame among botanists around the world grew. She began programs of plant breeding and developed many new lilies and other plants. Editing and writing for horticultural journals began taking up more and more of her time.

At the end of the 1930s, Mrs. Henry began to receive recognition for her achievements. She was elected president of the Philadelphia Botanical Club, became a director of the American Horticultural Society, and became a council member of the Pennsylvania Horticultural Society. When the Rock Garden Society began their bulletin in 1943, she was appointed associate editor and wrote the first article, "A Rock Garden of Natives."

Mary began to make her plants available to nurseries. The Upper Banks Nursery, operated by Fairman Furness, was a 50-acre garden and rare plant nursery along Ridley Creek, Pennsylvania. In 1940 Mary gave Furness permission to gather cuttings of many of the plants in her garden. When the plants were ready for distribution in 1942, he published a catalog, *Rare and Native Shrubs Collected by Mary Henry*, which included varieties of rhododendron, calycanthus, halesia, philadelphus, and syringa that she had developed. The Mayfair Nurseries, rock garden specialists in Hillsdale, New Jersey, also offered plants from Gladwyne, including many varieties of her phlox and penstemons.

In 1941 she became a research associate in the department of botany at the Academy of Natural Sciences, Philadelphia. That same year, the Pennsylvania Horticultural Society awarded her their Schaeffer Gold Medal for her notable contribution to horticulture: *Her keen eye has detected many species and varieties of horticultural value. These have been transplanted to or propagated in her garden at Gladwyne and her skill in their culture has made possible the demonstration that many highly attractive native plants can be grown far from their native haunts.*

Over the years her interest in collecting and breeding lilies had grown. In 1946 she was awarded the silver medal at a lily show organized by the Massachusetts Horticultural Society. The judges noted: *The most outstanding exhibit of lilies from the American wilds was the eight selections of Lilium philadelphicum now being cultured by Mrs. Henry at Gladwyne, Pennsylvania.*

Mary Gibson Henry on one of her many plant-hunting expeditions. *Royal BC*

During the last year of her life, between May and August 1966 she spent forty-two days in the field, traveling in Delaware, Maryland, Virginia, West Virginia, Kentucky, North Carolina, and Florida and collecting some seventy-five plants, including another *Lilium iridollae* and a *Styrax americanum* that still grows at Gladwyne. That same year, she filled orders from retail nurseries all over the United States and from individuals from Peru to Israel. She distributed Gladwyne material to the Morris Arboretum, the University of Arkansas, the Royal Botanic Garden, Edinburgh, Hilliers Nursery in England, and the Agricultural Experimental Station in Puerto Rico.

Mary Gibson Henry died at age eighty-two on a collecting trip in North Carolina in April 1967. Her years of devotion to horticulture had produced many solid achievements: more than a hundred articles had been published in journals such as *Herbertia*, *Bartonia*, and *National Horticultural Magazine*; herbaria in Scotland and North America had received thousands of specimen sheets from her collections; the hardiness and suitability of plants previously thought too tender for Philadelphia had been demonstrated; new species and varieties had been introduced to arboreta and nurseries; and interest in American flora for American gardens had been stimulated. The garden at Gladwyne has been preserved for future generations because her 50-acre private botanical garden was permanently endowed as the Henry Foundation for Botanical Research in 1950. It is a nonprofit foundation open to the public. The daylily *Hymenocallis henryae* is named in her honor.

4.54 FLORENCE BELL ROBINSON (1885–1973)

Author, prominent educator in landscape architecture, and a pioneer in introducing women into the field

Born in Lapeer, Michigan, in 1885, Florence Bell Robinson was the only child of Dr. and Mrs. William Robinson. In 1908 she graduated with a bachelor's degree in philosophy from Kalamazoo College in Kalamazoo, Michigan. In addition to this, she was awarded a second degree, bachelor of philosophy, as a result of taking correspondence courses from the University of Chicago. For the next eighteen years, Florence taught high school courses in Detroit, in subjects including drafting, botany, biology, chemistry, physics, and physiography.

She became fluent in French and German and obtained a third degree, a bachelor's in architecture, from the University of Michigan, leading to a master's in landscape design in 1924.

Florence arrived at the University of Illinois, Urbana-Champaign, in 1926 and spent the rest of her career there, developing a highly ranked landscape architecture department.

Florence Bell Robinson. *University of Illinois Urbana-Champaign*

She accepted an appointment at the University of Illinois as an associate in landscape design. Florence was expected to teach plant material and planting design—a typical subject reserved for women in most departments of landscape architecture. Schools established for the benefit of women, such as the Smith College Graduate School of Architecture and Landscape Architecture and the Cambridge School of Domestic Architecture and Landscape Architecture, granted degrees in both domestic architecture and landscape design to prepare their students for country estate work. The University of Illinois was rather rare in including in its undergraduate curriculum the subject of city planning.

Florence successfully broke the gender tenure barrier by becoming the first female tenure track faculty member in 1929. Women were still encountering many obstacles to progressing to tenure at the time, but Florence moved steadily up the ranks. In 1949 she was promoted to associate professor, and in 1951 she was made full professor in the Department of Landscape Architecture at age sixty-six—something that no other female landscape architecture teacher would accomplish until the 1970s.

During summers she traveled to remote areas of the world, including China, Japan, and Guatemala, visiting gardens and parks. Travels in Europe during summer 1928 expanded her growing interest in landscape architecture. Her tour of China and Japan in 1929 developed her knowledge of Chinese garden design, which she reinforced with a further trip to China and Japan in 1931.

In addition to teaching, Florence also ran a private landscape architectural practice. Her approach to garden design was based on the application of principles of composition derived from works of art—particularly paintings. A creative work, she maintained, must reflect unity and harmony and incorporate ideas of simplicity, balance, and scale. She designed about thirty small gardens, but she had developed a special interest in the design of large parks and school grounds. Conservation was also a major interest that continued even after her retirement.

An expert in the area of plants and planting design, she published and lectured extensively and developed a plant cataloging system for educating students that was later published. Florence was very influential throughout the 1950s and 1960s, partially as a result of her research on plants and ecology, and her emphasis on the interdependence of building and planting design.

Florence had a good knowledge of art, architecture, science, and engineering, and an encyclopedic knowledge of plant materials. She was recognized both as a teacher and author of textbooks. Her books included *Landscape Planting for*

Airports (Urbana: University of Illinois, 1948, Aeronautics Bulletin 2), as well as several articles in academic and popular magazines such as *Landscape Architecture Magazine*, *House & Garden*, and *Country Life*.

Useful Trees and Shrubs (Champaign, IL: Garrard) was published in 1938. When *Planting Design* was published by McGraw-Hill in 1940, it became a standard text in plant material courses throughout the USA, Australia, the Philippines, Russia, and England. Similarly, Florence's *Tabular Keys for the Identification of the Woody Plants* (Garrard, 1941) became the standard text in plant material courses.

Her final major publication was *Palette of Plants* (Garrard, 1950). It listed plants' "personalities" and included a section on the design of cemeteries, making Florence something of an expert on that specialized subject.

In 1950 she wrote, *As for my achievements, they are limited to my profession of landscape architecture. I have been too busy making-good my job here at the University of Illinois to give attention to foreign affairs. Here I have reached the top rank "full professor" for which I am rightfully proud. And I can say without boasting that I have worldwide fame, slight though it might be. I have written five textbooks in my subjects all of which have been used in a number of schools having landscape courses, and two of which have gained considerable distributions outside school circles.*

Through her teaching and publications, which reflected her background both in architecture and science, Florence was a stimulating influence for her students. She was also known for her card index system, which recorded the plants identified during weekly plant walks for her plant identification course. She frequently spoke to art leagues, to garden clubs, and on the local PBS radio station on topics including garden design, choosing shrubs, and the use of hybridized plants. She was also active in the American Planning and Civic Association and the National Conference of State Parks.

Florence Bell Robinson retired in 1953 and died in Hendersonville, North Carolina, in 1973 at age eighty-seven.

4.55 MARIE SELBY (1885–1971)

Creator of the Marie Selby Botanical Gardens, Sarasota Bay, Florida, which specializes in epiphytic plants

Marie was born Mariah Minshall in Wood County, West Virginia, in 1885. The Minshall family moved to Marietta, Ohio, where her father studied geology at Marietta College and invented parts for oil drilling equipment. The family went on camping and hiking trips along the Ohio River, and it was this early introduction to the great outdoors that gave Marie her love of nature and the environment.

She met William (Bill) Selby, a partner with his father in the Selby Oil and Gas Company, and they were married in 1908. Early in their marriage the young couple entered the country's first cross-country automobile race. As a result, Marie Selby became the first woman to cross the USA by car. They bought 7 acres of land bordering on Sarasota Bay and Hudson Bayou, and in the early 1920s the Selbys built a Spanish-style, two-story house there. Designing, landscaping, and the selection of trees, shrubs, and flowers for the garden were undertaken by Marie. Colorful flower borders were planted at the sides of the roadway leading to the tip of the peninsula. A major feature was an impressively large rose garden.

In 1946, Selby Oil and Gas merged with the Texas Company to form Texaco. William's oil company made him very wealthy and enabled Marie's passion for nature and gardening to flourish. She was a charter member of Sarasota's first garden club, the Founder's Circle. She was determined to keep Sarasota a beautiful and green place and was upset later in life by the proliferation of high rise buildings. She planted a row of tall bamboo canes on the bay side of her property to block the sight of the offending condominiums.

Marie Selby. Marie with her dog Riggles, ca. 1920. Photographer: Harold Wagner. *selby.org*

In 1955, William Selby established the William and Marie Selby Foundation. The impact of the Selby Foundation in the Sarasota community has been, and continues to be, significant. It supports initiatives in education, the arts, children, libraries, health services, and programs to support the aged. William Selby died in 1956, and Marie continued to live in the home and garden she loved until her death in 1971. Her will specified her wish to leave her property to the community as a botanical garden *for the enjoyment of the general public*. A board of directors was appointed to oversee this generous gift.

After consultation with the New York Botanical Garden and the University of Florida, it was decided that the garden should specialize in epiphytic plants. These are organisms that grow on the surface of a plant and derive moisture and nutrients from the air, rain, and water, or from debris accumulating around it. This specialization makes the garden unique among the more than 200 botanical gardens in the USA. It also features displays of orchids and bromeliads and their canopy ecosystems, with a focus on botany, horticulture, and environmental education.

Marie Selby Botanical Gardens was opened to the public on July 7, 1975. Since then, the property has more than doubled in size from 7 to nearly 15 acres, which includes 9 acres of display gardens. The historic Payne Mansion on the adjoining property was purchased in 1973 and now houses the gardens' museum. Ongoing research and exploration for tropical plants attracts worldwide attention, especially from international scholars and plant enthusiasts. Its plant collection has specimens collected from New World Tropic locations, many during research expeditions, and also has acquisitions from international institutions. There are more than 20,000 greenhouse plants, plus thousands more in the outdoor gardens and eight greenhouses, including the impressive Tropical Conservatory.

Marie was a conservationist and devoted her life to protecting the environment, as well as creating the botanical gardens. The Marie Selby Botanical Gardens has become a world class center for research and education, as well as a famous visitor attraction that brings more than 200,000 visitors each year.

The walkway at Selby Gardens.
Daderot

It is situated at 900 South Palm Avenue, in the heart of Sarasota, Florida, and is a very fitting memorial to Marie Selby's love of gardens and her generosity in donating her house and garden for the enjoyment of visitors and the continuation of specialized research by botanists.

4.56 LILLA LEACH (1886–1980)

Lilla was an independent field botanist who systematically collected plants throughout Oregon and other western states.

Lilla, whose family immigrated to Oregon over the Oregon Trail, was born on March 13, 1886, on her parents' farm in Barlow, Clackamas County. She developed her love of flowers while wandering the family acreage as a young child. She attended school in Barlow and Canby, then the Tualatin Academy in Forest Grove. There she met John Leach, the man who was to become her future husband. Lilla then moved on to the University of Oregon, where she studied with botanist Albert Sweetser. She then taught high school botany in Eugene for five years.

John Leach finally won her hand by assuring her he knew how to handle pack animals and *could take her where the cake-eating botanists could never get*. They were married in an outdoor ceremony on her parents' farm in 1913 and moved to Portland, where John established a pharmacy. She was particularly interested in the Siskiyou Mountains of Curry County, in southwestern Oregon. She and John spent nine summers there between 1928 and 1938, exploring the heart of that rugged range, where Lilla discovered several new species.

Lilla Leach. *Leach Collection, Leach Botanical Garden, Portland*

Lilla Leach hitches one of her mules to search for undiscovered flowers in the Kalmiopsis,1928. *Leach Collection, Leach Botanical Garden, Portland*

Lilla and John, with their burros Pansy and Violet, reportedly traveled more than 1,000 miles of primitive trails on their Siskiyou expeditions. It was there, on June 14, 1930, that Lilla made her most important discovery: a pink-flowered shrub in the heath family never before noted by botanists. Lilla later wrote that when she spotted the plant beside the trail, she *dropped to my knees . . . I had never seen anything so beautiful before*. She believed, at once, that she had discovered a new species. *Kalmiopsis leachiana* would be named in Lilla and John's honor. It blossoms briefly in the spring and grows only in a few pockets of these mountains. The hearty shrub started evolving before the ice age and is believed to be the oldest living member of the Ericaceae family, more commonly known as heather. The genus *Kalmiopsis* is endemic to southwestern Oregon and occurs nowhere else in the world.

It was not long after Lilla's discovery that nursery owners began to pillage the populations of *Kalmiopsis leachiana*, and it was soon clear that the small clusters of flowers were in peril. Lilla and John pressed the US Forest Service to create a protected area. In 1946 the Forest Service designated almost 77,000 acres to be protected for its biological diversity, and it is from Lilla's flower that the area gets its name. When Congress passed the Wilderness Act in 1964, the Kalmiopsis became one of the first areas to be protected under that status. In 1978 the area was expanded to encompass nearly 180,000 acres, making it Oregon's third-largest wilderness area.

Lilla and John bought property on Johnson Creek in southeast Portland. They built their cottage-style manor house there in 1936, which they called Sleepy Hollow. They lived in a stone cottage near Johnson Creek during the summer before the house was completed. Their collecting slowed during WWII, when Lilla began to suffer from arthritis.

In 1950, Lilla received the Eloise Payne Luquer Medal—the very first one to be awarded by the Garden Club of America. The medal honors distinguished achievement in botany.

John died in 1972 and Lilla eight years later, in 1980, in Portland, at age ninety-four. Her ashes and John's were scattered in the Kalmiopsis wilderness.

The Leaches' home and garden were bequeathed to the City of Portland in 1982, and today the Leach Botanical Garden has become a 16-acre botanical garden in outer southeast Portland, Oregon, near SE 122nd Avenue and Foster Road. It features a diverse collection of more than 2,000 hybrids, cultivars, and native and nonnative plants, including alpines, medicinal herbs, rock garden plants, camellias, and forty genera and more than 125 species of ferns.

4.57 ELSA REHMANN (1886–1946)

American landscape architect best known for her pioneering ecological approach to garden design

Elsa was born in Forest Hill, Newark, New Jersey, on April 11, 1886. Her parents were German-born architect Carl F. and Marie Rehmann. Elsa may have attended the Public Drawing School; her older sister, Antoinette, was a graduate and her father was principal of the school from 1882 until his death in 1906. She originally intended to become a professional writer and enrolled in Wells College in 1904. In 1906 she transferred to Barnard College, where she studied medieval architecture and geology, in addition to liberal arts. Having graduated from Barnard College in 1908, she studied at the Lowthorpe School of Landscape Architecture, Gardening and Horticulture for Women, in Groton, Massachusetts. She left the school in 1911, probably one of the first eight graduates.

In 1911, Elsa began working as an apprentice in landscape architecture firms. Her first employers were Charles N. Lowrie, who headed the system of parks of Hudson County, and Marian Cruger Coffin (see 4.46), who specialized in stately gardens. While working as an apprentice she started her writing career and had

Elsa Rehmann as a student at Barnard College, 1907. *Barnard Archives & Special Collections* magazine articles published in *Garden Magazine*, *Country Life in America*, *House Beautiful*, and *Better Homes and Gardens*.

Her first book, *The Small Place: Its Landscape Architecture*, was published by GP Putnam's Sons in 1918. It described and illustrated a diversity of residential designs made by contemporary American landscape architects.

In the book, Elsa reflected the common garden concepts and ideas of the time. She put forward the concept that a garden should be a *manifestation of distinctive individuality, an expression of personality*. It features designs for both formal and informal gardens, a hillside property, a property in the shade, two gardens on one property, the planting of an approach and drive turn, and a layout for a city property, among others.

From 1919, Elsa had her own practice, working from her home. Most of her clients were in Essex County, but she also designed gardens in other parts of New Jersey, as well as in Delaware, New England, New York, and Pennsylvania. By the 1920s her views had become fashionable, and gardens became seen as a vehicle for expressing the private self. Her second book, *Garden-Making* (Houghton Mifflin), came out in 1926. It included her own designs and examined then-current gardening theory. The book was praised for its scholarly value, poetic prose, and comprehensibility.

Elsa taught landscape gardening at Vassar College from 1923 to 1924 and landscape architecture from 1925 to 1927. Association with the botany department of the college in the 1920s changed Elsa's landscape philosophy. The head of the department was Edith A. Roberts (see 4.71), a forerunner in plant ecology. Roberts was developing an outdoor botanical laboratory for the study of New York's Dutchess County's plant communities and their biotopes. Elsa was asked to interpret the information gathered there from the point of view of an artist, with the intention to show that native plants could be *blended into an attractive landscape picture*.

Elsa Rehmann and Edith Roberts jointly published a series of articles titled "Plant Ecology" in the magazine *House Beautiful* in 1927, stating their aim to emphasize the role of plants as an integral part of the landscape and to outline the compositions that they had made. Striving to demonstrate how understanding plant communities could transfer to grounds and gardens, they stressed the role of ecology in naturalistic planting. Their findings were assembled into *American Plants for American Gardens*, published by University of Georgia Press in 1929 and republished in 1996. This pioneering book was among the first to promote the use of native plants in landscape design. Plant settings featured include open fields, hillside, wood and grove, streamside, ravine, pond, bog, and seaside. The design and management of a wide range of project types are featured, including residential properties, school grounds, corporate office sites, roadways, and parks.

Elsa's exposure to architecture in childhood via her architect father, and her early inclinations for writing, figured prominently in her books. Over her life, Elsa had come to consider plant communities to be the basis for design criteria and translated them very successfully into artistic compositions. The siting and characteristics of buildings were also key. Elsa retired from her practice around 1929, when she moved to live with her sister in Rockport, Massachusetts. During the 1930s she participated in a series of lectures with botanist Stephen Hamblin. While living in Rockport, Elsa dedicated most of her time to writing poetry. A volume called *First Poems* was published in 1933.

Elsa died in Rockport on May 30, 1946, at just sixty years old. Although she was a qualified landscape architect who started her own practice in 1919, her legacy is mainly as a teacher and an author, rather than her designs for clients' gardens. Her book *American Plants for American Gardens*, coauthored with Edith Roberts, remains a pioneering book for being among the first to promote the use of native plants in landscape design.

4.58 GANNA WALSKA (1887–1984)

Would be opera singer who created the Lotusland botanical garden at her mansion in Montecito, California

Ganna Walska was born Hanna Puacz in 1887 to Polish parents Napoleon Puacz and Karolina Massalska in Brest-on-the-Bug, Russian Empire. The area now known as Poland was, at the time, shared among Germany, Austria, and Russia; Ganna's town lay in the

Ganna Walska. Unknown photographer. *George Grantham Bain Collection (Library of Congress)*

Russian part. Her chosen stage name comes from the Russian form of Hannah (Ganna) and her favorite music, the walz (Walska). As a teenager she moved to St. Petersburg, where she met a Russian baron, officer Arcadie d'Eingorn, with whom she eloped in 1907. The marriage did not last long, but it did open doors for Ganna, causing her to take an interest in, among other things, opera. She took voice lessons in Paris, and it was there, in 1914, that she changed her name to better suit her chosen profession.

Despite her best efforts, she never had a successful vocal career. By all accounts she had a major problem—she could not sing in tune. Her few public performances seldom finished because she was booed off the stage. It is said that during one performance of Giordano's *Fedora*, she veered so persistently off-key that the audience pelted her with rotten vegetables. Ganna's failure as a vocalist is nearly legendary, inspiring, in Orson Welles's *Citizen Kane*, Kane's support of his second wife's hopeless vocal career. Even without becoming a diva, Walska attracted plenty of attention, being a great beauty and a femme fatale with abundant charisma. Ganna was married six times:

Baron Arcadie d'Eingorn in 1904 (the marriage was later dissolved). He died of tuberculosis in 1915.

New York endocrinologist Dr. Joseph Fraenkel in 1916. He died in April 1920.

Multimillionaire sportsman and carpet tycoon Alexander Smith Cochran in 1920. They divorced in 1922 and he died in 1929.

Wealthy Chicago press mogul Harold Fowler McCormick in 1922. They divorced in 1931 and he died in 1941.

English inventor Harry Grindell Matthews in 1938. He died in 1941.

Yoga and Buddhism scholar Theos Bernard in 1942. They divorced in 1946 and he died in 1947.

Ganna's wealthy husbands would provide for her extravagant lifestyle and enabled her endeavors, including a completely unprofitable line of perfumes and cosmetics, the ownership of a French chateâu and Paris's Theâtre des Champs Elyseés, and in 1926 her purchase of the Duchess of Marlborough's Fabergé egg. The egg had been offered by Consuelo Vanderbilt at a charity auction.

Until 1940, she spent most of her time between America and Europe, moving to the New World permanently just before the Nazis occupied France. It was here she met her fourth husband, Harold Fowler McCormick, who sponsored voice lessons for Ganna and, as a big supporter of the Chicago Opera Company, was able to install her as the star of its 1920 production of Ruggero Leoncavallo's *Zazà*. However, Ganna never got to perform. On the eve of the premiere the show was canceled. According to one story, the conductor refused to put up with Ganna's singing.

Ganna would try every sort of fashionable mumbo jumbo and spiritual teachings in search of creative fulfillment and personal enlightenment, attempting to conquer her nerves and salvage her voice, but nothing helped.

After immigrating to America, Ganna soon tired of New York and left to visit California in 1940. She wrote in a memoir: *One need not be in California long before he feels his soul beginning to stir. The air is magnetized . . . the consciousness awakens . . . the soul must speak.* After a six-week stay in Hollywood Hills, fifty-three-year-old Ganna Walska was convinced that her destiny lay in this "sunny land." In 1941, with the encouragement of her sixth husband, Theos Bernard, she purchased the historic 37-acre Cuesta Linda estate in Montecito, near Santa Barbara, intending to use it as a retreat for Tibetan monks. Because of restrictions on wartime visas, the monks were unable to travel to the United States. After eventually conceding that she lacked talent and giving up on her career as a singer, Ganna used the wealth she had amassed through her series of profitable marriages to embark on the development of her estate.

Ganna Walska posing in front of her home's signature landscape. *Ganna Walska Lotusland*

Ganna consulted with several of the best designers—interestingly, none of them female—but chose to tailor her gardens to suit her own fancy, often against their advice. She wanted the best and the most unusual plants and was often willing to pay high prices to get them. She was the author of her heavily landscaped and designed gardens, containing numerous beautiful, extraordinary, eerie, and rare plants, as well as eye-catching decorative features. It was after her divorce from Bernard in 1946 that she changed the name of her estate to Lotusland, after the *Nelumbo nucifera*, which is held sacred in Indian and Tibetan religions.

Lotusland became a collection of many gardens, including the Japanese Garden, Fern Garden, Bromeliad Garden, Australian Garden, Cactus Garden, Water Garden, and Aloe Garden. She said of her ambition that she hoped *to develop to its maximum capacity into the most outstanding center of horticultural significance and of educational use*.

A view of part of Lotusland. *Ganna Walska Lotusland*

She devoted the rest of her life to designing, expanding, and maintaining the estate's renowned, innovative, and extensive gardens, allocating $1 million from a 1971 auction of her famous jewelry collection.

Ganna Walska died at her estate in 1984 at age ninety-seven. She left the 37-acre gardens and remaining fortune to the Ganna Walska Lotusland Foundation, and Lotusland was opened to the public in 1993. Ganna Walska had an extraordinarily varied early life with a catastrophically failed singing career and six marriages, but this 37-acre estate would be her legacy.

Mirroring her own vibrant personality, Lotusland has some eccentric decorative features thanks to Ganna having taken little notice of professional advice and preferring her own instincts. Today Ganna Walska Lotusland receives around 15,000 visitors a year who get to witness Ganna's choice of unusual, rare, and exotic plants.

4.59 ROSE ISHBEL GREELY (1887–1969)

One of very few female landscape architects in the mid-Atlantic states in the first half of the twentieth century, she designed more than 500 city and suburban gardens and country estates.

Rose Ishbel Greely. *Jane Greely*

Rose was born on February 18, 1887, in Washington, DC. For her education she went to the National Cathedral School for Girls in 1905 before completing finishing school at the Finch School, New York City. In 1916 she enrolled at the Cambridge School of Domestic and Landscape Architecture for Women (later to become part of Smith College) and in 1919 completed the landscape architecture course. Rose also dabbled in metalworks and interior decorating but discovered a true love for architecture and landscape architecture at Smith College.

After completing her education, Rose found many different jobs: she wrote articles for *House Beautiful* while working as a draftsman in the office of prominent landscape architect Fletcher Steele. When Rose moved to DC, she was employed by architect Horace Peaslee. Still in Washington, in 1926 she opened her own firm situated at 1623 H Street, and later at 1701 I Street. She became the first licensed female architect in DC and established her own practice there. Rose's experience as a child and her education influenced her designs. She always sought to establish harmony between the interior and exterior of the home, blurring the threshold that divides landscape from architecture. She had more than 500 commissions as an architect and landscape architect, proving the success of the practice that she had built for herself.

Despite Rose's strict spatial organization for city homes and gardens, she applied a more organic, natural approach to country homes. She incorporated surrounding features of sites into her designs, smoothing the transition between the building environment and nature. The Jefferson Patterson Estate design, St. Leonard, Maryland, is a good example of this. Here her design is defined at the perimeter of the home but moves out into the landscape with less detailed features. In a 1934 interview, Rose said,

> *The whole question of landscape development—streets, parks, private places—is a matter of design. In order to create a successful whole, it is necessary to think, not so much of the individual plant, as of its place in the whole scheme. I think that the work of a landscape architect is interesting because he is dealing largely with living things that grow and change from year to year.*

Rose's garden at 1224 30th Street, Washington, was featured in the magazine *House Beautiful* in 1933 and remains a regular stop on Georgetown garden tours.

In a 2014 *Washington Post* story, gardening columnist Adrian Higgins called the garden *a masterpiece of spatial arrangement in a contained urban environment.*

Of Rose's major commissions, many were for some of the most powerful people in the Washington, DC, area. Highlights of an illustrious career include

1933: garden design, Jefferson Patterson Estate, St. Leonard, Maryland
1934: study of planting, Commanding Officers Quarters, Aberdeen Proving Grounds, Maryland
1938: general design plan for the grounds, Col. and Mrs. HP Le Clair, Friendship, Maryland
1940: design for Mrs. A. Lothrop Luttrell, Bethesda, Montgomery County, Maryland
1941: topographical survey for Mrs. C. G. Van Emon, Barnesville, Montgomery County, Maryland
1942–43, 1946, 1953–55: work for Mrs. L. Corrin Strong, Washington, DC, and Gibson Island, Maryland

After the end of WWII, Rose's commissions continued:

1949-51: garden design for Mr and Mrs Albert Walker, Westmoreland Hills, Montgomery County, Maryland
1950: work for Miss Mary Gore, Marwood Estate, River Road, Montgomery County, Maryland
1950–51: work on the swimming pool area for Miss Mary Gore, River Road, Potomac, Maryland
1951: general design plan for Mrs. Albert W. Walker, Westmoreland Hills, Maryland
1951–54: terrace and rose garden for Mrs. Philip Bard, Hurstleigh, 6 Meadow Road, Baltimore County, Maryland
1952–58: design for Miss Watkin's Garden, St. Timothy's School, Stevenson, Maryland
1953: design work for Admiral and Mrs. Ralph Riggs, Rockville, Maryland
1956: work for Mr. and Mrs. David Bruce, New Windsor, Carroll County, Maryland

In 1969, Rose Ishbel Greely passed away at her home in Washington, DC, after an illustrious, successful, and admired career. She had been the first licensed female landscape architect in Washington, DC, and had established her own highly successful practice there. She is remembered for having designed more than 500 city and suburban gardens and country estates for the movers and shakers of Washington, DC; Maryland; and Virginia.

4.60 ELIZABETH LORD (1887–1976) AND EDITH SCHRYVER (1901–1984)

Similar to the partnership of Florence Yoch and Lucile Council (4.69) in California, the work of Elizabeth and Edith is so inextricably intertwined that they share an entry in this book.

Born in Salem, Oregon, Elizabeth Lord was the daughter of William Paine Lord (1838–1911) and Juliet Montague Lord (1844–1924). William Lord was the Oregon governor from 1895 to 1899, when President William McKinley appointed him US minister to Argentina. The family spent four years in Argentina before returning to Oregon. Elizabeth attended grade school at Oregon public schools and in Buenos Aires, but her inspiration for pursuing a career in gardening was her mother, Juliet, who founded Salem Floral Society in 1915. The society, now called the Salem Garden Club, was Oregon's first organization dedicated to floral gardening. Spurred by her mother's interest in gardens, Elizabeth decided to pursue landscape architecture as a profession, and she entered the Lowthorpe School of Landscape Architecture in Groton, Massachusetts, in 1926.

While on a study tour of European gardens in 1927 sponsored by the Lowthorpe and Cambridge schools, Elizabeth met up with Edith Schryver, whom she knew from Lowthorpe. Born in Kingston, New York, in 1901, Edith had enrolled full time at Lowthorpe in 1920 while working part time in the Boston offices of landscape architects

Edith Schryver (*left*) and Elizabeth Lord (*right*). *gaietyhollow.com*

Harold Blossom, Elizabeth Pattee, and Elizabeth Strang. In summer 1922, Edith found work in the New Hampshire office of Ellen Shipman (see 4.41). Upon her graduation from Lowthorpe in 1923, she spent the next five years in Shipman's New York City office, where she assisted with the design of several significant estate gardens.

Discovering that they had similar aesthetic tastes and complementary skills, Elizabeth and Edith decided to form their own landscape architecture practice, Lord & Schryver, and moved to Salem, Oregon, where they started by living at the Lord family residence. By forming Lord & Schryver the two women became the first female landscape architects in the Northwest.

In *Space, Style and Structure: Building in the Northwest America* (Oregon Historical Society, 1974), architect Wallace Kay Huntington (1926–2015) describes the founding of Lord & Schryver as *one of the milestones in the history of Northwest garden design.*

Their first commission was a garden for Mr. and Mrs. D. B. Jarman in 1929, who wanted a Spanish design influence. Then, in 1932, they built their own house, Gaiety Hollow, on Mission Street with architect Clarence Smith, with whom they were to collaborate on many commissions. The design of the garden and house together as one entity put into practice Elizabeth and Edith's cardinal principle: their gardens are characterized by a formal structure—defined by hedges, fencing, and pathways—and planted with flowering trees, shrubs, perennials, biennials, and annuals to achieve an informal charm. At Gaiety Hollow, Elizabeth and Edith initiated an ambitious bulb planting program and extended the garden to the west, adding a pergola, brick paving, boxwood hedges, shrubs, and perennials.

A view of part of Gaiety Hollow, Salem, Oregon. *gaietyhollow.com*

Elizabeth would concentrate on planting design, while Edith was primarily responsible for design and construction drawings. The women liked to work with a client's architect to achieve an integrated house and garden. They planted outdoor spaces used for entertaining and dining with plants that would be in continuous bloom. They designed many gardens on challenging sloping sites and integrated existing trees, borrowing natural views into the design whenever they could. For four decades the partners designed and supervised work all over the Northwest, including the Deepwood

Estate in Salem (1935); Reed College in Portland (1939); the University of Puget Sound in Tacoma, Washington; various Salem parks; and the Asahel Bush House (now the Bush House Museum). From 1952 to 1968 they designed the grounds of the historic Minthorn House in Newberg, Oregon, the boyhood home of President Herbert Hoover.

In addition to their highly sought after garden designs, Elizabeth and Edith were regarded as consummate professionals, because they worked to raise the profile of landscape architects by involving an audience beyond their clients. The pair worked to educate the general public through newspaper articles and lectures and by participating in the regular regional radio broadcast *Home Garden Hour*. In a series of nine articles written in 1932 for the Portland newspaper *The Oregonian*, they outlined *the main points to consider in designing an attractive garden* for a small urban lot. While several of their projects involved large estates, many were for areas around a city home. Indeed, the Gaiety Hollow garden occupies only ⅓ acre.

During their career they were also busy with clubs and committees. Elizabeth was chairperson of the Willamette Valley Division of the State Federation of Garden Clubs, as well as continuing her public service as a member of the Salem Garden Club, where she was responsible for the plantings at Salem's Marion County Courthouse. In 1937 she was appointed to the Salem Parks Board, where she struggled with an inadequate budget and the problems of Englewood, Willson, and Pringle Parks. Elizabeth served on the Parks Board for nine years and also served on the Salem Parks Advisory Committee. As chairperson of Salem's Tree Committee, she fought for a curbside tree planting program that included city responsibility for the upkeep of trees in residential areas. Elizabeth was a member of the state's Capitol Planning Commission from 1949 to 1963. She was especially involved with the landscaping of the Capitol Mall and the salvage of Capitol Park's old plantings after the Columbus Day storm in 1962. During and after WWII, Edith taught classes at Oregon State University and was a member of numerous gardening clubs. Together with Elizabeth, she also served on the Oregon Roadside Council.

Historically, Edith and Elizabeth's work represented a transition from a formal, symmetrical style of garden design influenced by Gertrude Jekyll and Ellen Shipman (see 4.38) to one that responded in a distinctive way to the unique features of northwestern US climate, soil, topography, and plant material. Their work is characterized by subtle and creative plant combinations, rather than by use of exotics. They created a style often characterized as *informal formality*. They introduced many plant species from the East Coast into the northwestern palette by working with local growers, educating and encouraging them to propagate new varieties suited to the climate.

Nearly all the gardens designed by Edith and Elizabeth are in private ownership. Sadly, over time most of them have degraded for various reasons, including lack of knowledge or interest as ownership changes, the labor intensive maintenance requirement, and the increased growth of tree canopy altering growing conditions. One project that is still accessible to the public is the Deepwood Museum & Gardens. Developed on a 6-acre property that also contains a significant Queen Anne house, the garden is cared for by the City of Salem in cooperation with Deepwood Gardeners and the Lord & Schryver Conservancy.

Lord & Schryver ceased operations in 1969, when health issues prevented both women from continuing the practice. Following Elizabeth's death in 1976, Edith continued living at Gaiety Hollow until her death. She passed away in Salem in 1984 at age eighty-three. The legacy these women left is important, not only for its intrinsic historical value but also for its relevance for today. It is a composite of incorporating past influences, working within the realities of their time, and setting a new standard of garden design and professionalism.

The Gaiety Hollow garden was purchased and cared for faithfully by a family until 2013, when it came into the hands of the Lord & Schryver Conservancy for rehabilitation and preservation. The property is listed on the National Register of Historic Places.

4.61 ANNETTE HOYT FLANDERS (1887–1946)

Landscape architect whose commissions over a twenty-four-year period, mostly in the eastern and midwestern United States, included private estates, real estate subdivisions, the grounds of industrial plants, and public recreational developments

Annette Hoyt Flanders.
Cultural Landscape Foundation

Annette was born in Milwaukee, Wisconsin, the daughter of Frank M. Hoyt, a prominent attorney, and Hettie Pamelia Hoyt. Her early education was from tutors and at private schools. She majored in botany at Smith College, earning her a BSc in 1918, and got her MA in landscape architecture from the University of Illinois. She studied civil engineering at Marquette University, as well as design, architecture, and the history of architecture at the Sorbonne in France. She married lawyer Roger Yale Flanders in 1913, becoming Annette Hoyt Flanders. Toward the end of WWI, in 1918 and 1919 Annette served with the American Red Cross in France.

On her return to the USA she joined the landscape architecture firm Vitale, Brinckerhoff, and Geiffert in New York, where she was responsible for design and for supervising planting. She opened her own landscape architecture office in New York in 1922. Later, in 1943, she relocated her office to Milwaukee, Wisconsin. The scope of her practice included private estates, real estate subdivisions, the grounds of industrial plants, recreational developments, and exhibit gardens. Her designs emphasized minimizing the amount of grading required, stating that landscape designs should adhere to the natural form of the land. She drew inspiration from several different styles, including Beaux-Arts, midwestern naturalism, and modernism. Her fundamental edict was that any garden should be perfectly adapted to the terrain and to the use for which it was intended.

Annette worked primarily in the eastern and midwestern United States. Her commissions included estate gardens for Sigmund Lehmann and his sons, Tarrytown, New York; the Phipps Estate, Denver, Colorado; and Morven Farm Gardens, Charlottesville, Virginia.

Her design of the McCann Estate French Gardens, Oyster Bay, Long Island, New York, received the Architectural League of New York's Medal of Honor in Landscape Architecture in 1932.

Annette became a member of the American Society of Landscape Architects in 1923 and was elected a fellow in 1942. She was recognized in *House & Garden*'s hall of fame in 1930. In 1932 she was awarded a medal of honor by the Architectural League of New York. She wrote extensively for numerous publications, promoting simple, livable, and economical garden design. Her articles appeared in *House & Garden*, *Country Life in America*, and *House Beautiful*. In addition, she worked as consultant garden editor for *Good Housekeeping* from 1933 to 1934, as well as publishing a four-part series on suburban garden design. She also lectured to horticultural and botanical societies, schools, and garden and women's clubs and appeared often on radio talk shows.

Annette Hoyt Flanders continued to design and publish articles until her death in 1946.

4.62 CAROLINE "CARRIE" CORONEOS DORMON (1888–1971)

Respected botanist, horticulturist, ornithologist, historian, archeologist, preservationist, naturalist, conservationist, and author; considered the first woman employed in forestry in the United States

Caroline was born at Briarwood, the family home near Saline, in southern Bienville Parish, northern Louisiana, to James L. Dormon and the former Caroline Trotti. As a child, Caroline developed a keen interest in plants and wildlife. Her mother encouraged Caroline and her siblings to explore the longleaf pine forests of Kisatchie Wold, where they developed a deep, abiding love of the natural world. Caroline recalled: *We were rather delicate children, of a nervous temperament; so . . . our parents made it possible for us to spend every moment we were outside the schoolroom in the woods . . . and we didn't play Indians, we were Indians*. A passion for native plants and ancient forests, coupled with a strong feeling of kinship with Native Americans, shaped Caroline's life and work. The children were encouraged to read scholarly and governmental publications exploring the history and diverse cultures of ancient natives, as well as the myriad problems faced by a contemporary Native American population. Her lifelong interest was heavily shaped by her belief that contemporary tribes, like old-growth forests, were quickly disappearing.

Caroline "Carrie" Coroneos Dormon. *USDA Forest Service*

She was educated at Baptist-affiliated Judson College in Marion, Perry County, Alabama, from which she received a bachelor's degree in literature and art in 1907. She taught for several years in Louisiana schools, where Caroline was often referred to as Miss Carrie. She then reestablished her home at Briarwood in 1918, where she planned to *put into usable form the store of information which I had been gathering all my life*.

She joined the Division of Forestry and began to collect and preserve native trees and shrubs. Although she considered herself in no sense a clubwoman, Caroline became active in the Louisiana Federation of Women's Clubs, where she served as state chairman of conservation. Through avid letter writing, she extended and strengthened networks among those who could advance her efforts to gain public support for natural resource conservation.

After leaving the Division of Forestry in 1941, she joined Louisiana's Board of Public Welfare and the state's Highway Department (later the Louisiana Department of Transportation and Development), where she worked as a landscape beautification consultant. She was later a landscape consultant for Huey P. Long Charity Hospital in Pineville, in Rapides Parish, east of the Red River from Alexandria. A self-taught landscape designer, Caroline's garden designs would always emphasize the wild landscape. She corresponded frequently with Elizabeth Lawrence (see 4.81) and worked with Ellen Shipman (see 4.38) on the gardens at Longue Vue in New Orleans. Other projects included Hodges Gardens, Louisiana, and her own gardens at Briarwood. Caroline was also a keen horticulturalist and began growing irises in the 1920s, helping to popularize their use. She was also involved with the establishment of the Louisiana Iris Society.

Caroline was a consultant for popular Hodges Gardens State Park near Many, in Sabine Parish. The park opened as a private development in the 1950s, but it came under the operation of the State of Louisiana in April 2007. Caroline proposed what became the Louisiana State Arboretum, some 8 miles north of Ville Platte, the seat of Evangeline Parish, as part of nearby Chicot State Park. The 301-acre site was dedicated in 1964. The Caroline Dormon Lodge opened in 1965 and serves as a visitor center, library, and herbarium of native plants that grow within the boundaries of the arboretum.

Lured out of her self-imposed retirement in 1920, she joined the Louisiana Department of Conservation to coordinate a program of educational outreach and public relations, a program that she designed. That same year she also joined the Society of American Foresters. From her platform as the chairman of forestry for the Louisiana Federation of Women's Clubs and the first female member of the Society of American Foresters, she was instrumental in the campaign to save and designate the Kisatchie National Forest in Louisiana in 1930, a 600,000-acre forest of longleaf pines.

By now widely known for her work with forestry and native plants, Caroline was also a passionate advocate for Louisiana's cultural resources, spearheading efforts to identify and protect archeological sites throughout the state. Seeking to support local Native Americans, she sought out tribal artists and traditionalists and recorded stories in native languages. She promoted the work of Choctaw, Koasati, and Chitimacha basket weavers, bringing crucial support to struggling families and fostering a new appreciation for these ancient, enduring traditions.

Caroline campaigned on national and state levels for recognition and assistance for Native Americans and promoted traditional arts as an economic base to support tribal communities.

Her books, many of which she illustrated, include *Wild Flowers of Louisiana* (Doubleday, Doran, 1934), *Forest Trees of Louisiana* (Ramires-Jones, 1941), *Flowers Native to the Deep South* (J. Horace McFarland, 1958), *Natives Preferred* (1965), *Southern Indian Boy* (Claitors, 1967), and *Bird Talk* (Claitors, 1969). She was a frequent contributor to *Home Gardening for the South*.

In 1965 Caroline was presented with an honorary doctor of science award from Louisiana State University in Baton Rouge. Briarwood, her family home, is the headquarters of the Caroline Dormon Nature Preserve. Natchitoches attorney and philanthropist Arthur C. Watson organized the Foundation for the Preservation of the Caroline Dormon Nature Preserve and served as its treasurer until his death in 1984.

The Caroline Dormon Trail extends 10.5 miles in the Kisatchie Bayou Recreation Complex within the national forest. It is popular for horseback riding, hiking, and bicycling. The trail starts at the Longleaf Scenic Byway. In August 2012 the Rapides Parish School Board opened Caroline Dormon Junior High School in Woodworth, Louisiana. Land for the school was donated by the United States Forest Service from the Kisatchie National Forest.

Caroline willed her home, Briarwood, to the public. It is open for tours and other events. More information is available on her in *The Gift of the Wild Things: The Life of Caroline Dormon* (University of Louisiana at Lafayette, 1990), written by Dr. Fran Holman. Also available is *Adventures in Wild Flowers: The Timeless Writings of Caroline Dormon*, a compilation of fifty articles edited by Dr. Holman. The Dormon Collection is at the Eugene P. Watson Memorial Library of Northwestern State

University in Natchitoches. She was awarded the Eloise Paine Luquer Medal for special achievement in the field of botany by the Garden Club of America.

Caroline never married and died, aged eighty-three, in 1971 in Shreveport, Louisiana. She was interred at the Briarwood Baptist Church Cemetery near her Briarwood home.

4.63 RUTH BRAMLEY DEAN (1889–1932)

Landscape architect specializing in designing Long Island gardens

Ruth was born in Wilkes-Barre, Pennsylvania, in 1889. She attended the University of Chicago from 1908 to 1910. She then went to work in the Chicago office of prominent landscape architect Jens Jensen but left to go to New York City, where she worked for various architects, including Aymar Embury II. Ruth specialized in thoughtfully designed urban and rural gardens and designed gardens for many distinguished Long Island, New York, residences. Her designs featured simple yet functional divisions, well-chosen garden details, and a harmonious relationship with architectural elements.

Her design for Grey Gardens, a 4-acre estate in East Hampton (around 1913), included a 70-by-40-foot walled garden, beyond which stretched the Atlantic Ocean. Anna Gilman Hill and her husband, Robert Carmer Hill, lived at the property, and in Anna's book *Forty Years of Gardening* (Fredrick A. Stokes, 1938) she writes, *It was truly a gray [sic] garden. The soft gray of the dunes, cement walls and sea mists gave us our color scheme as well as our name ... nepeta, stachys, and pinks... . clipped bunches of santolina, lavender and rosemary made gray mounds here and there. Only flowers in pale colors were allowed inside the walls, yet the effect was far from insipid... I close my*

Ruth Bramley Dean. *Staline Rosario*

eyes and sense again the scent of those wild roses, the caress of the hot sun on our backs as we sauntered to and fro from our bath and lazy mornings on the beach.

In 1915 Ruth opened her New York office and maintained an independent office adjacent to her residence upon her marriage to architect Aymar Embury II in 1923. The two collaborated with architect Lusby Simpson, landscape architect Gilmore Clarke (of Clarke & Rapuano), and landscape architect Betty Sprout on the redesign of Bryant Park in 1934. In 1929 Ruth became the first woman to be awarded the Architectural League of New York's gold medal for three gardens she had designed in Grosse Pointe, Michigan. These gardens featured a series of enclosed garden *rooms*, thoughtfully composed mixtures of trees and shrubs (evergreen, deciduous, and native species), and simple shrub and flower color combinations. Ruth also contributed to such periodicals as *The Garden*, *House & Garden*, *House Beautiful*, and *Country Life*. In 1917 Moffat, Yard and Company published her book *The Livable House, Its Garden*.

Looking west to the pergola in Grey Gardens, designed by Ruth Dean. *Library of Congress Prints and Photographs Division*

Sadly, few of Ruth's gardens still survive today. She passed away at age forty-three and was buried in Cedar Lawn Cemetery in East Hampton, New York. Ruth's designs had featured simple yet functional divisions, well-chosen garden details, and a harmonious relationship with architectural elements. She had contributed to many influential magazines and is remembered for her thoughtfully designed urban and rural gardens, including many for distinguished Long Island residents.

4.64 ETHEL ZOE BAILEY (1889–1983)

Botanist, author, and first curator of the Liberty Hyde Bailey Hortorium at Cornell University. She also created an assemblage that would later be labeled the Ethel Z. Bailey Horticultural Catalogue Collection.

Ethel was born in 1889. Her father was a huge influence on her as a teacher, administrator, lecturer, and world traveler in search of botanical specimens. Liberty Hyde Bailey (1858–1954) was cofounder of the American Society for Horticultural Science and a world-renowned plantsman, utilizing his abilities as a botanist, taxonomist, horticulturist, and writer. He is sometimes referred to as the father of modern horticulture, as well as the father of rural sociology and rural journalism. He is also credited with being instrumental in starting agricultural extension services, the Nature Study movement, parcel post, and rural electrification.

Liberty Hyde Bailey came to Cornell University, Ithaca, New York, in 1888 and set about building a herbarium specializing in preserving material of horticultural origin. The Liberty Hyde Bailey Hortorium was named in his honor.

Ethel graduated from Smith College in 1911 with a bachelor's degree in zoology and immediately went to work at Cornell alongside her father. She was the hortorium's first curator from 1935 to 1957. Her father's prolific writings, some coauthored with Ethel, provided a wealth of horticultural information, not only to botanists but also to farmers and gardeners. Ethel edited several of his publications, including *The Standard Cyclopedia of Horticulture* (Macmillan, 1914) and *Manual of Cultivated Plants* (Macmillan, 1924).

Ethel traveled to several countries on research expeditions with her father, serving as his field assistant in China, Japan, Panama, Venezuela, and Trinidad.

Ethel Zoe Bailey and her father on a collecting trip in Panama, 1931. *Division of Rare and Manuscript Collections, Cornell University Library*

Her father's passion for his work, particularly Nature Study, is evident in this extract from one of his publications:

> *Nature-study not only educates, but it educates nature-ward; and nature is ever our companion, whether we will or no. Even though we are determined to shut ourselves in an office, nature sends her messengers. The light, the dark, the moon, the cloud, the rain, the wind, the falling leaf, the fly, the bouquet, the bird, the cockroach—they are all ours. If one is to be happy, he must be in sympathy with common things. He must live in harmony with his environment. One cannot be happy yonder nor tomorrow: he is happy here and now, or never. Our stock of knowledge of common things should be great. Few of us can travel. We must know the things at home.*

Ethel coauthored two reference books with her father, both published by the Macmillan Company: *Hortus: A Concise Dictionary of Gardening and General Horticulture* in 1935, and *Hortus Second: A Concise Dictionary of Gardening and General Horticulture* in 1947. While at Cornell, Ethel edited the first eight volumes of the academic journal *Gentes Herbarum*. She also coauthored *Dictionary of Gardening and General Horticulture*, last published by Biotech Books in 2003.

In its introduction the dictionary is described as follows:

> *This book is designed to account for all the Species and Botanical Varieties of Plants in Cultivation, together with brief directions on Uses, Propagation and Cultivation. It is a source—book and record of the plant materials with addition of common names, descriptive terms and definitions, inventories of families of plants, and abundant cross-references. This volume is intended to be useful as a handbook of ready reference, rapid aid to nomenclature and to spelling of names, help in labelling, medium of suggestions on the main or standard requirements in the cultivation of plants. It is hoped the book will contribute to the understanding and the dignity of plant-growing.*

After her father's death, Ethel revised and oversaw, with the staff of the Liberty Hyde Bailey Hortorium, the publication of a third, updated volume: *Hortus Third: A Concise Dictionary of Plants Cultivated in the United States and Canada*. This was last published by Barnes & Noble as a two-volume box set in 1997.

In addition, when her father had first arrived at Cornell, in 1888 he had begun acquiring seed and nursery catalogs from around the world, using them for his research on cultivated plants. In 1911 this collection was turned over to Ethel, and she took care of it for more than seventy years. It now numbers over 134,000 items. Ethel used this collection to retrieve information on cultivated plant material and recorded it on index cards, creating a master index that was the basis for several of the reference works written by her father. Over the years it has been used in garden restoration projects as a source of appropriate varieties. It provides a vast amount of historical data and is useful to document the introduction (and loss) of plant varieties. The collection also documents modern sources for seeds and plants, cultivars available, and tools used, as well as chemicals and pesticides available to gardeners. For academic research the collection can sometimes provide dates and places of introduction of particular plant cultivars and species. Since new catalogs are still being received each year, the collection is also useful in locating current seed or plant source information for both the nursery trade and the general public.

Ethel retired from Cornell in 1957 but continued to volunteer at the hortorium and work on her catalog collection until her death. She died in 1983 at ninety-three years old. She had a long and distinguished career in botany and horticulture, and in recognition of this she was awarded the George Robert White Medal in 1967 from the Massachusetts Historical Society and the Smith College Medal in 1970. Ethel is still best known for her three-volume work, *Hortus*, and her name graces the garden catalog collection she started. The Ethel Z. Bailey Horticultural Catalog Collection is now part of the College of Agriculture and Life Sciences at Cornell University.

4.65 EMMA LUCY BRAUN (1889–1971)

A prominent botanist, ecologist, and expert on the forests of the eastern United States. She was an environmentalist before the term was popularized and a trailblazing woman in her field, winning many awards for her work.

Known by her middle name, Emma Lucy Braun was born in 1889 in Cincinnati; she would live in Ohio for the remainder of her life. She was the daughter of George Frederick Braun and Emma Moriah Wright, and her early interest in nature was encouraged by her parents, who took her and her older sister, Annette, into woodlands to find and identify wildflowers. Her mother kept a small herbarium to preserve and identify her plant finds. In high school Lucy began collecting plants for study, the beginning of a huge personal herbarium that she assembled over her lifetime, eventually totaling 11,891 specimens. This collection is now a part of the herbarium at the Smithsonian National Museum of Natural History in Washington, DC.

Lucy studied botany and geology at the University of Cincinnati, earning a bachelor's degree in 1910, a master's degree in geology in 1912, and a PhD in botany in 1914. She became the sixth woman to earn a PhD from that institution; her sister was the first. Annette was an entomologist and authority on microlepidoptera (micromoths).

Lucy's teaching and research career at the university began as an assistant in geology from 1910 to 1913. Between 1914 and 1917, she taught as an assistant in botany, then advanced her career through the titles of instructor, assistant professor, and associate professor. Lucy achieved full professorship as a professor of plant ecology in 1946, two years before her retirement.

Emma Lucy Braun. Photographer unknown. *LuEsther T. Mertz Library at the New York Botanical Gardens*

As a professor Lucy had thirteen MA students and one PhD student, nine of whom were women; the mentorship of graduate students was uncommon for female professors at the time. She held the title of professor emeritus of plant ecology from 1948 until her death in 1971.

Lucy was especially enthusiastic and active in fieldwork, both during her active professorship and in retirement. She loved exploring, and it has been estimated that she traveled more than 65,000 miles in the USA during twenty-five years of investigations, most of it driving her own car. In addition to research nearby in Adams County, Ohio, and more widely in the East, Lucy made thirteen trips to the western United States. She was sometimes assisted in her work by Annette.

Lucy (*left*) fords a stream with an unknown assistant during field research in 1910 at Beechwood Camp, Hueston Woods, Ohio. *Courtesy of Willard Sherman Turrell Herbarium, Miami University*

Lucy took numerous color photographs of the flora she encountered in her fieldwork and displayed them as slides to illustrate her very popular lectures, both to university classes and the general public. In the hills of Kentucky during the period of Prohibition, Lucy and her sister sometimes explored areas where moonshining was active. They maintained the trust of local inhabitants, honoring local customs and not reporting illegal stills to authorities.

In the 1940s, Lucy described as new to science four species and four varieties of vascular plants, all from localities in Kentucky, as well as a hybrid fern. Over her career, Lucy wrote four books and 180 articles published in more than twenty journals. In the 1920s and 1930s, Lucy's taxonomy work included a new catalog of the flora of the Cincinnati area, with a comparison to the flora during the previous 100 years. Her study, one of the first of its kind in the United States, provided a model for analyzing changes to a flora of a region over time. Building from the understanding that the southern Appalachian mountains were a refugium for communities of forest plants during intervals of glaciation, Lucy proposed two migrations of prairie flora from the western grasslands during warming periods: a pre-Illinoian movement and a post-Wisconsinan one.

She summarized her thinking in her article "The Phytogeography of Unglaciated Eastern United States and Its Interpretation." This appeared in the *Botanical Review* 21, no. 6 (June 1955), published by Springer on behalf of New York Botanical Garden Press.

Lucy fought to conserve natural areas and was active in campaigns to set up nature reserves, particularly in Adams County. She founded the Cincinnati chapter of the Wild Flower Preservation Society in 1924, contributed to its journal *Wild Flower*, and served as the journal's editor from 1928 to 1933. Her efforts to protect a 22-acre xeric limestone prairie (Lynx Prairie) led to the establishment of the Richard & Lucile Durrell Edge of Appalachia Preserve System and ultimately to the creation of the Nature Conservancy.

Lucy was perhaps the foremost botanist in the field of deciduous forests. Her descriptions of the deciduous forest associations, from mixed mesophytic to beech-maple, are wonderful, a classic title in plant ecology. Lucy's commitment to conservation led to the eventual preservation of more than 10,000 acres in Ohio. Much of this land was carefully studied by her and her students, and the plant life was professionally cataloged for posterity. Her devotion to land preservation was one of the pivotal influences in the developing field of ecology. Her extensive research on plants was a major impetus in establishing plant ecology as an academic discipline. Not surprisingly, the Ecology Society of America elected Lucy its first woman president in 1950.

As a researcher with the University of Cincinnati, Lucy contributed to and published many articles and books over her life, including her most influential work, *Deciduous Forests of Eastern North America* (Blakiston, 1950). The book was the culmination of Lucy's research into vascular plant floristics and the composition of various deciduous forest plant communities, which had begun with her investigations of glaciated and unglaciated regions of southern Ohio. The book discusses both the current condition of the biome and its development after the end of the ice age. It also classifies forest regions, offering a map depicting an "original" forest pattern. The book describes in detail the trees and shrubs in the deciduous forests of Kentucky, Tennessee, Ohio, Virginia, West Virginia, and Pennsylvania. *Deciduous Forests of Eastern North America* is still widely used as a reference work today.

Francis Raymond Fosberg was an American botanist, a prolific collector, and an author. He said of her book, *One can only say that it is a definitive work, and that it has reached a level of excellence seldom or never before attained in American ecology or vegetation science, at least in any work of comparable importance.*

Lucy received many scientific prizes and held several notable positions over her career. She was the president of the Ohio Academy of Science from 1933 to 1934—the first woman—and was awarded Guggenheim fellowships in the field of plant sciences in 1943 and 1944. Lucy was also elected president of the Ecological Society of America in 1950—another first for a woman. There is even an award in her name; the E. Lucy Braun Award for excellence in ecology is awarded to a student for an outstanding poster presentation at the society's annual meeting. In 1952 the Cranbrook Institute of Science awarded her the Mary Soper Pope Memorial Award in botany. In 1956 she was awarded a certificate of merit by the Botanical Society of America, and she was declared one of sixty-nine distinguished American botanists by this society in 1961. In 1966 she received the Eloise Payne Luquer Medal for special achievement in botany from the Garden Club of America. Another first for a woman was when Lucy was inducted into the Ohio Conservation Hall of Fame in 1971.

Apart from the aforementioned *Deciduous Forests of Eastern North America*, Lucy's published papers, articles, and books include

"The Physiographic Ecology of the Cincinnati Region," 1916, *Ohio Biological Survey Bulletin*

"Ohio," coauthored with Jones and Lynds, in V. E. Shelford's *Naturalist's Guide to the Americas*, 1926, Williams & Wilkins Company. Lucy was also an associate editor.

"The Lea Herbarium and the Flora of Cincinnati," 1934, in *American Midland Naturalist*

An Annotated Catalog of Spermatophytes of Kentucky, 1943, John Swift Co.

"The Phytogeography of Unglaciated Eastern United States and Its Interpretation," 1955, in *Botanical Review*

The Monocotyledoneae: Cat-tails to Orchids, 1967, Ohio State University Press

The Woody Plants of Ohio: Trees, Shrubs, and Woody Climbers, Native, Naturalized, and Escaped, 1969, Hafner Publishing Co.

Lucy is remembered in the names of four plants: *Ageratina luciae-brauniae*, *Erigeron pulchellus* var. *brauniae*, *Silphium terebinthinaceum* var. *luciae-brauniae*, and *Viola* × *brauniae*.

She had a laboratory and experimental garden at the home she shared with her sister; she was never married. She died in her home at age eighty-one of congestive heart failure and is buried in Cincinnati with her parents and sister in Spring Grove Cemetery.

4.66 ALICE ORME SMITH (1889–1980)

With a long and distinguished career in architecture and landscape design, Alice was known for bringing men and nature into harmony in landscape.

Alice was born in 1889 to prominent local philanthropists Dudley Smith and Bernadine Orme, and the family lived at 501 South University Street in Normal, Illinois. She attended Smith College in Northampton, Massachusetts, earning a BA in 1911. She then trained as a nurse at New York Presbyterian Hospital, working there until WWI intervened. Alice joined the American Red Cross in the year prior to her mobilization and served as the first secretary of the Bloomington Chapter. When duty called in May 1917 to serve, the unit, consisting of twenty-three doctors and sixty-five nurses, most of whom were residents of New York, was sent to France. Upon arrival, the unit was attached to No. 1 General Hospital, British Expeditionary Force, at Etretat, France. The hospital was based out of Etretat until January 1919. The hospital sent out mobile hospitals to various battlefields throughout the course of the war. Alice came under fire at Bussy le Chateau.

Due to the proximity of the mobile hospitals to the front lines, Alice's experiences under fire and in the air have been said to *rival those of any man who was in the thick of the fight*. Alice's unit received a commendation from General John J. "Black Jack" Pershing for courage when coming under shellfire. In the letter of commendation sent to her unit, General Pershing wrote he was "proud to have them" in his command. Alice was one of only twenty-eight nurses to receive the Croix de Guerre, a French military decoration for bravery in the field of battle. She was discharged in February 1919 after spending two years in France.

Alice Orme Smith in a nurse's uniform. Photographer unknown. *mchistory.org*

Upon her return she enrolled at the Armour Institute's College of Architecture in Chicago (today known as the Illinois Institute of Technology), receiving a master's degree in 1922. From 1920 to 1923 she worked for architect Earl Reed and landscape architect Ralph Rodney Root. From 1923 to 1925 she attended Cambridge School of Architecture and Landscape Architecture. In 1926, Alice earned an MLA (master's of landscape architecture), which was officially awarded to her in 1935 upon the school's merger with Smith College to create an MLA program.

Alice was employed by landscape architect Harold Hill Blossom from 1925 to 1926 and moved to New York City after graduating from the Cambridge School. For the next four years she worked with Beatrix Farrand (see 4.45) on plans for Dumbarton Oaks in Washington, DC, and the walled Chinese garden at John D. Rockefeller's estate in Mount Desert, Maine.

From 1930 to 1932, Alice worked in Peking, China, where she produced measured drawings of Chinese gardens for Swedish architect Oswald Siren.

In 1932 Alice returned to America to open an office in New York City, before eventually establishing a private practice in Fairfield, Connecticut. Most of her commissions were in the northeastern United States. Throughout the course of her postwar career, she won awards for her designs, including an award from the *New York Times* for her designs of the Main Vista and the Garden of Religion at the 1939 World's Fair in New York.

Alice's other designs include the grounds of the American Shakespeare Theatre (now the American Shakespeare Centre) in Stratford, Connecticut, and the Bridgeport Museum of Art, Science and Industry (now Discovery Museum and Planetarium), in Bridgeport, Connecticut.

In addition, Alice designed gardens for the estates of Joshua Logan, US senator William Benton, and Lawrence Langer. In 1973 Alice was awarded the Smith College Medal for *bringing men and nature into harmony in landscape* and, in 1974, she was elected a fellow of the American Society of Landscape Architecture.

Alice Orme Smith died in Fairfield, Connecticut, in 1980 at age ninety-one. She is buried in the Orme Smith family plot at Evergreen Memorial Cemetery in Bloomington, Illinois. She is remembered for being a respected landscape architect in the northeastern United States, where, as well as for private commissions, she was known for her important public projects.

4.67 FLORENCE YOCH (1890–1972) AND LUCILE COUNCIL (1898–1964)

These talented landscape architect partners (Lucile, **right**, *and Florence,* **left**) *worked mostly in Southern California, starting their own firm. Because of their close life and work association, like Elizabeth Lord and Edith Schryver (see 4.60), they are coupled together for this book.*

Florence was born in Santa Ana, California, in 1890 to Joseph and Catherine Yoch. The youngest of six girls, she spent much of her time outdoors, including horse-and-buggy trips from the family home in Santa Ana to the beachfront hotel her parents owned and operated on Laguna Beach. Florence was surrounded by the cultural opportunities available in Laguna Beach, including art, drama, and gardening. Close friends of her parents and frequent visitors to the Laguna Hotel were Madame Modjeska and her husband, Count Karol Bozenta Chlapowski, whose house and garden in Santiago Canyon, California, inspired Florence to pursue a career in landscape design.

Florence's college education began in 1910 at the University of California, Berkeley, and then at Cornell's College of Agriculture. She would go on to earn her degree from the University of Illinois at Urbana-Champaign, Illinois, in 1915. Florence began practicing in 1918 and after graduation immediately went to work designing gardens in Pasadena and Orange County.

In 1921 she hired as apprentices Katherine Bashford, who would leave to found her own solo practice in 1923, and Lucile Council.

Lucile was born in Illinois in 1898 to parents William H. Council and Francis Bloomfield Council. She had studied at both Oxford University, England, and the Cambridge School of Domestic and Landscape Architecture (CSDLA) in

Florence Yoch (*left*) formed a very close design relationship with Lucile Council (*right*).
Cultural Landscape Foundation

Massachusetts, where she earned a master's degree. The CSDLA was the first school to offer women graduate training in the professions of architecture and landscape architecture under a single faculty. It was affiliated originally with Harvard University and later with Smith College. Other alumni include Rose Ishbel Greely (see 4.59).

In 1925, Florence and Lucile became work and life partners, forming a business partnership, Yoch & Council. They set up shop in the garden studio at Lucile's home in South Pasadena, and from there they would enjoy a thriving business creating landscaping for a large number of clients. Together they helped develop a casual but distinctively Californian interpretation of classic European gardens.

The pair made several trips to Europe, often sketching great gardens to provide inspiration for their designs at private residences, parks, campuses, public spaces, a botanical garden, and more. Over a period of fifty-three years the women completed more than 250 projects. Prestigious commissions included the residence of Mrs. Howard Huntington in Pasadena, the Wilshire Country Club in Los Angeles, and the garden of Il Brolino in Montecito, California.

The latter was inspired by an Italian villa, and the grounds feature a labyrinth of hedges for children to explore and play in. Florence insisted that the height of the hedges was determined by referring to the mountains that form a backdrop to the garden.

Through Dorothy Arzner—the first female movie director—the pair were introduced to distinguished Hollywood people such as Jack Warner and David Selznick, for whom they would design residential garden landscapes. However, Los Angeles clients could be impatient. Mrs. Selznick observed of her Beverly Hills garden: *Miss Yoch didn't stint there* [on soil preparation], *or on any of the sensible priorities. Money was sunk where it didn't show, so we had a grand new house, a splendid tennis court, a few nice trees, and many tiny plants. Miss Yoch said we were to practice patience and let them grow—a big order in that overnight town.*

Florence said that a successful garden is one in which every plant is significant and happily used.

A view of part of Thornton Gardens, San Marino, Los Angeles, California, designed by Yoch and Council. *Beverly Willis Architecture Foundation*

Working for the Hollywood elite would also lead to film set work, including the Tara set for David Selznick's *Gone with the Wind*.

Yoch & Council designed sets for five films besides *Gone with the Wind*: *Romeo and Juliet*, *The Garden of Allah* (Florence and Lucile traveled to North Africa to research this set), *How Green Was My Valley*, and *The Good Earth*. For this last film, the women turned the sloping hills of San Fernando Valley into terraced rice fields.

More information on their portfolio of work can be found in *Landscaping the American Dream: The Gardens and Film Sets of Florence Yoch: 1890–1972* (Sagapress, 1989). It was written by Florence's (much younger) cousin James J. Yoch, professor of English at the University of Oklahoma.

With the advent of WWII, Florence and Lucile's work greatly reduced. They had smaller commissions, largely in the Pasadena region. Their designs were noted for the combination of informal, wild plantings and formal geometry. They focused on plantings of native trees, shrubs, and flowers indigenous to California. Florence specialized in creating illusions in gardens. Those of half an acre or less were a real challenge to her ingenuity and were made to appear much larger and grander. On the back of a photograph of a garden for Misses Davenport (1922), she typed a note: *The garden illustrates what may be accomplished on a narrow city lot. The house and garden are on a lot only 60 ft wide*.

Florence and Lucile kept practicing until Lucile died in 1964. Florence died in 1972.

In their lifetimes, Florence and Lucile completed more than 250 projects. They are remembered for their casual but distinctively Californian interpretation of classic European gardens, including the villas of Italy, the Moorish gardens of Spain, formal gardens of France, colorful flower gardens of England, and Mediterranean landscapes.

4.68 LOUISE KLEIN MILLER (1890–1967)

Through her writing and the establishment of school gardens across North America, Louise was at the forefront in developing the love of gardening, nature, and the outdoors in children.

Much like Frances "Fannie" Griscom Parsons (see 4.17), Louise was dedicated to instilling the love of gardening in children and inspiring the establishment of school gardens. Throughout her career, her writing, teaching, and lectures inspired many to establish school gardens across North America. Louise was born in Montgomery County, Ohio. When she was two years old the family moved to Miamisburg, Ohio, where she attended the village school. Inefficient teachers gave direction to her whole life because at times they were so incredibly dull that she took to the woods, where she learned the songs and nesting habits of the birds, the color of butterflies' wings, and when and where the first spring flowers bloomed. Louise's later training at Central High School, Dayton, Ohio, organized the knowledge that she had been accumulating from nature. After graduation she taught in the city schools. In 1893 Louise went to Cook County Normal School, where she came under the influence of Colonel Parker and Mr. Jackman, both of whom were the exponents of nature study. After a postgraduate course she went to East Saginaw, Michigan, as supervisor of nature study in the schools, as well as assistant in the training school. After two years she was called to fill a similar position in Detroit, Michigan, and remained there four years. During the summer months, Louise taught at the Bay View, Michigan, Summer School, and with Dr. John M. Coulter of the University of Chicago studied the evolution of plants. At Cornell University, Professor L. H. Bailey gave a more practical direction to her work in agriculture

Photo of Louise, age eighty-six, from *As I See It* by Louise, published by Falmouth Publishing House, Portland, Maine, 1941. Photographer unknown. *thedailygardener.org*

and horticulture (see 4.64). Under his tutelage, she studied forestry, geology, entomology, chemistry, and other subjects that would be fundamental to her career development.

From Cornell University she was appointed to a teaching position at Briarcliff Manor, New York, where some of the millionaires of New York City had established a School of Practical Agriculture and Horticulture. Later she attended the Lowthorpe School of Horticulture and Landscape Gardening for Women in Groton, Massachusetts. This gave her the opportunity for study at the Arnold Arboretum of Harvard University.

The work of the children of the Village Improvement Association of Groton was placed under her direction, and she began to develop school gardens. After two years at Groton she went to Cleveland, Ohio. There she established school gardens, and the board of education created the position of curator of school gardens and appointed her to fill the position—at that time unique in the country. Louise's duties were to supervise the school gardens, give illustrated lectures on gardening in the public schools, extend home garden work, arrange for autumn flower shows, and superintend the improvement of school grounds. Under her leadership this school garden work was recognized as being among the best in the country, inspiring countless children to love gardens, plants, and nature.

The influence of Louise's work in Cleveland was marked. Each schoolyard and garden became an inspiring center for civic improvement. Areas of previous refuse dumping and fly breeding were cleaned up, and the city made them more sanitary and more beautiful. Children were taught the vegetable growing capacity of a small plot of ground, succession of crops, and harmonious color effects; they became interested in gardening, and many made the decision to pursue country life. Louise had always emphasized the physical, mental, and moral influence of this work in the fresh air and sunshine and was a great advocate of the power of gardening to inspire, especially children with behavioral or learning difficulties.

In 1904, D. Appleton of New York published her book *Children's Gardens: For School and Home*, a manual of cooperative gardening. The preface reads:

> *Miss Miller is an inspiration to all who know her and a living example of a truly beautiful soul. Such a crown of understanding makes the years sit lightly on the brow of such women as Louise Klein Miller. The eagerness of a never-failing interest in life shines from her young eyes—and the light of her serenity radiates upon all who know her. Grateful indeed are we that she has had the desire to give this little booklet to the world.*

An excerpt from the foreword to *Children's Gardens: for School and Home* reads:

> *A Manual of Cooperative Gardening: cooperative gardening is one of the newer movements for the education of the young and for the elevation of neglected and unfortunate classes; yet it has already become an important factor in the school and home life of many places under the auspices of school authorities, civic leagues, improvement associations, women's clubs, settlement houses, libraries and other bodies. This movement has two motives—the transforming of barren, dreary, ill-kept school grounds and other uncared-for public places into bowers of beauty and good taste; and developing in children love of Nature, appreciation of her beauties and ability to enhance for their own enjoyment and the public good the aesthetic effect of their immediate surroundings. This book has been written especially in the interest of children's gardens, but it contains much that may prove of value to all who care for this noble art.*

Louise's 1941 book *As I See It* by Falmouth Publishing House are reminiscences of her life and work. She was also the author of the courses *Nature Study for Pennsylvania Schools* and *Nature Study for Detroit Schools*. Louise was also a contributor to many magazines, always basing her articles on the benefits of gardening for children.

During her life, Louise lectured widely on the benefits of children's gardens, appearing at Chautauqua adult education and social movement assemblies, in front of civic associations, women's clubs, and teachers' associations in many parts of the United States and Canada.

Awards and positions were also forthcoming. She was elected a fellow of the American Association for the Advancement of Science; member of the executive board of the American Civic Association; vice president of the National Plant, Flower and Fruit Guild; and vice president of the School Gardening Association of America.

After a lifetime dedicated to instilling the love of gardening in children and inspiring the establishment of school gardens all over North America, Louise Klein Miller died in 1967.

Through her writing and the establishment of school gardens across North America, Louise was a model of developing children's love of gardening, nature, and the outdoors, always emphasizing the physical, mental, and moral influence of work in the fresh air and sunshine.

4.69 MARJORIE SEWELL CAUTLEY (1891–1954)

Landscape architect who was influential in the conception and development of visionary twentieth-century American Garden City communities

Marjorie spent her youth in Asia and the Pacific, where her father was stationed in the Navy. She was orphaned at age twelve, at which point she was sent to live with relatives in Brooklyn, New York. While there, she studied at the Packer Institute for Collegiate Studies. She went on to receive a BSc degree in landscape architecture in 1917 from nearby Cornell University and, much later, an MA in city planning from the University of Pennsylvania in 1943. She was employed shortly after her graduation from Cornell by architect Julia Morgan in Alton, Illinois, who was best known for her designs at Hearst Castle. Situated in San Simeon, California, this is a national historic landmark and California Historical Landmark. It was the joint concept of Julia Morgan and publishing tycoon William Randolph Hearst and was built between 1919 and 1947. The primary project Marjorie worked on with Morgan during WWI was a hotel for war workers.

Setting up her own New Jersey practice, Marjorie's first project undertaken as an independent practitioner—when only thirty-seven years old—was a public park in Tenafly, New Jersey, called Roosevelt Common in 1925. One of the interesting aspects of the design of the park at Tenafly was Marjorie's use of native plants, a theme that she applied extensively in her later work.

Marjorie was raised in New York and New Jersey at a time when architects were beginning to see the need to address the problem of housing. Also during her time with Morgan, Marjorie had been exposed to designing communal spaces. The growing popularity and affordability of the car and more sophisticated

Marjorie Sewell Cautley. *Division of Rare and Manuscript Collections, Cornell University Library* infrastructures resulted in the move of many middle-class Americans to bedroom communities outside more crowded urban areas. Unchecked, poorly designed housing and infrastructure growth would create problems unless addressed responsibly. One solution came from the Garden City movement—integrating the townscape with communal landscapes—and Marjorie was a prime supporter, looking to design well-planned and well-planted affordable housing.

Marjorie's professed interest in these neighborhood spaces, combined with her strong interest in the use of local plant species, came to the notice of architects/planners Clarence Stein and Henry Wright. They had already been experimenting with innovative housing design, and when Marjorie joined their office in 1924 they began working on a now-well-known housing project in the Sunnyside neighborhood of Queens in New York City, not far from the Brooklyn neighborhood where Marjorie had spent much of her childhood. Sunnyside Gardens was built in response to the post-WWI housing shortage and was intended for families of modest income. The great achievement of Sunnyside was its 200-by-900-foot *superblocks*, where all the houses were oriented toward rear courts. Only 28 percent of each block was developed, allowing for a large middle expanse to be devoted to community garden plots and public grassed areas. Some believe that Marjorie should be largely credited for devising this housing configuration. Marjorie's planting plans filled the rear court of each house with sycamores and flowering shrubs enclosed by low hedgerows that delineated each parcel while still fostering a communal sensibility among neighbors.

After Sunnyside Gardens, Marjorie went on to work on the Phipps Garden Apartments in Sunnyside (1930) and Hillside Homes (1935). Her best-known commission with Stein and Wright was at Radburn in Fair Lawn, New Jersey, where she continued to experiment with the lessons learned at Sunnyside.

Marjorie wrote in detail about the planting plan for Radburn in a 1930 issue of *Landscape Architecture* magazine. She explained that she had envisioned a community with no backyards, but simply small lawns or plots that did not encumber the extended view from the porch of each house out to the large central park, which was accessible only to neighborhood residents. Marjorie was also sensitive to the need for a greater sense of ownership within the community. As part of this concept, each resident had the option of personalizing their garden with different choices of trees, hedges, and shrubs. She held a keen appreciation for what she saw as the rapidly disappearing natural landscape of New Jersey, and in her designs, local plants were selected, particularly those with minimal maintenance and attractive display in all seasons.

After her tenure with Stein and Wright, Marjorie accepted a position as landscape consultant to the State of New Hampshire in 1935 and went on to oversee the construction of ten state parks, including Kingston and Wentworth Parks. At the same time, she taught extensively at Columbia University and the Massachusetts Institute of Technology. Marjorie was also a prolific writer, publishing often in *House & Garden*, *American City*, and the *Journal of the American Institute of Planners*. In 1935, Dodd, Mead & Company of New York published her book *Garden Design: The Principles of Abstract Design as Applied to Landscape Composition*.

Marjorie suffered a nervous breakdown in 1937 and was institutionalized. After she was released, she earned a master of fine arts in city-planning degree from the University of Pennsylvania in 1943. Her thesis was on urban planning, titled *How Blighted Areas in Philadelphia and Boston Might Be Transformed* (published by American City, 1943). In 1946 she suffered a relapse and was institutionalized again. Marjorie Sewell Cautley passed away in 1954.

4.70 MAY PETREA THEILGAARD WATTS (1893–1975)

Educator, naturalist, illustrator, scientist, teacher, author, artist, and poet

May was the daughter of Danish immigrants. Her father, a trained landscape gardener, helped develop her interest in gardening and plants at a young age. She grew up in the Ravenswood neighborhood of Chicago, Illinois. After attending Lakeview High School and teaching public school in Midlothian, Illinois, she went on to study at the University of Chicago, where she was inspired by the work of Henry C. Cowles, whom

May Theilgaard Watts. *Sterling Morton Library, the Morton Arboretum*

she referred to as *a great and first American ecologist*. May graduated with a BSc in botany and ecology and was elected to America's most prestigious honor society, Phi Beta Kappa, in 1918. She then taught at Lakeview High School until 1924, the year she married Raymond Watts. In 1925, May was a student at the Art Institute of Chicago.

Soon after moving to Ravinia, Illinois, with her husband and young family in 1927, May became involved in nature-related activities, and she urged her *city-dweller* neighbors to embrace native plants and trees. Through Henry Cowles she became associated with Friends of Our Native Landscape, a group working to preserve the natural landscape in the Midwest. This was led by architect Jens Jensen, who was also a neighbor and whose philosophies inspired May.

Jens was one of the most influential designers to popularize native gardens. He showed that not only could beautiful gardens have native species, but they could have native species in their respective places, as they would be without human integration or involvement. He taught that beauty does not have to come from a tulip from Holland or a maple from Japan; it can come from the wild reaches of our backyards or state parks. He summed up his philosophy by saying, *Every plant has fitness and must be placed in its proper surroundings so as to bring out its full beauty. Therein lies the art of landscaping.*

May began speaking about ecology at local garden clubs. She was invited to teach classes at the Morton Arboretum in Lisle, Illinois, and in 1942 she became an arboretum staff naturalist. In this role she developed programming that included botany, ecology, and geology, as well as gardening, sketching, nature literature, and creative writing. This was followed by productive years as a working naturalist, giving lectures, writing newspaper articles, and producing pamphlets to promote the responsible stewardship of the environment.

May authored several books and guides that helped nonscientists interpret the landscape. It was during this time that she wrote *Reading the Landscape: An Adventure in Ecology*, published by the Macmillan Company in 1957. This is an important work in the field of ecology that was among the most widely read and commonly used as a course book for decades by teachers.

In her book, May described places ranging from backyard gardens to the Indiana Dunes to the Rocky Mountain timberline. She wrote, *The most beautiful single aspect of the entire forest was, surely, the insteps of the trees. A more suitable union of tree in earth could hardly exist. Those arched and clutching roots wore lichens and mosses, liverworts, ferns, and fungi tucked into crannies, enshrouded curves, and lushly molded to muscular bulges.*

May wrote a similar volume, *Reading the Landscape of Europe* (Harper & Row, 1971). She also spread her knowledge and her passion for the natural world to the public in a column written regularly for the *Chicago Tribune* and had an educational horticulture program on public television. Another of her books was *Tree Finder: A Pocket Manual for Identification of Trees by Their Leaves* (Nature Study Guild, 1939). This was followed by *Flower Finder: A Guide to Identification of Spring Wild Flowers and Flower Families* (Nature Study Guild, 1955). The dust jacket of *Flower Finder: A Guide to Identification of Spring Wild Flowers and Flower Families* reads:

> *Evolution, climate, animals and man all have their effects on the growing things of an area. May Theilgaard Watts, the distinguished naturalist, recreates the history of many regions by their revealing plant life. In every chapter, she describes a different location—a neighbor's yard, a forest in the Great Smokies, a mountain top and other sites. In each instance, she explains the plants she sees and what they mean, skillfully building up evidence for a picture of the place's past.*

May also wrote books for children to encourage their love of nature and the outdoors. One example is *My Nature Book: Fun in the Outdoors*, published by Artists and Writers Guild, Whitman Publishing Company, in 1938.

May became the first director of education for the Morton Arboretum in 1942. Situated in Lisle, Illinois, it is a public garden and outdoor museum with a library, herbarium, and program in tree research, including the Center for Tree Science. It was a distinctive position, making her one of the first interpretive naturalists in the United States. Her nature programming at the Thornhill Education Center merged the old and young, the beginner and experienced student. She also shared her vision and passion by helping students see more through chalk talks, songs, games, and long outdoor rambles in the woods. Although May had to retire from the arboretum after suffering a stroke in 1961, she continued her campaigns for nature preservation throughout the remainder of her lifetime, including efforts to establish the Illinois Prairie Path on an abandoned railroad line that was once the right-of-way for the defunct Chicago, Aurora, and Elgin Railroad.

May retired in 1961 and died in 1975. She has the May T. Watts Nature Park in Highland Park, Illinois, and the May Watts Elementary School in Naperville, Illinois, named in her honor. Her house in Highland Park is listed on the National Register of Historic Places.

4.71 EDITH A. ROBERTS (1881–1977)

Botanist, author, professor of plant science, pioneer, and ecologist

Edith was born in 1881, a farmer's daughter in Rollinsford, New Hampshire. There she received an AB (artium baccalaureus) from Smith College in 1905 and an AM (artium magister) and PhD from the University of Chicago. After three years as an associate professor at Mount Holyoke, she worked as a field representative for the US Department of Agriculture during WWI. Traveling throughout the forty-eight states, Edith advised women who were managing farms while their men were away fighting the war. She once told an interviewer that she thought, *All women [who are] going to run a family should have plant science. It is basic to living.*

After the end of WWI, in 1918 Edith was appointed associate professor of botany at Vassar College, a private coeducational, liberal arts college in Poughkeepsie, New York. This was a time before it was popular to study native plant species. Two years later she was made a full professor and chairman of the department, at a time when there were very few women professors. At her suggestion, the department was renamed plant science.

The word "ecology" may seem to have originated in the early 1970s, but at Vassar, half a century earlier, Edith was already popularizing the term. She focused on studying the interrelationship between organisms and their environment. In a 1948 paper presented to the Electron Microscope Society of America, it was Edith who proved (along with fellow faculty member Mildred Southwick) that young green and yellow plants are the original source of vitamin A. This being so, the *New York Times* reported, fish livers can no longer be regarded as the main source of vitamin A. People who prefer to get this vital

Edith A. Roberts. *Vassar College Archives*

nutrient from vegetables such as carrots or spinach, rather than the previously prescribed doses of cod liver oil, have reason to be grateful to Edith.

One of Edith's main achievements as head of plant science was the creation of the Dutchess County Outdoor Ecological Laboratory, the first of its kind in the country. Located in upstate New York, it contained 675 different species of trees, shrubs, vines, flowers, ferns, and mosses. A 1948 article in the *Poughkeepsie New Yorker* reads:

> *At its start, the laboratory comprised four acres of poison ivy, two oak trees and a gleam in the eyes of Vassar plant scientists. Under Roberts's guidance, and thanks to her determination, the outdoor laboratory grew to the point that it contained nearly all of the 2,000 or more plants that are native to Dutchess County, growing under the natural conditions of soil, light, temperature, and moisture.*

The department's funds were inadequate to maintain this venture and were sometimes supplemented by fees obtained from outside lectures given by Edith. With Margaret F. Shaw, Edith wrote a book about the plants of Dutchess County.

Edith was an early advocate of gardening and landscaping using native species, which require less water and fewer pesticides than imported plants. She wrote about them first in a series of articles in *House Beautiful* magazine and then in her book *American Plants for American Gardens*. Published in 1929 by Macmillan, it was one of the first popular books to promote the use of native plants in gardening and landscaping. It was written by Edith with landscape architect Elsa Rehmann (see 4.57). Emphasizing the strong links between ecology and aesthetics, and nature and design, the book shows the basic, practical application of ecological principles to the selection of plant groups or *associations* that are suited to a particular climate, soil, topography, and lighting.

American Plants for American Gardens focuses on the vegetation concentrated in the northeastern United States, but extends from the Atlantic Ocean west to the Alleghenies and south to Georgia. The plant community settings featured include the open field, hillside, wood and grove, streamside, ravine, pond, bog, and seaside. Plant lists and accompanying texts provide valuable information for the design and management of a wide range of project types: residential properties, school grounds, corporate office sites, roadways, and parks.

In his introduction to a reprint of this book by University of Georgia Press published in 1996, Darrel G. Morrison identifies *American Plants for American*

Gardens as being among a handful of influential early books advocating the protection and use of native plants. This is now a major area of interest among gardeners, landscape architects, nursery managers, and students of ecology, botany, and landscape design, but the book was ahead of its time in many ways. Included is an appendix of plant name changes that have occurred since the book's original publication in 1929.

Edith A. Roberts died in 1977, having been in the forefront of a group of women who blazed trails in academia just as the suffrage movement won them the right to vote. She is remembered for being a true pioneering botanist, author, professor of plant science, and ecologist.

4.72 WANDA KIRKBRIDE FARR (1895–1983)

Botanist known for her discovery of the mechanism by which cellulose is formed in the walls of plant cells

She was born Wanda Kirkbride near New Matamoras, Ohio, in 1895 to parents Frederick Kirkbride and Clara Nicolaus, and her father died when she was just four years old. She and her mother went to live with Wanda's grandparents, who lived locally. Her great-grandfather Dr. Samuel Richardson was a physician who lived in the same town, and he helped cultivate Wanda's interest in science, particularly plants. Wanda received a bachelor's degree in biology from Ohio University at Athens in 1915 and a master's degree in botany from Columbia University in 1918. After graduating from Columbia she taught botany at Kansas State University and Texas A&M University.

Wanda Kirkbride Farr at her microscope. Unknown photographer and date. *Smithsonian Institution Archives*

Around 1928, after marrying botanist Clifford Farr, Wanda postponed enrolling in a PhD program to move with her husband to Washington University in St. Louis, Missouri. There she began working as a researcher under Dr. Montrose Burrows at the Barnard Skin and Cancer Clinic. Clifford began working as an assistant professor in botany at the same university. Wanda performed microscopy on live animal and plant cell cultures.

In February 1928, Clifford Farr died and the university asked Wanda to take over his classes. She also began research related to her late husband's work, studying the growth of root hairs in plants. Within a few years, Wanda was hired by the US Department of Agriculture as a cotton technologist on the strength of her previous root hair research. She moved to the Boyce Thompson Institute in Yonkers, New York. After approximately ten years of research, she was appointed director of the Cellulose Laboratory of the Chemical Foundation at the same institute, until she was called to the laboratories of the American Cyanamid Company to do WWII-related research.

Wanda answered a question that had puzzled researchers for a hundred years. Cellulose, a primary component of cell walls, was known to be constructed from cellulose granules. These granules had appeared to microscopists prior to this time to emerge fully formed in the cells' protoplasm. By contrast, the formation of starch, which is composed of the same elements (carbon, hydrogen, and oxygen), could be seen to occur in stages, in structures called plastids inside the cell protoplasm. Wanda discovered that cellulose-manufacturing plastids do exist in the protoplasm of the cell, but that such plasmids had been invisible because they have a light-refractive index similar to that of the protoplasm in which they are located. She made the plasmids visible in cotton cells by mounting the cells in a new bath derived from the juices of the cotton plant, rather than in water, which had been used previously.

In 1956 she started her own research firm, Farr Cytochemical Laboratories. The Royal Microscopical Society elected her a fellow. She was also a member of the Botanical Society of America and the Torrey Botanical Club. Wanda Kirkbride Farr died in 1983 at eighty-eight years old. She is immortalized for her important research work on plant fibers and is best remembered for her important, breakthrough discovery of the mechanism by which cellulose is formed in the walls of plant cells.

4.73 HELEN ELISE BULLARD (1896–1987)

Landscape architect who excelled in the management of city planning, housing, garden design, and gardening issues throughout her career

Helen was born in 1896 in rural Schuylerville, New York. She attended Schuylerville Public School before graduating in 1918 from Cornell University with a BSc in landscape architecture (then landscape art) from the College of Agriculture. She worked briefly for the American Locomotive Company, later becoming director of the Small Home Grounds Department at the Wagner Park Nursery Company in Sidney, Ohio. In 1921 she became the chief plantsman and planting designer in Warren Manning's Boston office. He was an American landscape designer and promoter of the informal and naturalistic wild garden approach to garden design. An advocate for the conservation of the American landscape, Manning was a key figure in the formation of the American Society of Landscape Architects and a proponent of the National Park System.

Helen then moved on in 1927 to work as an assistant to landscape architect Annette Hoyt Flanders (see 4.61) in New York City, where she was recorded as supervising at least fifty men—not an easy challenge at a time when men still dominated the world of horticulture.

As a result of the Great Depression private garden design commissions declined, so Helen moved to the public sector. After meeting Robert Moses, she went to work for him. He was an American public official who worked mainly in the New York metropolitan area. Known as the master builder of mid-twentieth-century New York City, Long Island, Rockland County, and Westchester County, he was one of the most prominent figures in the history of urban development in the United States.

Helen created the planting designs for the new Long Island parkways and organized and oversaw the spring and summer flower bedding programs for Long Island state parks. She became assistant landscape supervising engineer for the New York City Department of Parks in 1935. She played a significant role in the creation of the colonial revival garden at the Morris-Jumel Mansion in Upper Manhattan.

Helen also executed the design and construction of New York City's first nature trail, designed and supervised flower-bedding programs for all five boroughs, oversaw city flower shows, and served as one of the several landscape architects for the 1939 New York World's Fair. She was appointed junior landscape architect for the New York State Department of Public Works in 1938, remaining there until her retirement in 1964.

Helen Elise Bullard died in 1987 at age ninety-one in Schuylerville, New York, and was buried in Prospect Hill Cemetery there.

4.74 GENEVIEVE GILLETTE (1898–1986)

An early conservationist who dedicated more than sixty years of her life to establishing public parks and preserving natural beauty for future generations

Genevieve was born on a farm in Lansing, Michigan, in 1898 to David and Kitty Beal Gillette. From her grandmother she acquired her love of plants and appreciation of nature, and from her father came her deep sense of respect and stewardship for the environment. The beauty of nature, the outdoors, and landscape that Genevieve enjoyed with her father on spring walks in the family's farm woodlot on the banks of the Grand River made a lasting impression.

Genevieve Gillette. *Michigan State University*

Genevieve's father died during her teenage years, and this forced the family to sell the farm and move into town. She enrolled at Michigan Agricultural College, Michigan State University, in 1916. She became rather bored by the traditional women's studies in home economics, and her mentors saw this. Consequently, she was encouraged by professors to enroll in agriculture and chemistry classes. Genevieve did not see this as an improvement and had no heart for her new studies. Then something occurred that was to change her life and really inspire her. News came that classmates had been killed during WWI, and she volunteered to help a project to commemorate the student soldiers. It was a task that brought a new study interest.

Genevieve chose the memorial site and plaque as well as participated in the planting of trees—one for each soldier lost—near Williams Hall, on the west campus. She recalled: *It was my first landscaping project on campus, but not the last.*

In 1920 she was the only woman to graduate from Michigan in the college's first landscape architecture class. After graduation she made many job applications but found few prospects of employment. Luckily she persevered and eventually accepted the only job offer she had received. For $25 a week, she answered phones and made teas in the Chicago office of famed landscape architect Jens Jensen. It was through this employment that Genevieve became involved with Jensen's followers, an organization called Friends of Our Native Landscape.

During her two years of employment with Jensen, Genevieve continued to increase her landscaping knowledge, met many influential people, and accompanied the Friends group on many of their surveying expeditions, focusing on finding possible parklands. Jensen encouraged Genevieve to get a state parks system going in her native Michigan.

After leaving Jensen's office, Genevieve spent part of a year in Lakeland, Florida, working for the chamber of commerce as a consultant on city development. She soon returned to Michigan, this time to Detroit in 1925, to work at prestigious florist shop John Breitmeyer & Sons, assisting with landscape work originating from their nursery. She was responsible for advising developers on the landscaping of subdivision homes and suggested that landscaping be done for several demonstration homes at a time to make them more appealing to buyers. This concept was published in the realtor's magazine. It was considered a brilliant marketing idea.

Through working for John Breitmeyer & Sons, Genevieve established contact with many wealthy Detroit residents, who later contributed funds to her various park and conservation causes. It led to Genevieve developing a close friendship with

P. J. Hoffmaster, who was superintendent of state parks (1922–1934), and later director of the Department of Conservation. He enlisted the aid of Genevieve to scout the state for areas of land having state park potential. It was an assignment she gladly made her life's work.

Beginning in 1924, Genevieve helped locate and raise public support and funding for parks at Ludington, Hartwick Pines, Wilderness, and Porcupine Mountains. Porcupine Mountains, in the Upper Peninsula, contains the largest virgin hardwood and hemlock forests east of the Rocky Mountains. Other parks included Sleeping Bear Dunes National Lakeshore, Pictured Rocks National Lakeshore, the Huron-Clinton Metroparks system, and what was to become P. J. Hoffmaster State Park in the sand dunes area of Lake Michigan, between Grand Haven and Muskegon. In campaigning for the establishment of these parks, Genevieve faced opposition from the timber industry, mining companies, and summer cottage owners.

One of the things that set Genevieve apart from other women volunteers was that she had to earn her own living. At this difficult time, she obtained work managing the development of Westacres, a low-cost government housing project with community gardens near Pontiac.

Genevieve was responsible for the implementation of the housing project, from the large-scale grading of the site and development of a lake to the selection of street trees. Genevieve kept this job for eight years, then serving as a community consultant for the next seventeen. She served as a garden instructor for the Detroit Park and Recreation Department with the public school system and helped thousands of city residents with their thrift gardens during the Great Depression.

During the years that she assisted Hoffmaster, she also supported herself by working on landscaping projects for the City of Lakeland, Florida. She also ran her own private practice in Ann Arbor, which she maintained for more than thirty years. Her major clients were Albion College, Ferris State College, the City of Big Rapids, the sponsors of Westacres, and Starr Commonwealth, a nationally prominent educational center for troubled children.

From 1951, Genevieve gathered together active citizens and conservation groups concerned with the neglect of state parks. From these modest meetings in her living room the Michigan Parks Association was founded, and she acted as president. She asked every organization with an interest in parks to join, including the American Automobile Association, the League of Women Voters, the Federated Garden Clubs of the State of Michigan, the Federated Women's Club, the Park and Forestry Associations, the Michigan Botanical Club, and the Natural Areas Council.

Established to influence the direction and funding for the future of state parks and to assist in encouraging public support for her projects, this collective was instrumental in promoting a large state bond issue for parks and recreation in 1969. Genevieve worked hard on the bond issue for ten years.

Genevieve Gillette on one of her many expeditions to locate suitable parkland. *Cultural Landscape Foundation*

In 1959, at age sixty-one, Genevieve set out on a tireless lobbying effort in the state legislature to pass a $100 million bond to rebuild a deteriorating state park system. She was mainly responsible for securing federal funding for the Michigan state parks system in the 1960s, arguing that substantial numbers of park users were from out of state and that these users should share in the cost of upkeep of the state system. She said, *Parklands are something we should insist on while we're building, not after cement covers the ground. After all, aren't we the only people who can leave those following us any heritage of natural beauty?*

Genevieve's volunteer efforts and exhaustive written reports were instrumental in making Hoffmaster's vision of an expanded park system become a reality. When Hoffmaster was promoted to director of conservation in 1934, Michigan had seventy-two state parks and nine million annual visitors. Realizing the need for thorough research and detailed reports as her quest for high-quality parklands continued, Genevieve relied on the expertise of friends in the Michigan Botanical Club. She later formed the Natural Areas Council. The council is still active today, studying and recommending properties worthy of state protection.

Genevieve became a fellow of the American Society of Landscape Architects (ASLA) in 1968. She was a guest lecturer at both the University of Michigan and Michigan State University. In 1964, Michigan's Senator Phillip Hart invited her to Washington, DC, to help lobby for a land and water bill, and to establish Sleeping Bear Dunes as a national lakeshore. It is in Michigan's Lower Peninsula and hugs the northeastern shore of Lake Michigan. It includes South and North Manitou Islands, and the park is known for the huge scalable dunes of the Dune Climb. It is an area of 57,000 acres of spectacular dunes rising up to 500 feet above Lake Michigan.

Genevieve also helped establish Pictured Rocks as national lakeshore. The following year, President Johnson invited her to serve on the Citizen's Advisory Committee on Recreation and Natural Beauty, chaired by Laurance S. Rockefeller. She served on many other important boards and committees over the years. As late as 1981, she was also serving on the Wilderness and Natural Areas Advisory Board of Michigan by appointment of the governor.

Genevieve Gillette died in 1986. In her obituary the *Detroit Free Press* called her *a saving angel to Michigan's natural beauty and a miracle worker*. She was a selfless individual who took the words *stewardship of the land* to heart. She gave management and direction to the conservation movement in Michigan and saw the state's park system grow from a few small parcels to more than eighty parks, proving that her efforts had made a real difference. Her estate provided a $300,000 trust for acquiring land exhibiting certain natural and scenic qualities and giving the property to the public. Thompson's Harbor State Park, near Roger City in Presque Isle County, was her last gift to the people of Michigan. The E. Genevieve Gillette Visitor Center at P. J. Hoffmaster State Park was dedicated in 1976 and is a tribute to a woman whose determination helped to preserve the state's natural heritage for future generations to enjoy. Located 5 miles north of Grand Haven, it educates citizens of Michigan in ecological principles—a concept that was dear to her heart.

4.75 KATHERINE ESAU (1898–1997)

German American botanist who received the national medal of science for her work on plant anatomy

Katherine was born in 1898 in Yekaterinoslav, in the Russian Empire (now Dnipro, Ukraine), to a family of Mennonites of German descent. She began studying agriculture in Moscow, but after a year her family was prompted by the Bolshevik Revolution to move to Germany, where she completed her studies at the Agricultural College of Berlin. The Esau family moved to California in 1922, where Katherine worked for the Spreckels Sugar Company on sugar beet resistance to curly-top virus.

Katherine Esau by her electron microscope. *UCSB Natural History Collections*

She resumed her education at the University of California, Davis, where she achieved her doctorate in 1931. She joined the faculty and remained there until her retirement at age sixty-seven.

Her early work in plant anatomy focused on the effect of viruses on plants, specifically on plant tissue and development. She worked at the University of California, Davis, as a teacher, and later a professor of botany. While teaching, she continued her research on viruses and specifically phloem, the living tissue in vascular plants that transports the soluble organic compounds made during photosynthesis and known as photosynthates, in particular the sugar sucrose, to parts of the plant where needed. Her treatise *The Phloem* was published in 1969 as volume 5 of the *Hand-buch der Pflanzenanatomie* (Histologie Band 5, Teil 2, Gebrüder Borntraeger, Berlin). This volume has been recognized as the most important of this series and a definitive source of information about phloem.

Katherine was an influential plant anatomist, and her books *Plant Anatomy* (McGraw-Hill, 1953) and *Anatomy of Seed Plants* (John Wiley & Sons, 1977) have been key plant biology texts for decades. She published 162 articles and five books in total during her career, including *Plants, Viruses, and Insects* (Harvard University Press, 1961). She was elected a fellow of the American Academy of Arts and Sciences in 1949. In the 1950s she collaborated with botanist Vernon Cheadle on more phloem research. In 1957 she was the sixth woman elected as a member of the National Academy of Sciences. In 1963 she was promoted to full professor at the University of California, Davis. After retiring from Davis, she moved to the University of California, Santa Barbara, in 1965, and continued her research well into her nineties.

Esau tending beet plants. *UCSB Natural History Collections*

Elga Ruth Wasserman (1924–2014) had remarkable careers in science, university administration, activism, family law, and publishing. She wrote, *Women students need an unusual sense of self to persevere in a predominantly male setting.* A graduate of Smith College (BA, 1945, summa cum laude and Phi Beta Kappa), Harvard (PhD, 1949, organic chemistry), and Yale (JD, 1976), Wasserman was an expert on issues facing women and other minority populations in academia, and was most famous for overseeing the entrance of the first coeducational class at Yale College in 1969. When Elga Wasserman asked her to reflect on her education and career, Katherine wrote, in 1973, that scientific activities dominated her career and added, *I found ways of maintaining spiritual independence while adjusting myself to established policies. . . . I have never felt that my career was being affected by the fact that I am a woman.* Her dedication to her work might explain why she, unlike many of her contemporaries, was able to deal with the pressures of working in environments often considered by men as their exclusive territory.

In 1989, President George H. W. Bush awarded Katherine the National Medal of Science, an honor bestowed to individuals in science and engineering who have made important contributions to the advancement of knowledge in the fields of biology, chemistry, engineering, math, and physics.

Katherine Esau died in 1997 in Santa Barbara, California. She had published 162 articles and five books, including *Plant Anatomy* and *Anatomy of Seed Plants*, both of which have been key plant biology texts for students. Many of Katherine's publications are currently housed at the Cornelius Herman Muller library at the Cheadle Center for Biodiversity and Ecological Restoration, University of California, Santa Barbara. In memory of her contributions as a lecturer, author, and scientist, the Katherine Esau Award was created. It is awarded to the graduate student who presents the best paper in structural and developmental biology at the annual meeting of the Botanical Society of America.

4.76 CYNTHIA WESTCOTT (1898–1983)

Plant pathologist, author, and expert on roses; nicknamed the Plant Doctor

Cynthia Westcott pictured in her rose garden. Photographer: Molly Adams. *Smithsonian Gardens, Smithsonian Institution, Archives of American Gardens, Maida Babson Adams American Garden Collection*

Cynthia was born in North Attleboro, Massachusetts, in 1898. Her early interest in the outdoors was enhanced by two farms owned by the family. One farm was about a mile from their home in North Attleboro. The other, on Chopmist Ridge, was 30 miles away in Scituate, Rhode Island. The Chopmist Ridge farm consisted of 300 acres, and this gave her an early initiation to the world of nature. Cynthia's first exposure to lime sulfur, which would become so important to her as dormant sprays in her plant doctoring experiences, was its use for dipping goats in the spring. She acquired a love of roses from the great fragrant bunches of hybrid perpetuals that a neighbor brought whenever she was sick as a child. She was valedictorian of her North Attleboro High School class in June 1916.

Cynthia's ambition was to go to the private women's liberal arts college in Wellesley, Massachusetts. Her high school English teacher (a graduate of Wellesley in 1913) encouraged her to choose botany as a course. She did so and fell under the tutelage, inspiration, and guidance of Margaret Ferguson (see 4.35), who stimulated her interest in botany.

Cynthia wanted to continue in advanced studies at Cornell University, New York, but only a few women were conducting graduate work at that time, and Cornell had few assistantships available for women. Accordingly, Cynthia taught science for one year at Northboro High School in Massachusetts. Her persistence was finally rewarded when she received an assistantship offer in Cornell's Department of Plant Pathology. She would have preferred to go to the Cornell botany department, but because they had nothing to offer, she accepted it. Her entry into plant pathology was pure chance, but she was soon entranced by the subject.

Professor Whetzel at Cornell later offered her a full-time job as a research assistant in Cornell, paid for by funds provided by the Heckscher Research Foundation. She held this appointment on the university's plant pathology staff for ten years. Cynthia was the only woman in a department of forty men, and she confessed that she rather liked that. It was there that she planted her first rose garden and conducted her first tests on garden sprays to counteract and prevent plant diseases.

Cynthia's research for her doctoral dissertation related to brand canker of roses, caused by *Coniothyrium wernsdorffiae*. She was awarded her PhD from Cornell in 1932.

She soon realized that realistically, outside academia, there were few, if any, jobs available for women. She finally took a part-time assistantship as a bacteriologist with the New Jersey Experiment Station at Rutgers University. In her spare time she took courses at Rutgers, one of which was on microbiology. She decided to go into business, offering her expertise in practical plant doctoring. Her good friend Irene Dobroscky did not have a permanent job either, and they decided to open a partnership called Plant Doctors at 96 Essex Avenue, Glen Ridge, New Jersey, in 1933. It was North America's first ornamental-disease-diagnosis business.

That same year, Cynthia bought a garden in Glen Ridge, New Jersey, for use as a laboratory. She described it as *equipped with all the common plant diseases*. The business was operated in the same manner as a medical doctor's was in those days, in that she made house calls to diagnose problems, treating roses and other ornamentals in her clients' gardens, as well as inviting gardeners with plant problems to visit her house as a clinic. During winter months she wrote, lectured, and traveled. Her expertise in diseases of roses and other ornamentals was highly regarded. She was among the first to successfully use bisdithiocarbamates for plant disease control.

During her thirty years as a plant doctor, Cynthia gave nearly 1,000 lectures, traveling to every state in the United States and collecting specimens along the way. In her own words, *I like my specimens, for I've had so much fun getting them. The aphids on oleander recall a lovely week in Savannah. They were from the patio of the comfortable Hotel de Soto. . . . The bagworms came from dead evergreens put out for the trash man to collect on a sidewalk in Houston. The earwig is my memento of a beautiful garden in Seattle; the cottony-cushion scale is from a rose bush beside a lake in Winter Park; the rose rust means happy days in California*.

Cynthia felt that a basic ingredient of a good plant pathologist is recognizing how to learn from plants. She said, *I think there has not been a day in all the years I have been working in gardens when plants have not taught me something*.

She taught garden courses at department stores Macy's and Bamberger's and also conducted special courses at the New York Botanical Garden and the Brooklyn Botanic Garden. Her articles appeared in numerous garden magazines; she wrote regular columns in the *New York Times* and *Home Garden* and contributed to the book published by *Home Garden* titled *10,000 Garden Questions Answered*.

Cynthia willingly shared what she learned from plants, and particularly how to treat and identify plant diseases, in several books:

The Plant Doctor: The How, Why, and When of Disease and Insect Control in Your Garden (Frederick A Stokes, 1937)
The Gardener's Bug Book (American Garden Guild and Doubleday, 1946)

Westcott's Plant Disease Handbook (Van Nostrand, 1950)
Anyone Can Grow Roses (Van Nostrand, 1950)
Garden Enemies (Van Nostrand, 1953)
Are You Your Garden's Worst Pest? (Doubleday, 1961)

She also wrote her autobiography, *Plant Doctoring Is Fun*, published in 1957 by Van Nostrand.

During WWII she lectured on pest control for victory gardens. Victory gardens, also called war gardens or food gardens for defense, were vegetable, fruit, and herb gardens planted in private gardens and public parks during WWII. The government encouraged people to plant victory gardens not only to supplement their rations but also to boost morale, because gardeners could feel empowered by their contribution of labor to the war effort and also be rewarded by the produce they grew. It was an important initiative, and Cynthia's efforts to teach amateur gardeners about control of plant diseases was an important contribution to the program.

Cynthia's interests in horticulture were widely spread, but her special passion was roses. She was the first president of the North Jersey Rose Society, serving from 1954 to 1956, and for six years she was a director of the American Rose Foundation. She was a fellow of the American Association for the Advancement of Science and a member of the American Entomological Society, the American Phytopathological Society, and other organizations. Among her honors were a citation in 1955 from the American Horticultural Council and gold medals from the American Rose Society in 1960 and the Garden Club of New Jersey in 1963. The Northeast Division of the American Phytopathological Society honored her with their award of merit in 1969, and the American Phytopathological Society appointed her a fellow in 1973. She served on the board of directors of the American Horticultural Council, on the board of directors of the National Council of State Garden Clubs, and as director-at-large and consulting rosarian of the American Rose Society. In recognition of her successful books, she was elected to the hall of fame of the Garden Writers of America. The Garden Club of New Jersey gave her its horticulture award for 1956 (silver medal) for promoting the rose and its culture all over the United States. In 1975 the American Rose Society honored her at their national convention with a presentation called *This is Your Life, Dr. Cynthia Westcott*, and the Jackson and Perkins Company named a hybrid tea rose 'Cynthia Westcott' in her honor.

Every year on Rose Day, Cynthia would open her gardens to the public to view her test plots and admire her roses during their peak of bloom. She would serve punch and cookies for her guests, who sometimes numbered more than 700. She freely shared her knowledge and her hospitality with the general public, and what she learned about gardens, and especially plant diseases, she passed on to gardeners throughout North America.

Cynthia continued as a plant doctor until retirement in 1962, when she moved to a retirement community near Croton-on-Hudson, New York. Cynthia Westcott died of a heart ailment in 1983 in North Tarrytown, New York. She will long be remembered for her dedicated efforts to help people keep their plants healthy. However, it was her magazine articles and several bestselling books that had made her a national personality, earning her the name the Plant Doctor. The Cynthia Westcott Papers, an archive of her research notes and business correspondence, is at Cornell University Library.

4.77 ETHEL GRANGER MCDOWELL EARLEY CLARK (1899–1976)

Ethel established herself in American horticulture history as the first president of the nationally influential Negro Garden Clubs of Virginia. A self-taught gardener, she was a skilled flower show judge and a horticultural educator keen to spread her love of gardening to others.

Ethel was born in 1899 in Roanoke, Virginia, the daughter of Phoebe Ragland Granger and William Granger, a laborer on the railroad. In 1916 she married David McDowell, a laborer from North Carolina. It did not last and they had no children. For most of the following decade, Ethel lived with her parents or alone and made a living as a cook. An uncontested divorce was granted on October 18, 1927, on the grounds of desertion.

In 1929, in Roanoke, she married James Earley, a widowed railway hostler for the Norfolk and Western Railroad. They also had no children. They lived in a home with a large garden, and she was listed in the 1930 census as a "homemaker with no occupation" so, apparently, James was able to support her without the need for her to work.

She began her garden club career as a leader of the Big Lick Garden Club (named after the original name of Roanoke). The club was successful and attracted a large membership, becoming a powerhouse of community improvement. She served as president from 1930 to 1938, again 1939–1940, and also 1951–1953. The club was very active in beautifying the city with flowers and shrubs and tidying unsightly, untended roadsides and patches of land, which was greatly appreciated and noted by the residents of the city. Their reputation grew and membership and volunteers increased. This persuaded the city council to donate an old post office building to the club, which the club promptly converted into a community center. Working directly with the chamber of commerce, Ethel and the club took charge of weed elimination in vacant lots and alleys in the city's Black section, later known as Gainsboro, and collaborated with the white president of the Roanoke Valley Garden Club to beautify the nearby highway entrance. Inspired by the work of the Black women's garden clubs, city officials in Roanoke began to improve street conditions in other segregated neighborhoods.

In 1931, Ethel invited Hampton Institute horticulturalist Asa C. Sims to lecture on landscaping at her home. Impressed by her accomplishments, he invited her to attend the founding meeting of the Negro Garden Clubs of Virginia (later known as the Virginia Garden Clubs). Eighteen club representatives met at Hampton Institute (later Hampton University) in April 1932. Ethel outlined the Big Lick Garden Club's impact on Roanoke, and the impressed members present that day elected her the first state president. She was reelected to a second one-year term in 1933.

By 1942 the Negro Garden Clubs of Virginia had grown from seven chapters to sixty-five, and by 1955 more than 100 clubs from across the state had joined. Annual conferences featured local mayors and dignitaries and botany experts from Virginia State College (later Virginia State University) and Hampton Institute, as well as lecturers from the National Park Service. These garden clubs were effective in spreading the joys of gardening to many, especially in deprived areas, and were a driving force in improving local environments.

Through the leadership of Ethel and other officers, the Negro Garden Clubs of Virginia provided *effective programs for community improvement, opportunities for leadership by women*, and furnished examples of *interracial cooperation*, as noted approvingly by a writer in Hampton's *Southern Workman*. Club members beautified neighborhoods and increased property values in racially segregated neighborhoods, whose residents were denied the loans and financial support that white homeowners received, and they encouraged home and school garden initiatives and urged members to register and vote. The Negro Garden Clubs included interracial cooperation into its mission, and its chapters bridged racial gaps by planning and hosting interracial garden club events during the Jim Crow age of segregation. The Negro Garden Clubs of Virginia offered networking, artistic expression, and education for women (who were ordinarily excluded from such opportunities). In 1955 the *Roanoke Tribune* celebrated their work by noting that *the efforts of this organization can be felt all over the State of Virginia. Wherever there are garden clubs there is beauty. The* Southern Workman agreed that *this movement, simple in its inception, has in many instances become the center of community progress* and called it contagious. As women member gardeners moved from Virginia, they took their focus with them and established flourishing club networks in many other states. They were trailblazers of giving often deprived people of color from all walks of life a mission to improve the lot of others through nature and gardening initiatives.

In addition to her garden club work, Ethel remained active in local affairs throughout the 1950s and served her community's practical needs as a notary public. She was elected the founding vice president of Section II of the Virginia School Food Service Association and became president in 1957. She supported the temperance movement, encouraged early literacy as a member of the Gainsboro Branch Library reading club, and financially supported the Lula Williams Branch of the Young Women's Christian Association (YWCA), which assisted Black working women. She actively supported the United Nations' 1948 Universal Declaration of Human Rights and in 1950 wrote to state legislators to support civil rights legislation in Virginia.

Widowed on January 1, 1957, at age sixty-one she married Roanoke resident Claude Lee "Cordie" Clark in 1960. He was a veteran of WWI and a retired coal miner. He died on June 16, 1972. Ethel Granger McDowell Earley Clark died in a Salem nursing home on September 22, 1976, following a stroke. She was buried beside her third husband at C. C. Williams Memorial Park in Roanoke. She had been an important influencer of African American garden clubs and did much to foster and encourage interracial harmony, largely through gardening activities and channels. Serving her community in many ways, she demonstrated emphatically how gardening can be a healing, effective, joyful, and pleasing way of improving the environment, especially in deprived areas.

4.78 GLADYS IOLA TANTAQUIDGEON (1899–2005)

Gladys was a Native American Mohegan tribe medicine woman, herbalist, anthropologist, author, and tribal council member. She helped Native American artisans preserve their traditional skills, culture, and arts, and published several books in her lifetime about traditional herbal medicine.

While her achievements were noteworthy, she is also included as a representative and as a tribute to the many Native American women who taught their contemporaries about the benefits of herbal medicine and the power of plants. In addition to this valuable contribution, Native American women usually oversaw the cultivation, nurturing, and harvest of crops and vegetables. See Buffalo Bird Woman (4.14) for a good example of this. Knowledge about the medicinal benefits of plants was an integral part of Native American culture, and by sharing this with early settlers, there is little doubt that this, together with advice on vegetables and crops to grow successfully, helped the settlers survive the formative years, in what was often difficult environmental, climatic, and horticultural situations. Medicine women like Tantaquidgeon were essential to their tribes and to the survival of the settlers.

Gladys Tantaquidgeon. *Connecticut Women's Hall of Fame, New Haven, Connecticut 06515*

Gladys was the third of seven children born to Mohegan Native American parents John and Harriet Fielding Tantaquidgeon. In the Mohegan language the family name translates as *fast runner*. They lived on Mohegan Hill in Quinnetucket (Uncasville, in New London County, Connecticut). In childhood she learned traditional practices, beliefs, and lore from *nanus*, the respected women elders. By age five the tribal *nanus* had chosen her to be schooled in the traditions of Mohegan pharmacology and culture. She started studying with her aunt in 1904, specializing in traditional herbal medicine and attending classes in local schools.

Anthropologist Frank Speck met Tantaquidgeon as a child, and, impressed with her intelligence and curiosity, when she was old enough he invited her to study anthropology with him at the University of Pennsylvania. He arranged housing with foreign students at his home in Swarthmore, enrolled her in classes, and enlisted her as a fieldwork assistant to broaden her knowledge and her understanding of Native American cultures. Later she did fieldwork among the Lenape and other eastern Algonquian tribes. She further expanded her knowledge of traditional Native American pharmacopeia by researching herbal medicine practices in many different East Coast tribes.

During the time of the Indian Reorganization Act and the Indian New Deal under the administration of President Franklin D. Roosevelt, from 1934 to 1947 Tantaquidgeon began work with the US Bureau of Indian Affairs. In 1938 she was transferred to the Indian Arts and Crafts Board to serve as a *native arts specialist*. Working mostly in the Dakotas, Montana, and Wyoming areas, she helped Native American artisans preserve their traditional skills, culture, and arts. In addition, she helped them form cooperatives and other institutions to sell and manage their crafts. She developed ways for tribes to revive cultural practices and skills that were gradually being eroded away and forgotten.

In 1931 she worked with her brother Harry, a former chief, and her father, John, to found the Tantaquidgeon Indian Museum. It is the oldest such museum to be owned and operated by Native Americans. After ending her government service in 1947, she returned to Mohegan Hill, Uncasville. She worked full time at the museum for the next fifty years, until her retirement from there in 1998.

As a librarian in the Niantic Women's Prison in Connecticut in the late 1940s, she helped minority women by advising them of their rights and offering legal counsel. During the 1970s and 1980s she served on the Mohegan Tribal Council, encouraging the preservation and revival of their endangered tribal customs and language.

Tantaquidgeon published several books in her lifetime about traditional herbal medicine. Her best-known work, *A Study of Delaware Indian Medicine Practices and*

Folk Beliefs (1942), was reprinted in 1972, 1995, and 2000 as *Folk Medicine of the Delaware and Related Algonkian Indians*. In 1992 she was elected the tribal medicine woman of the Mohegan. She preserved numerous records and tribal correspondence in boxes under her bed, which proved to be critical evidence as documentation to aid the tribe's case for federal recognition. The tribe proved community continuity and was eventually federally recognized as a sovereign tribal nation of the Mohegan people in 1994. This recognition was part of a settlement linked to their claim for the lands that make up the present-day Mohegan reservation on the Thames River by the town of Montville, near Uncasville, New London County, Connecticut.

Tantaquidgeon received the National Organization for Women's Harriet Tubman Award in 1996, as the citation said, *for consistent endeavor in the area of social justice*. She received honorary doctorates from the University of Connecticut (doctor of humane letters degree, 1987) and Yale University (1994). In 1994 she was inducted into the Connecticut Women's Hall of Fame.

Gladys Tantaquidgeon died in 2005 at age 105. She had helped preserve and record many Native American skills, crafts, language, and heritage that might well have disappeared without her enthusiasm and work.

4.79 ISADORE SMITH (ANN LEIGHTON, 1902–1985)

Ann Leighton was the professional name of Isadore Smith, a renowned garden historian, scholar, author, designer, and landscape architect. She used her expertise to write three books that give us a valuable resource of information about seventeenth- and eighteenth-century American gardens and colonial life.

Isadore Smith (a.k.a. Ann Leighton)

Isadore was a native of Portsmouth, New Hampshire. She was a graduate of Portsmouth High School and the National Cathedral School, Washington, DC, and graduated from Smith College in 1923. She married Colonel A. William Smith, a British army veteran of WWI. They moved to Ipswich, New Hampshire, in 1934, and she lived most of her life there.

While living on Argilla Road in Ipswich during WWII, she wrote *While We Are Absent*, published by Little, Brown & Co. in 1943, a book about the challenge of maintaining a home and raising children while her husband, who once again answered his country's call in wartime, was serving in Europe.

Her love of nature led her to a passion for gardening, and she began to design gardens for friends in her locality. Her particular interest was the history of colonial gardens, and she re-created many that were attached to historic houses in New England that had lost their originality, either through neglect or overplanting with designs and plants that were not authentic.

Isadore worked tirelessly to preserve Ipswich's natural and architectural history. An ardent conservationist, she proposed and persuaded the Ipswich town meeting to designate the Town Farm poorhouse as a park, thereby preserving it from development. During the 1960s she served on the Ipswich Salt Marsh committee, which was concerned with the preservation of the town's coastal wetlands, and was a member of the Hall-Haskell House committee, which assumed the task of restoring the town's Little Red House, a federal house next to the Town Hall. In addition, she is credited with the inspiration to create what is known as Sally's Pond in the center of town, which reflects the two historic houses owned by the Ipswich Historical Society on the town green.

A member of the Ipswich School Committee in the 1950s and a longtime sponsor of the Essex County Greenbelt Association of Massachusetts, she also was a dedicated member of the Ipswich Historical Society. A member of the American Society of Landscape Architects, she designed period gardens for the Lee Mansion of the Marblehead Historical Society; the Colonial Dames in Swansea; the Weeks Family Homestead in Greenland, New Hampshire; the Paul Revere House in Boston's North End, and at the 1677 Whipple House, Ipswich, also owned by the Ipswich Historical Society.

Over many years, Isadore combined her encyclopedic knowledge of early gardens with New England history. She used this to design her historic colonial period gardens with authentic layout, features, and plants. She also put her expertise to excellent use by writing three books, the first of which, *Early American Gardens: For Meate or Medicine*, was published under the pseudonym Ann Leighton by Houghton Mifflin in 1970. When this was published, the late Walter Muir Whitehill, Boston historian and director of the Boston Athenaeum, said, *What a perfectly enchanting book! Why has no one ever had the wit and imagination to combine a taste for gardening and 17th-century New England history until now? Because, I suspect, few people read as widely, garden as enthusiastically, or write as engagingly.*

A second volume, *American Gardens in the Eighteenth Century: For Use or For Delight*, was published in 1976. A third volume, *American Gardens of the Nineteenth Century: For Comfort and Affluence*, was published posthumously in 1987 by the University of Massachusetts Press. The trilogy of 1,350 pages of scholarship is still in print today. Isadore summed up the staying power of her subject matter in a brief book jacket teaser: *While buildings may decay and crumble, the plants of every age are still with us and need only to be collected and replanted to speak for the time and its people.* Isadore also wrote many articles and short stories that appeared in such magazines as *House & Garden* and in such collections as *The American Woman's Garden*.

One of Isadore's commissions was the re-creation of the garden at the Brick House, off Route 33 in Greenland, New Hampshire. The garden was designed in 1977 by Isadore, supported by Katharine C. Weeks—author of the book *Gardening with New England Colonial Plants: Their History, Uses & Culture*.

The garden beds at the Brick House comprise a typical housewife's garden of the late seventeenth century. This was functional and practical, focusing on the vegetable plots containing all the herbs and plants essential for a New England household. The concept of a *pretty* garden emphasizing flowers and shrubs would have been alien to a woman of the seventeenth century. The garden was there to feed the family and, if possible, produce a surplus that could be sold to supplement the family's income. Plants were not in neat, even rows. Every inch of available space would be used, not only to yield as many vegetables and herbs as possible but also to act as a weed repellent. Sometimes small fruit trees were planted in these gardens. Because there was no order, every garden was different, planted according to the needs of the woman of the household. Every herb and plant fell into one of three categories: medicinal, household, or culinary.

On September 9, 2012, the colonial-era herb garden beds at the Brick House were formally dedicated to Katharine C. Kitty Weeks in appreciation for her efforts in collaboration with Isadore Smith to conceive, create, and nurture the gardens for the enjoyment and edification of present and future generations.

The garden at Brick House, showing typical raised beds. *weeksbrickhouse.org*

Isadore Smith died in 1987 in the home of her sister, Mrs. Wallace Niles, in Tallahassee, Florida, after a long illness. She had designed gardens for friends in her locality, but her special interest and focus had been the history of colonial period gardens, and she re-created many that were attached to historic houses in New England that had fallen into disrepair. Her re-created gardens give us an opportunity today to visit several authentic examples of how they were designed and planted, and indicate how essential they were to the survival of a family.

4.80 BARBARA MCCLINTOCK (1902–1992)

Scientist and cytogeneticist who was awarded the 1983 Nobel Prize in Physiology or Medicine for the discovery of genetic transposition. She specialized in researching the genetic structure of maize.

Barbara was born in 1902 in Hartford, Connecticut, the third of four children born to homeopathic physician Thomas Henry McClintock and Sara Handy McClintock. The family moved to Brooklyn in 1908, and Barbara completed

Barbara McClintock examining samples of maize.
Carnegie Institution for Science Administrative Archives C017055

her secondary education at Erasmus Hall High School, where she discovered her love of science. She wanted to continue her studies at Cornell University's College of Agriculture, but her mother resisted sending her to college for fear that she would be unmarriageable. Fortunately her father intervened and she began her studies at Cornell's College of Agriculture in 1919. She studied botany, receiving a BSc in 1923. Her interest in genetics began when she took her first course in that field in 1921.

The course was taught by C. B. Hutchison, a plant breeder and geneticist who, impressed by Barbara's interest, telephoned to invite her to participate in the graduate genetics course. She said later that Hutchison's invitation was the reason she continued in genetics: *Obviously, this telephone call cast the die for my future. I remained with genetics thereafter*.

Although it has been reported that women could not major in genetics at Cornell, and therefore her MS and PhD (earned in 1925 and 1927, respectively) were officially awarded in botany, recent research has revealed that women did earn graduate degrees in Cornell's Plant Breeding Department during the time that Barbara was a student at Cornell.

At Cornell, Barbara started her career as the leader in the development of maize cytogenetics, the focus of her research for the rest of her life. From the late 1920s, she studied chromosomes and how they change during reproduction in maize. She developed the technique for visualizing maize chromosomes and used microscopic analysis to demonstrate many fundamental genetic ideas.

One of those ideas was the notion of genetic recombination by crossing over during meiosis—a mechanism by which chromosomes exchange information. She produced the first genetic map for maize, linking regions of the chromosome to physical traits. She demonstrated the role of the telomere and centromere regions of the chromosome, which are important in the conservation of genetic information.

Barbara became recognized as among the best in the field. Her cytogenetic research focused on developing ways to visualize and characterize maize chromosomes. She was credited with making ten of the seventeen significant advances in the field that were made by Cornell scientists between 1929 and 1935. She published the first genetic map for maize in 1931. This information provided necessary data for the crossing over study she published with a colleague, Harriet Creighton; they also showed that crossing over occurs in sister chromatids, as well as homologous chromosomes. In 1938, Barbara produced a cytogenetic analysis of the centromere, describing the organization and function of the centromere, as well as the fact that it can divide.

Despite her progress at Missouri—ahead of her time in many ways—Barbara was excluded from faculty meetings and was not made aware of positions available at other institutions. In 1940 she wrote to her superior, Charles Burnham: *I have decided that I must look for another job. As far as I can make out, there is nothing more for me here. I am an assistant professor at $3,000 and I feel sure that that is the limit for me.*

In early 1941 she took a leave of absence from Missouri in hopes of finding a position elsewhere. She accepted a visiting professorship at Columbia University, where her former Cornell colleague Marcus Rhoades was a professor. Rhoades offered to share his research field at Cold Spring Harbor on Long Island. In December 1941 she was offered a research position at the Carnegie Institution of Washington's Department of Genetics, Cold Spring Harbor Laboratory. After her yearlong temporary appointment, Barbara accepted a full-time research position at Cold Spring Harbor Laboratory. There she was highly productive and continued her work with the breakage-fusion-bridge cycle, using it to substitute for x-rays as a tool for mapping new genes. She would work on transposition to demonstrate that genes are responsible for turning physical characteristics on and off all the way through to the 1950s, developing theories to explain the suppression and expression of genetic information from one generation of maize plants to the next.

Barbara's breakthrough publications, and support from her colleagues, also led to her being awarded several postdoctoral fellowships from the National Research Council. This funding allowed her to continue to study genetics at Cornell, the University of Missouri, and the California Institute of Technology. In 1944, in recognition of her prominence in the field of genetics, Barbara was elected to the National Academy of Sciences—only the third woman to be elected. The following year she became the first female president of the Genetics Society of America.

In 1944 she undertook a cytogenetic analysis of *Neurospora crassa* at the suggestion of George Beadle, who used the fungus to demonstrate the one-gene-one-enzyme relationship. He invited her to Stanford to undertake the study. She successfully described the number of chromosomes, or karyotype, of *N. crassa* and described the entire life cycle of the species. Beadle said, *Barbara, in two months at Stanford, did more to clean up the cytology of Neurospora than all other cytological geneticists had done in all previous time on all forms of mold.*

Examples of the diversity of maize. *Sam Fentress*

In 1947, Barbara received the achievement award from the American Association of University Women. In 1957, McClintock received funding from the National Academy of Sciences to start research on indigenous strains of maize in Central America and South America. She was interested in studying the evolution of maize through chromosomal changes, and being in South America would allow her to work on a larger scale. Barbara explored the chromosomal, morphological, and evolutionary characteristics of various races of maize.

After extensive work in the 1960s and 1970s, McClintock and her collaborators published the seminal study *The Chromosomal Constitution of Races of Maize*, leaving their mark on paleobotany, ethnobotany, and evolutionary biology.

Barbara officially retired from her position at the Carnegie Institution in 1967 and was made a distinguished service member of the Carnegie Institution of Washington. This honor allowed her to continue working with graduate students and colleagues in the Cold Spring Harbor Laboratory as scientist emerita; she lived in the town.

In reference to her decision twenty years earlier to stop publishing detailed accounts of her work on controlling elements, she wrote in 1973: *Over the years, I have found that it is difficult if not impossible to bring to consciousness of another person the nature of his tacit assumptions when, by some special experiences, I have been made aware of them. This became painfully evident to me in my attempts during the 1950s to convince geneticists that the action of genes had to be and was controlled. It is now equally painful to recognize the fixity of assumptions that many people hold on the nature of controlling elements in maize and the manners of their operation*.

Even late in the twentieth century, Barbara's contribution to biology was still not widely acknowledged as amounting to the discovery of genetic regulation. It was not until the late 1960s and 1970s, after biologists had determined that the genetic material was DNA, did members of the scientific community begin to verify her early findings. Other awards received include being elected a fellow of the American Academy of Arts and Sciences in 1959, and in 1967 the Kimber Genetics Award. Three years later she was given the National Medal of Science by Richard Nixon in 1970—the first woman so awarded.

Cold Spring Harbor named a building in her honor in 1973. She received the Louis and Bert Freedman Foundation Award and the Lewis S. Rosenstiel Award in 1978. In 1981 she became the first recipient of the MacArthur Foundation Grant and was awarded the Albert Lasker Award for Basic Medical Research, the Wolf Prize in Medicine, and the Thomas Hunt Morgan Medal by the Genetics Society of America. In 1982, Barbara was awarded the Louisa Gross Horwitz Prize from Columbia University for her research in the *evolution of genetic information and the control of its expression*.

Most notably, Barbara received the Nobel Prize for Physiology or Medicine in 1983, the first woman to win that prize individually and the first American woman to win any unshared Nobel Prize. It was given to her by the Nobel Foundation for discovering *mobile genetic elements*. In her press statement about the Nobel Prize, Barbara noted: *It might seem unfair to reward a person for having so much pleasure, over the years, asking the maize plant to solve specific problems and then watching its responses*.

She was elected a foreign member of the Royal Society in Great Britain in 1989. She received the Benjamin Franklin Medal for distinguished achievement in the sciences of the American Philosophical Society in 1993. She was awarded fourteen honorary doctor of science degrees and an honorary doctor of humane letters. In 1986 she was inducted into the National Women's Hall of Fame. An anthology of her forty-three publications, *The Discovery and Characterization of Transposable Elements: The Collected Papers of Barbara McClintock*, was published by Routledge in 1987.

Barbara's own words best describe what sustained her lifelong enthusiasm for research: *I just have been so interested in what I was doing and it's been such a pleasure, such a deep pleasure, that I never thought of stopping . . . I've had a very, very, satisfying and interesting life*.

Barbara spent her later years as a key leader and researcher in the field at Cold Spring Harbor Laboratory. She remained a regular presence in the Cold Spring Harbor community and gave talks on mobile genetic elements and the history of genetics research for the benefit of junior scientists.

Barbara McClintock died of natural causes in Huntington, New York, on September 2, 1992, at age ninety; she never married or had children. A great role model for young women in terms of persistence, intellect, drive, and a grand curiosity that fueled all her research, Barbara is perhaps the most highly honored woman in this book. It is unfortunate that her work was not immediately understood or accepted by her contemporaries, and it took decades for her groundbreaking work to be recognized. However, Barbara did not let the scientific community's reaction discourage her. She once commented, *It didn't bother me, I just knew I was right. Anybody who had had that evidence thrown at them with such abandon couldn't help but come to the conclusions I did about it*.

4.81 ELIZABETH LAWRENCE (1904–1985)

Internationally known, award-winning author and practicing landscape architect

Elizabeth was born at the home of her paternal grandparents in Marietta, Georgia, in 1904. Having graduated from Barnard College in New York City and taking a long trip abroad, after her father's death in 1936 Elizabeth returned to the large family house in Raleigh, North Carolina. The Raleigh garden, which her mother had maintained in her absence, was so beautiful that she decided never to leave it again, at least not for long. Her mother was a passionate gardener and inspired Elizabeth to go back to school. She became the first female graduate of the very first landscape architecture program at State College (now North Carolina State University). After completing her studies, she embarked upon her career as a garden designer, lecturer, and writer.

Her first article was published in *Garden Gossip* in 1932, a magazine of the Garden Club of Virginia. Four years later, a publication in *House & Garden* launched her as a national garden writer. She continued to work as a freelance garden journalist up to the publication of her first book, *A Southern Garden*, in 1942, and through WWII. *A Southern Garden* was published by the University of North Carolina Press and was reissued in three editions. It is regarded as a classic in garden literature. Elizabeth writes that gardening in the Middle South, where seasons have no definite boundaries but merge imperceptibly, could and should be a year-round pleasure. She takes the reader through the cycle of seasons, telling which plants are most suitable to which season. The book includes tables giving blooming dates of more than 800 varieties of plants, which were meticulously recorded by her over a period of years.

Elizabeth collected scientific information, much of it from her copious records of several thousand plants she had grown in her own gardens, and then personalized it. She was a popular lecturer at garden clubs, where audiences thought her the most *charming* speaker they had ever had and a *plants woman* of encyclopedic knowledge. She was a passionate letter writer with a steady flow of correspondence over more than half a century, and she collected bloom dates (when flowers bloomed) for her records. Although books about gardening were important, she believed that the most valuable source of information was other gardeners who had themselves grown the plants in all places and conditions, and she wrote to them across the country, from Maine to California. When they wrote back, she assembled their collective knowledge and put it in her books. The results were the firsthand experiences of practicing gardeners sharing their thoughts.

Elizabeth was already an award-winning author and practicing landscape architect when she moved from Raleigh to Charlotte, North Carolina, in 1948. She had struggled to make a career for herself in Raleigh at a time when there was little work for landscape designers, especially women, and especially in the South. The following year she started her new garden—a well-designed, dynamic *living laboratory*—where she tested a miscellaneous variety of plants to find out what grows well in the Middle South. Soon after the publication of *A Southern Garden* she purchased a lot on Ridgewood Avenue, in the historic district of Charlotte. There she built her house and began to lay out a garden. The house was a small, five-bay colonial revival–style frame dwelling set on landscaped grounds, including paths, beds, and borders. She believed passionately that gardeners should experiment with plants and with design features, that they should try something new. She certainly followed this credo, because she introduced hundreds of exotic plants into her garden. Elizabeth's garden was an inspiration for her writing for the next thirty-five years and was frequently referred to in her work.

Elizabeth Lawrence in her garden in Raleigh, August 1957. *southerngardenhistory.org*

Elizabeth wrote six manuscripts and numerous articles for various regional and national publications. Her books *The Little Bulbs* (1957) and *Gardens in Winter*

(1961) became favorites with her growing fan base, but nothing gave her and her readers more pleasure than her Sunday columns for the *Charlotte Observer*. She wrote more than 700 columns for the newspaper. Many of these columns were posthumously collected in *Through the Garden Gate* and *Beautiful in All Seasons*, published by University of North Carolina Press.

Each of her books had its own following, both among gardeners, who applied to Elizabeth for information and advice that remains relevant today, and readers who regarded Elizabeth as a gifted literary writer who knew poetry as well as she knew plants. During her lifetime, along with being a much-respected gardening author and a talented landscape architect, Elizabeth was active on many civic commissions and boards, including seven years on the Berkeley Civic Art Commission. She was a founding member of the California Horticultural Society (1935), joined the American Society of Landscape Architects (ASLA) in 1937, and was elected an ASLA fellow in 1972. She served on the ASLA task force on women in landscape architecture from 1974 to 1975 and served on the San Francisco Housing and Planning Commission. Elizabeth moved away from the Charlotte property in 1984 and died shortly afterward in 1985.

In 1986, Mary Elizabeth "Lindie" Wilson purchased the property and immediately started resurrecting the garden, which had fallen into disrepair during two years of neglect. Lindie would later collaborate on a book about Elizabeth. Lindie's stewardship for the next twenty-three years ensured the survival of a significant number of plants original to Elizabeth—most still thrive in the garden to this day. During her ownership, Lindie engaged the help of many regional and national experts to figure out the best way to preserve the property, out of which was born the Friends of Elizabeth Lawrence in 2003. In 2005 the house and garden were designated a historic site by the Charlotte-Mecklenburg Landmarks Commission and entered into the Archives of American Gardens, and in 2006 the property was listed on the National Register of Historic Places. In 2008 the property was purchased by the Wing Haven Foundation.

The Elizabeth Lawrence House and Garden remains open to the public as a horticultural and historic resource. It is maintained in Elizabeth Lawrence's spirit—as a vibrant, dynamic, and undeniably inspiring *living laboratory*. Using Elizabeth's writings, many of her favorite plants are still being reintroduced in her garden.

In 2004, on what would have been her 100th birthday, Elizabeth was featured as one of the twenty-five greatest gardeners in the world by *Horticulture* magazine. That same year, Beacon Press published *No One Gardens Alone: A Life of Elizabeth Lawrence* by Emily Herring Wilson. It tells Elizabeth's life story and establishes her as one of the premier gardeners and writers of the twentieth century. In 2008, Duke University Press published the book *Beautiful in All Seasons: Southern Gardening and Beyond with Elizabeth Lawrence*, which includes 132 gardening columns by Elizabeth Lawrence edited by Ann L. Armstrong and ex-owner of Elizabeth's garden, Lindie Wilson.

Written by Emily Herring Wilson, in 2010 *Becoming Elizabeth Lawrence: Discovered Letters of a Southern Gardener* was published by John F. Blair. It includes a treasure trove of Elizabeth's letters. Through these readers can read what life in a southern town was like for women, especially during the 1930s and 1940s. Elizabeth discusses family, friends, plays, travels, ideas, and, of course, her garden and her writing. Along with her garden and books, Elizabeth's letters remain an inspiration for future generations of gardeners.

4.82 GERALDINE KNIGHT SCOTT (1904–1989)

Prominent Californian landscape architect and lecturer at the University of California

Geraldine was born in Wallace, Idaho, and moved to the San Francisco Bay Area to live with relatives after her parents died. In high school she decided to become a landscape architect and enrolled in UC Berkeley's College of Agriculture in 1922. She received a degree in landscape architecture there in 1926. She then attended art and architecture classes at Cornell University from 1926 to 1928. In 1928 she began her professional career in Southern California in the office of AE Hanson. Over the next two years, she worked on various residential gardens and estates, including, in 1928 and 1929, the Harold Lloyd Estate in Beverly Hills.

A postcard depicting part of the Harold Lloyd estate's garden in Westwood Hills, California. *Boston Public Library, Tichner Brothers Collection*

In 1930, Geraldine started a tour of Europe. She spent nearly two years visiting historic Italian villas and the famous gardens of France and Spain. She returned to California in 1932 but was unable to find work due to the Great Depression. In 1939 she married Los Angeles journalist Mellier G. Scott, with whom she shared a strong interest in urban and regional planning issues. After a trip to view housing projects in Europe, they returned to Los Angeles, and Geraldine became the director of the Citizens Housing Council to promote public housing. She also became the first female member of the Los Angeles Regional Planning Commission, where she worked on recreational planning and war housing. In 1941, Geraldine and her husband moved to Berkeley, California, where they served on the San Francisco Housing and Planning Commission. Geraldine opened a private landscape architecture practice in 1948 with a focus on site planning and integrating the existing landscape into the project. With her expertise covering botany, soils, agronomy, forestry, and plants, her work included housing, schools, and office park landscapes, as well as private gardens. Her talent for visual combinations of plants and knowledge of Californian flora led landscape architect Daniel Urban Kiley to invite Geraldine to join his design team for the Oakland Museum of California Garden in 1963. Geraldine was in charge of plant selection and numerous other horticultural and construction related details.

In 1952, Geraldine began a long association with her alma mater, the University of California, Berkeley, as a part-time lecturer. At first she taught courses in site planning, but a more significant contribution came at the end of the 1950s, when she took responsibility for two courses in plants and design subjects. These were, she claimed, *deemphasized in favor of broad analysis concerns in both office practice and course content*. Her classes covered planting and design, as well as site planning. She stressed the need to see and arrange plants according to their physical characteristics: color, texture, size, and shape. Her combinations of plants were often unexpected, but always appropriate. In 1962 the Landscape Architecture Department asked Geraldine to manage the newly acquired Blake Garden estate.

Blake Garden is a 10.6-acre landscape laboratory and public garden at 70 Rincon Road in Kensington, California. It is a teaching facility for Berkeley and offers a spectacular panoramic view of San Francisco Bay and the Golden Gate Bridge. Geraldine completed a long-range plan for the gardens in 1964 and developed them into an important field education resource.

In addition to the Oakland Museum of California Garden and Blake Garden, her other notable projects include the Pacific House at the Golden Gate International Exposition (1939) and the Daphne Funeral Home in San Francisco (1953).

Geraldine was active on many civic commissions and boards, including seven years on the Berkeley Civic Art Commission. She was a founding member of the California Horticultural Society (1935), joined the American Society of Landscape Architects (ASLA) in 1937, and was elected an ASLA fellow in 1972. She served on the ASLA task force on women in landscape architecture in 1974–75.

Geraldine had a hugely successful career. When she died in 1989, she left behind not only a lasting legacy, but a signature style that had at its core a detailed knowledge of California flora.

4.83 MILDRED ESTHER MATHIAS (1906–1995)

Botanist, plant hunter, and conservationist with expertise in umbellifers (the carrot family), which earned her international recognition in taxonomy

Mildred was born in 1906 in Sappington, Missouri, south of St. Louis. Her father, Oliver John Mathias, was a teacher, and the family moved around eastern Missouri as Mildred was growing up. Despite moving houses often, she showed an early

Mildred Mathias examining a vanilla vine in Costa Rica in 1984. *Jepson Herbaria Archives, University of California, Berkeley*

interest in gardening. In Desloge, where her father was school superintendent, Mildred graduated in 1923 from high school. She then enrolled at the State Teachers College in Cape Girardeau and then registered, in fall 1923, at Washington University in St. Louis.

Her family relocated to St. Louis so that Mildred could live at home while attending WU. There Mildred majored in mathematics until her junior year but switched to botany when classes for her major were unavailable, and when the dean of engineering would not give permission to a woman to take a math course in his male-only institution. Luckily, Mildred was soon fascinated with botany and at Washington University earned an AB (1926), MA (1927), and PhD (1929) while conducting her graduate research at the Missouri Botanical Garden.

Taxonomy is a branch of biology that encompasses the description, identification, nomenclature, and classification of organisms. For her doctoral dissertation, Mildred, at age twenty-two, produced a very fine taxonomic paper on *Cymopterus* and relatives of the carrot family (Umbelliferae). Umbelliferae is a family of mostly aromatic flowering plants and is commonly known as the celery, carrot, or parsley family. New World umbellifer genera and species then were poorly researched, but Mildred was about to change that. During summer 1929, in her Model T Ford and with two female companions, she traveled across the western United States to visit numerous localities of Umbelliferae.

After marrying Gerald L. Hassler (a PhD in physics) in Philadelphia in 1930, Mildred carried on independent research on umbellifers during various research appointments, often without pay. In 1939, Dr. Lincoln Constance at the University of California, Berkeley, joined in the study, and together, from 1940 to 1981, they published more than sixty scientific papers on "Umbelliferae of the New World," including descriptions of about 100 new species, hundreds of new combinations, and several new genera.

In 1944, Mildred and her husband permanently settled in Southern California. Now a mother of four, Mildred accepted a staff position in fall 1947 as herbarium botanist at the University of California, Los Angeles—a public research university in the Westwood district of Los Angeles. In 1951 that position was elevated to lecturer so that her talents could be utilized to teach plant taxonomy. Four years later, Mildred was appointed as assistant professor in the department of botany, one of very few women who then held a faculty position at UCLA. She was also appointed vice chair of the department.

In 1951, Mildred published her first articles on California horticulture. She began introducing nurseries and gardeners to a diverse range of botanically and horticulturally interesting, sometimes nonconventional, subtropical plants that would thrive in coastal and desert terrain in Southern California. This improved the quality of landscape planting in Los Angeles. She published and spoke often on the importance of correct scientific identification and naming of horticultural materials, and her educational exhibits at garden shows won several awards. In 1954 an umbellifer from northeastern Mexico was named as the genus *Mathiasella* in her honor.

In 1959, Mildred joined Dermot Taylor, chair of pharmacology at UCLA, to collect and screen plants of tropical forests that had potential for new medicines. She studied, classified, and led groups to discover plants across the world, from Southeast Asia to Australia, to Tanganyka and Zanzibar in Africa, to Amazonian Peru and Ecuador in South America and in the western United States. She learned a lot about drug plants from native herbalists and medicine men. Her pioneering efforts in the tropics in the period from 1959 to 1964 earned the great admiration of her colleagues and helped her growing reputation as a foremost botanist.

Since her early research days, Mildred appreciated natural areas in California, and that interest grew at UCLA. Her earliest successful conservation effort in 1957 helped establish Rancho Las Tunas in San Gabriel as a state park. She used her influence to save historic oaks, and she assumed leadership in the Southern California chapter of the Nature Conservancy. In recognition of her work, she was awarded the merit award of the California Conservation Council in 1962 and the Nature Conservancy National Award in 1964.

Aloe species in the Mildred E. Mathias Botanical Garden. *Jepson Herbaria Archives, University of California, Berkeley*

During the early 1960s, Mildred, together with several other professors, worked diligently to establish the University of California Natural Land and Water Reserves System (now called the Natural Reserve System), the main objective being to set aside important parcels of undisturbed California habitats and acquire and manage them by the University of California for university teaching and research. These visionaries helped this to become a national model for conserving natural ecosystems. Mildred reveled in taking people on hikes through natural areas and converting them to the cause. One of her many personal crusades was her conservation effort on Santa Cruz Island, California. Mildred served as chair of the university-wide advisory committee for twenty-two years and held many other positions of leadership on advisory boards for other conservation programs.

UCLA's Botanical Garden was started in 1929 on 7 acres reserved for that purpose as an academic laboratory shortly after the Westwood, Los Angeles, campus opened. By 1947 the garden hosted approximately 1,500 different species and varieties of plants. In 1956 Mildred was appointed director of the Botanical Garden; she would serve as such until retirement in 1974.

During the 1960s, Mildred helped develop the garden into the *university garden* and opened it for public tours. It was later named the Mildred E. Mathias Botanical Garden in her honor as a recognition of her immense contribution to its development.

In 1963, Mildred spoke critically about the careless destruction of tropical forests, which are where many promising drugs from plants are being lost for all time. She turned to the tropics and became a major conservation voice in the establishment of the Organization for Tropical Studies (OTS), formed to obtain protected field sites for conducting scientific research in the tropics. For her dedication, Mildred was chosen as president of OTS from 1969 to 1970 and was a critical leader during its first ten years of existence, when funding was very minimal. She was the motivator to incorporate botanical gardens of Costa Rica in the master plan for OTS and helped formalize the Las Cruces Biological Station there.

Beginning in the mid-1960s, demand for Mildred's time increased dramatically, as she willingly and enthusiastically served as an officer for, or on advisory boards of, numerous horticultural programs. She once wrote, *Life is a series of intermittent meetings*. Among awards Mildred received are the American Horticultural Society scientific citation (1974); the Award of Merit by the American Association of Botanical Gardens and Arboreta (1976); the Liberty Hyde Bailey Medal (1980), awarded to an outstanding horticulturist who has made a contribution in the fields of research and education; the Medal of Honor from the Garden Club of America (1982); and the Charles Lawrence Hutchinson Medal of the Chicago Horticultural Society (1988). She was the first executive director of the Association of American Botanical Gardens and Arboreta (1977–1981), which under her tenure created a certification program in horticulture that linked universities with hands-on training at a network of horticultural gardens. Mildred also received the Botanical Society of America Merit Award in 1973 and was elected president in 1984. Her achievements in ethnopharmacology were rewarded when, in 1993, she was named distinguished economic botanist by the Society of Economic Botany.

Mildred provided unstinting service to many horticultural organizations in California and around the world, as well as generating an enthusiastic following of professional landscapers and amateur gardeners. She placed a strong emphasis on education for the general public, especially on conservation issues. She costarred with Dr. William Stewart in a weekly gardening show, *The Wonderful World of Ornamentals*, on NBC television from 1962 to 1964, and she published dozens of book reviews in popular magazines. She published more than 100 articles and books about her findings. When she retired in 1974, UCLA Extension persuaded Mildred to lead a natural history trip to Costa Rica. As a result of this expedition she established a new career as a tour guide for adult education.

Annually she visited Costa Rica and the Peruvian Amazon, and she immersed her students in native culture, as well as all aspects of tropical biology. La Selva Biological Station, a protected area encompassing lowland tropical rainforest in northeastern Costa Rica, was a standard stop on her tours. In 1974 she led fifty-three groups, with a thousand participants, to foreign natural areas, gardens, and museums in more than thirty countries. Her last tour, at age eight-eight, was in November 1994 to Chile.

Mildred Esther Mathias died in 1995 as a result of a stroke suffered while gardening at home in Westwood, California. Taxonomy specialist; explorer of tropical forests for potential new medicines; instigator of botanical gardens, state parks, and study centers; and trailblazing tour guide, Mildred left behind a remarkable legacy of botanical and conservation achievements and a wide trail of friendships around the globe.

4.84 ELSA UPPMAN KNOLL (1906–2000)

Prolific gardening book author, including The Sunset Western Garden Book

Elsa was born in Santa Clara, California, the daughter of Swedish immigrants. She was a graduate of Stanford University and of the California School of Gardening for Women. Started by Judith Walrond-Skinner in 1924, the school was the first to teach horticulture to women in the West. After joining the staff, Elsa became its owner-director in 1936 and moved the school from its site in Hayward, California, to the Stanford University Campus in Stanford, renaming it the California School of Gardening. The school became coeducational, and it was here that, in 1939, *Sunset* magazine discovered Elsa. She began to work on their publications.

Samson Benjamin Knoll, a Polish historian and educator, married Elsa in 1940. In 1942, *Sunset* magazine appointed Elsa garden editor. Using the gardening school as a laboratory for her writing, she continued running the California School of Gardening until 1947, when it closed its doors. *Sunset* then became her sole occupation. In 1961, Elsa was made senior editor and, after her retirement in 1971, continued as editorial consultant for the magazine's garden department.

In November 1933, *Sunset* published a book called the *All-Western Garden Guide*. The ninety-six-page paperback's main claim to fame was a dictionary encyclopedia, the first of its kind published for gardening west of the Continental Divide. The guide was illustrated with panel drawings called Western Garden Movies, on topics such as "Diary of a Dahlia," written from the point of view of a flower as it progresses from a seedling to pruning and progressing to winning first prize at the San Leandro flower show. In the book was a coupon offering a two-year subscription to *Sunset*, plus the guide, for $1.

In 1941, Elsa authored the *Sunset Visual Garden Manual: How to Do It—Illustrated Step by Step*, which went through sixteen printings. Elsa stated her philosophy of gardening in the introduction to this book: *Yes, the soil gives us much more than flowers that are beautiful to look at or fruits and vegetables that are good to eat. It gives us hope, courage, patience and quiet joy. It anchors us to something solid, fundamental, timeless and constructive*. The book is regarded as a classic, down-to-earth guide to gardening, dedicated to keeping it simple, enjoyable, and understandable. It included sections on Garden Techniques; Annuals; Perennials, Bulbs; Shrubs & Trees; Special Plants; and Special Gardens.

Sunset's biggest success was the *Sunset Western Garden Book*. Elsa, together with twenty other staff members, worked for a year to put together the 384-page spiral-bound book.

It was an immediate hit. Selling for $2.95, it sold 100,000 copies in the twenty-one months after its publication on March 5, 1954. This book and its subsequent editions sold nearly six million copies. This also spawned the *Sunset National Garden Book* and the *Sunset Southern Garden Book*.

Since it was first published, novice and professional gardeners alike have come to regard the *Sunset Western Garden Book* as the essential reference guide on plants and planting. It included a compendium of plants suited for the various climatic zones and microclimates of the western United States, and gave practical advice on gardening guidelines for the region. The book included a twenty-five-page section on perennials and thirteen pages on California natives, although drought-tolerant plants were seldom used in the 1950s and 1960s. Often referred to as the gardeners' bible, the *Sunset Western Garden Book* has been updated about once a decade since the first edition.

Elsa was responsible for many of Sunset's other publications, such as *How to Grow and Use Bulbs*, released in 1962. Another popular paperback book published by *Sunset* was *Basic Gardening Illustrated*, which contained 822 how-to drawings and photographs.

Elsa Uppman Knoll died in 2000 at age ninety-four of complications from lung infections. She left behind her a huge list of achievements. Elsa's main legacy is that she helped introduce countless thousands of people to the joys of gardening, giving down-to-earth, practical advice and helping them achieve success in their endeavors.

4.85 PAMELA CUNNINGHAM COPELAND (1906–2001)

Leader in the native plant naturalistic garden movement and an active proponent of conservation efforts and proper stewardship of our natural resources. Celebrated horticulturist known for establishing the Mount Cuba Center for the Study of Appalachian Piedmont Flora.

Pamela was born in 1906 in Litchfield, Connecticut. She attended boarding schools in the United States and, in 1920 and 1921, in France. In 1924 she graduated from the Knox School of Cooperstown, New York. While in Paris in 1929, Pamela met Lammot du Pont Copeland. They married in 1930. From 1930 to 1935 they lived in Bridgeport, Connecticut, and in 1935 they moved to Wilmington, Delaware. They purchased 126.7 acres—the beginning of what eventually became a 250-acre estate. In 1937 they built Mount Cuba at 3120 Barley Mill Road, Greenville, New Castle County, Delaware, not far from Wilmington. The house, in neo-Georgian style, had extensive gardens.

An initial plan for formal gardens at Mount Cuba was drawn up by Thomas Warren Sears when the house was built, but it was not completed. Pamela was instrumental in the design of the estate grounds and was particularly interested in native plants from the Piedmont region of the United States. In the 1940s she created a small wildflower garden at Mount Cuba, which was later expanded.

In 1951, Marian Cruger Coffin (see 4.49) designed an eighteenth-century-style garden for her. In the 1960s, Pamela worked with landscape architect Seth Kelsey in developing a system of ponds, paths, and plants. Pamela envisioned that the elegant gardens they cultivated on their estate since the 1930s would someday inspire a community of conservation. As she put it, *I want this to be a place where people will*

Pamela Cunningham Copeland pictured in the Round Garden at Mt. Cuba Center, April 16, 1960. Photographer unknown. *Mt. Cuba Center Library and Archives*

learn to appreciate our native plants and to see how these plants can enrich their lives so that they, in turn, will become conservators of our natural habitats.

In 1979 her work at Mount Cuba was recognized when the Pennsylvania Horticultural Society awarded her their certificate of merit. Pamela established the Mt. Cuba Center for the Study of Appalachian Piedmont Flora in 1983. It was added to the National Register of Historic Places in 2003. The center was endowed in 2003 as a foundation for preserving and propagating native plants from the Piedmont region.

Pamela was listed in *Forbes* magazine in 1985 as one of the wealthiest people in America, with a fortune of $150 million on the basis of holdings in the DuPont Company. She competed for many years in the Philadelphia Flower Show, repeatedly winning the Pennsylvania Horticultural Society's horticultural sweepstakes trophy for points in the horticultural classes. The trophy has since been named in her honor as the Mrs. Lammot du Pont Copeland Horticultural Sweepstakes Trophy *for the individual accumulating the greatest number of points in the Horticulture Classes*. In 1991 she was awarded the Pennsylvania Horticultural Society's Distinguished Achievement Award, being recognized as *a leader in the native plant naturalistic garden movement and an active proponent of conservation efforts and proper stewardship of our natural resources*. In 1987, Pamela received the Achievement Award Medal of the Garden Club of America for her establishment of the Mount Cuba Center, for her vision in preserving rare and endangered plants, and for her understanding of horticulture and conservation. Among other awards, she received the Edith Wharton Women of Achievement Award for Garden Design in 1997. In 1996 a variety of trillium was named for her, *Trillium grandiflorum Pamela Copeland*.

Pamela was involved in land conservation and historical preservation at a number of important sites, including the Red Clay Reservation in Hockessin, Delaware; Winterthur; Gunston Hall Plantation; and the White House in Washington, DC. She and her husband donated lands and money in the 1950s to create the Red Clay Reservation, preserving open lands that would otherwise have been developed. She was a charter member of the board of trustees at Winterthur Museum and Gardens and the first regent of Gunston Hall Plantation, the home of the George Mason family, from 1951 to 1960. She was a member of the committee for the preservation of the White House from 1970 to 1977 and worked with the White House Preservation Fund from 1984 to 1990. She was a trustee at the National Trust for Historic Preservation from 1958 to 1967, receiving the National Trust's President's Award in 2000.

She served in a variety of positions with other organizations, including Historic Deerfield, the Peabody Essex Museum, the council of the American Association of Museums, the Historical Society of Delaware, and the Decorative Arts Award Committee of the Henry Francis du Pont Award Committee. She received the Decorative Arts Award in 1986.

Pamela coauthored, with Richard K. MacMaster, *The Five George Masons: Patriots and Planters of Virginia and Maryland*, published by University of Virginia Press in 1975. A new edition of the book was published in 2016. She also wrote a memoir of growing up in Litchfield, *Recollections of Pamela Cunningham Copeland*, published in 1996.

After a lifetime dedicated to plant and land conservation and the preservation of historic gardens and houses, Pamela Cunningham Copeland died in 2001. She is remembered for having donated her 250-acre estate garden at Mount Cuba, Delaware (and with it a large financial endowment), and establishing the Mount Cuba Center for the Study of Appalachian Piedmont Flora.

4.86 FLORENCE BELLIS (1906–1987)

Extraordinary horticulturist who, in the early 1930s, developed Barnhaven primroses—supremely colorful and vigorous, and named for her Oregon home

Florence Hurtig was born in New Orleans in 1906 but later moved with her family to Oregon, where her mother had a market garden. She trained as a pianist, but the Great Depression prevented her from following that career, and she ended up stuck without work or money and her health deteriorating. She decided to move

Florence Bellis in 1953; photographer unknown. *American Primrose Society, published in their 2007 Winter Journal*

with her husband, Lou Levy, to a leaky old barn in Gresham, Oregon, belonging to a wealthy acquaintance. She describes the first time she saw it: *It was nothing to look at with its ochre-colored paint faded into the wood, but circumstances made it the most beautiful thing in the world. It was a haven and when I crossed the creek and stepped into the lane leading to it, I had a strange feeling of destiny. It was to become the site of Barnhaven gardens.*

Florence decided to spend her last $5 on a few packets of Suttons seeds she had seen sometime earlier in the English seed catalog belonging to a friend. She sowed the seeds the following spring, and germination was excellent. She planted the seedlings under the alders along the creek at the back of the barn. A year later, over a thousand plants bloomed—the whites and yellows of the *Munstead* strain and the reds of Suttons *Brilliance* and *Crimson King*.

Word got around about her colorful garden and visitors began to arrive, so she started to grow plants for sale. She also started sending out hand-painted mailing lists. The first catalog had a rather fundamental problem, in that she forgot to include prices.

In the first batch of seedlings from Suttons was a Chinese red polyanthus with a small gold-star center and an almost-black stem. It was named *Kwan Yin* because *its elegance of form and grace suggest China's goddess of mercy*. Its pollen was used to produce several of the strains of polyanthus. With rigorous selection and hand pollination she created many other strains, such as her *Marine Blues*. These strains became known as the silver dollar primroses because the size of each flower equaled or exceeded that of the then dollar coin. The only other outside blood used was from the *Linda Eickman* pink polyanthus, which were bred over ten years into the *New Pinks* strain and from the famous *Cowichan* strain, offered for the first time as plants and seeds in 1949. These originated in the small community in Cowichan station near Victoria. Florence managed to obtain some pollen and introduced a range of hardy *Cowichans*.

Amazingly, when she started experimenting with plants, Florence had never grown a plant or read a gardening book, let alone a botany text. Despite this, she made hybridizing history, perhaps because she did not have the scientific background that would have bound her to accepted procedures. Instead she relied on instinct, which led her to pass up the paintbrush most hand hybridizers use to transfer pollen, and to do it with her fingers, something that had never been done with primroses before. Florence wrote in her book *Gardening and Beyond* (a collection of her essays published after her death): *By observation I had escaped the tediousness of the traditional brush with its slowness. Instead of each stigma being lightly brush-touched with pollen, my fingers transferred a heavy load, making the seed set phenomenal.*

That early discovery was, as she put it, *the wings on which the operation flew*, and it is a practice widely used today. From there, Florence took off on a thirty-year odyssey to improve the acaulis and polyanthus groups of primulas. Color was her first objective, though size, form, and fragrance were not forgotten. She despised the muddy colors of many primroses and set out to emphasize clear, clean colors, according to one of Florence's long-standing friends, Anita Alexander. Anita said, *Until she started, there were blues or yellows or reds or whites. She separated them into strains by selecting two that best typified the color she wanted, crossed those, planted their seeds and kept doing that until the gene pool was pure.*

Florence's interest in primroses was developing, and she enrolled at Oregon State University to research the subject. She wrote about her work and published a series of articles in the *Oregon Journal*. This led to the founding of the American Primrose Society in 1941, and she became editor of the *Society Journal* for the following nine years. Meanwhile, she continued developing her Barnhaven plant propagation and sales business, and for thirty years she worked as a mail order wholesaler and retailer specializing in primroses and received visitors from all over the world.

After years of patient hand-crossing, Florence did what no one else had been able to do: breed primrose hybrids that would come true to seed. Traditionally propagated by cuttings, original primula lines got weaker and more disease prone as time went on. Florence not only was able to improve polyanthus and acaulis primroses but also succeeded in separating the colors into strains and keeping them true to seed at least half the time.

Florence's marriage to Lou Levy ended in divorce in the mid-1950s, and she had married Bob Bellis in 1959. But when Bob died in 1966, she was devastated and decided she could no longer run the nursery without him. Florence sent her stock of seeds to Jared and Sylvia Sinclair in Brigsteer, in the Lake District of northern England. The Barnhaven company still exists today, although in a totally different location, because it then crossed the English Channel, where it settled in a small village in Brittany, France. The nursery is situated in Plestin-les-grèves, in the Côtes d'Armor, North Brittany.

When Florence decided to withdraw from the business, the fame of Barnhaven was worldwide, but, sadly, Florence had made very little money from running the nursery, so she was obliged to work in a small health-food store for as long as she was able. Florence Bellis died peacefully in her sleep in 1987. She is an excellent example of a woman with no formal horticultural training achieving prominence in her field by developing expertise in one species of plant, primroses.

4.87 ANNE OPHELIA TODD DOWDEN (1907–2007)

Renowned and popular botanical artist whose subjects ranged from the flowers found in Shakespeare's works to the weeds found in New York City

Anne was born in Denver, Colorado, in 1907. She grew up in Boulder, where she walked the foothills of the Rocky Mountains, collecting and drawing nature specimens. Even at age five, Anne knew that she would become an artist. Her first illustrations were for a book by her father, who was a pathologist at the University of Colorado. She said, *I collected and drew any living thing that came my way, especially insects and flowers, and the study of nature was my absorbing hobby.*

Anne was educated at the University of Colorado, the Carnegie Institute of Technology (now Carnegie Mellon University), and the Beaux-Arts Institute of Design and the Art Students League. She was awarded a BA degree in art in 1930 from Carnegie Institute of Technology in Pittsburgh, moving shortly after to New York. As a young artist in New York, Anne hoped to become a book illustrator but initially met with little success. She supported herself for almost two decades as a drawing instructor at the Pratt Institute and then became chairman of the art department at Manhattanville College, New York. She earned a living as a freelance textile designer in New York, designing floral-printed wallpaper and drapery. In 1934 she married Raymond Baxter Dowden. He was also an artist, and she had met him while studying at Carnegie. For many years he was on the faculty of the Cooper Union School of Art and Architecture.

It was in her forties that Anne began her botanical career as a regular freelance illustrator with commissions for *Life*, *House Beautiful*, *Natural History*, and other magazines.

Anne had found her life's calling and made the transition to full-time botanical illustration and writing. She was in her fifties when she began publishing books. Her books—more than twenty of them—were a result of a friend's introduction to Crowell Publishers of New York. The first book was intended for seventh graders, and all were for young adults. She had a passion for understanding the interdependency of plants and their pollinators, and she considered it her greatest mission to educate young readers about nature. Anne said, *Art teaches young people. I wanted to present ideas myself pictorially and in words. We're lucky to be artists. I always found it a very satisfying field.*

Along with her own books, Anne also illustrated books written by others. An example of this is *Shakespeare's Flowers*, which was written by Jessica Kerr and illustrated by Anne. Atlantic Books issued a reprint edition in 1997.

Anne was recognized for the anatomical accuracy and beauty of her art. She worked mainly in watercolor, producing detailed images by using only living specimens as models; this meant she hoarded extensive collections of preserved flowers and insects as her reference material. She refers to the pleasure, fun, and joy of being an artist and learning about the most beautiful world of intricate relationships in her books *From Flower to Fruit* (1984) and *The Clover and the Bee: A Book of Pollination* (1990). Her other subjects for her books included poisonous plants, flower pollination, and state flowers, as well as flowers mentioned in the Bible.

Anne's book *Look at a Flower* (1963) remained in print for twenty-two years. Two of her books won awards from the American Library Association. Among them was *Wild Green Things in the City: A Book of Weeds* (1972), about native weeds that grow in New York City, where she had lived for more than fifty years. She spent three years scouring the city in search of specimens to illustrate, investigating warehouse areas, parking lots, docks, sites of torn-down buildings, and the edges of railroad yards.

Her work was shown in museums and at botanical gardens, including the Smithsonian, the New York Public Library, and the Denver Art Museum. The Hunt Institute for Botanical Documentation at Carnegie-Mellon University in Pittsburgh holds a major body of her original artwork and most of her correspondence. The Hunt Institute specializes in the history of botany and all aspects of plant science and serves the international scientific community through research and documentation.

Anne's husband, Raymond, died in 1982, and they had no children. After sixty years in New York City, she moved back to Boulder, Colorado, in the early 1990s to be near family and her beloved mountains. She set up a studio there and published her last book, *Poisons in Our Path: Plants That Harm and Heal,* in 1994, when she was eighty-seven years old. Paintings from her final book were shown at the Denver Botanic Gardens in 2002. The same year, the Hunt Institute mounted a retrospective of her work to coincide with her ninety-fifth birthday.

A print by Anne Dowden. *Crab Apple, Malus Silvestris. Carnegie Mellon University*

Anne Ophelia Todd Dowden died in Boulder in 2007 at age ninety-nine. She was a widely acclaimed botanical artist and writer who had produced more than twenty books and was recognized for the anatomical accuracy and beauty of her paintings. Anne is remembered by many, including James White, curator of art and principal research scholar at the Hunt Institute for Botanical Documentation at Carnegie-Mellon University in Pittsburgh. He described Anne as such: *Surely among America's leading botanical artists of the 20th century, and probably the most popular*.

4.88 RACHEL CARSON (1907–1964)

Marine biologist and conservationist whose book Silent Spring *was credited with advancing the global environmental movement, particularly with a campaign to ban harmful pesticide use*

Rachel Carson, author of *Silent Spring*. Unknown photographer. *Smithsonian Institution Archives*

Rachel was born in 1907 on a small family farm near Springdale, Pennsylvania, just up the Allegheny River from Pittsburgh. She was the daughter of Maria Frazier McLean and Robert Warden Carson, an insurance salesman. An avid reader, Rachel spent a lot of time exploring around her family's 65-acre farm. The natural world, particularly the ocean, was the common thread of Rachel's favorite literature. She began writing stories (often involving animals) at age eight and had her first story published at age ten. She attended Springdale's small school through tenth grade, then completed high school in nearby Parnassus, Pennsylvania, graduating in 1925 at the top of her class of forty-five students. At the Pennsylvania College for Women (today known as Chatham University) she began by studying English but switched her major to biology in January 1928. Though admitted to graduate standing at Johns Hopkins University in 1928, she was forced to remain at the Pennsylvania College for Women for her senior year due to financial difficulties; she graduated magna cum laude in 1929. After a summer course at the Marine Biological Laboratory, she continued her studies in zoology and genetics at Johns Hopkins University in fall 1929.

After her first year of graduate school Rachel became a part-time student, taking an assistantship in Raymond Pearl's laboratory, where she worked with rats and drosophila (flies) to earn money for tuition. After false starts with pit vipers and squirrels, she completed a dissertation project on the embryonic development of the pronephros (a kidney) in fish. She earned a master's degree in zoology in June 1932. She had intended to continue for a doctorate, but in 1934 Rachel was forced to leave Johns Hopkins to search for a full-time teaching position to help support her family back in Pennsylvania during the Great Depression. In 1935 her father died suddenly, worsening their already critical financial situation and leaving Rachel to care for her aging mother.

She accepted a temporary position with the US Bureau of Fisheries writing radio copy for a series of weekly educational broadcasts titled *Romance under the Waters*. The series of fifty-two seven-minute programs focused on aquatic life and was intended to generate public interest in fish biology and in the work of the bureau. At this time Rachel also began submitting articles on marine life in the Chesapeake Bay to local newspapers and magazines, on the basis of her research. Her supervisor, pleased with the success of the radio series, asked her to write the introduction to a public brochure about the fisheries bureau. He also worked to secure her the first full-time position that became available.

Sitting for the civil service exam, she outscored all other applicants and, in 1936, became only the second woman the Bureau of Fisheries hired for a full-time professional position as a junior aquatic biologist.

Rachel attempted to leave the bureau (by then transformed into the Fish and Wildlife Service) in 1945, but few jobs for naturalists were available because most funding for science was focused on technical fields. In mid-1945 she first encountered the subject of DDT (dichlorodiphenyltrichloroethane), a new pesticide that was beginning to undergo tests for safety and ecological effects. DDT was only one of her many writing interests at the time, and editors found the subject unappealing; she published nothing on DDT until 1962.

Rachel rose within the Fish and Wildlife Service, by 1945 supervising a small writing staff and in 1949 becoming chief editor of publications. Though her position provided increasing opportunities for fieldwork and freedom in choosing her writing projects, it also entailed increasingly tedious administrative responsibilities. By 1948 she was working on material for a book and had made the conscious decision to begin a transition to writing full time.

Her widely praised 1951 bestseller *The Sea around Us*, published by Staples, won her a US National Book Award, which gave her recognition as a gifted writer and financial security.

Her next book, *The Edge of the Sea*, and the reissued version of her first book, *Under the Sea-Wind*, were also bestsellers. This sea trilogy explores the whole of ocean life, from the beaches and shores to the depths. Through 1955 and 1956, Rachel worked on a number of projects, and her interests were turning to conservation. She considered an environment-themed book project tentatively titled *Remembrance of the Earth* and became involved with the Nature Conservancy and other conservation groups. She also made plans to buy and preserve from development an area in Maine she called the Lost Woods.

Early in 1957 she moved to Silver Spring, Maryland, and focused on specific environmental threats, turning her attention to problems that she believed were caused by synthetic pesticides. For the rest of her life, Rachel's main professional focus would be the dangers of pesticide overuse; many synthetic pesticides had been developed through the military funding of science since WWII. Rachel was closely following federal proposals for widespread pesticide spraying; the USDA planned to eradicate fire ants, and other spraying programs involving chlorinated hydrocarbons and organophosphates were on the rise. It was the US federal government's 1957 gypsy moth eradication program that prompted Rachel to devote her next book to pesticides and environmental poisons.

The gypsy moth program involved aerial spraying of DDT and other pesticides (mixed with fuel oil), including the spraying of private land. Landowners on Long Island filed a suit to have the spraying stopped, and many in affected regions followed the case closely. Though the suit was lost, the Supreme Court granted petitioners the right to gain injunctions against potential environmental damage in the future; this laid the basis for later successful environmental actions.

Rachel's four-year project, gathering examples of environmental damage attributed to DDT, resulted in *Silent Spring*, and by 1958 she had arranged a publishing deal. As her research progressed, she found a sizable community of scientists who were documenting the physiological and environmental effects of pesticides. She also took advantage of her personal connections with many government scientists, who supplied her with confidential information. From reading the scientific literature and interviewing scientists, Rachel found two scientific camps when it came to pesticides: those who dismissed the possible danger of pesticide spraying, barring conclusive proof, and those who were open to the possibility of harm and willing to consider alternative methods, such as biological pest control.

By 1959 the USDA's Agricultural Research Service responded to her criticism and others with a public service film, *Fire Ants on Trial*. Rachel characterized it as flagrant propaganda that ignored the dangers that spraying pesticides (especially dieldrin and heptachlor) posed to humans and wildlife. That spring Carson wrote a letter, published in the *Washington Post*, that attributed the recent decline in bird populations—in her words, the *silencing of birds*—to pesticide overuse. That was also the year of the Great Cranberry Scandal: the 1957, 1958, and 1959 crops of US cranberries were found to contain high levels of the herbicide aminotriazole, which caused cancer in laboratory rats. The sale of all cranberry products was halted.

Rachel attended the ensuing FDA hearings on revising pesticide regulations; she came away discouraged by the aggressive tactics of chemical industry representatives, which included expert testimony that was firmly contradicted by the bulk of the scientific literature she had been studying. She also wondered about the possible financial inducements behind certain pesticide programs. By 1960, Rachel had more than enough research material, and her writing was progressing rapidly. In addition to thorough literature search, she had investigated hundreds of individual incidents of pesticide exposure and the human sickness and ecological damage that resulted. Health troubles slowed the final revisions in 1961 and early 1962.

Silent Spring was published by Houghton Mifflin in September 1962. The book described the harmful effects of pesticides on the environment and is widely credited with helping launch the environmental movement. It was difficult to find a title for the book; *Silent Spring* was initially suggested as a title for the chapter on birds being killed by insecticide spraying. By August 1961 she finally agreed to the suggestion of her literary agent Marie Rodell: *Silent Spring* would be a metaphorical title for the entire book, suggesting a bleak future for the whole natural world, rather than a literal chapter title about the absence of birdsong. Though *Silent Spring* had generated a fairly high level of interest based on prepublication promotion, this became much more intense with the serialization in the *New Yorker*, which began in the June 16, 1962, issue. This brought the book to the attention of the chemical industry and its lobbyists, as well as a wide swath of the American populace.

Around that time, Rachel also learned that *Silent Spring* had been selected as the Book of the Month Club's book for October. It had a first print run of 150,000 copies, two and a half times the combined size of the two conventional printings of the initial release. As Rachel put it, this *would carry it to farms and hamlets all over that country that don't know what a bookstore looks like, much less The New Yorker*.

Silent Spring brought environmental concerns to an unprecedented number of Americans. Although it was met with fierce opposition by chemical companies, it spurred a reversal in national pesticide policy that led to a nationwide ban on DDT and other pesticides, and it inspired a grassroots environmental movement that led to the creation of the US Environmental Protection Agency. Rachel had managed to galvanize conservationists, ecologists, biologists, social critics, reformers, and organic farmers to join in the American environmental movement. Her bestselling book helped transform and broaden the older conservation movement into more comprehensive and ecologically informed environmentalism. Moreover, through dozens of translations, *Silent Spring* affected events abroad and prepared the way for the rise of environmental and green movements worldwide.

The overriding theme of *Silent Spring* is the powerful, and often negative, effect humans have on the natural world. Rachel's main argument is that pesticides have detrimental effects on the environment; they are more properly termed biocides, she argues, because their effects are rarely limited to the target pests. DDT is a prime example, but other synthetic pesticides come under scrutiny as well, many of which are subject to bioaccumulation. Rachel also accuses the chemical industry of intentionally spreading disinformation, and public officials of accepting industry claims uncritically. Most of the book is devoted to pesticides' effects on natural ecosystems, but four chapters also detail cases of human pesticide poisoning, cancer, and other illnesses attributed to pesticides. Rachel predicted increased consequences in the future, especially as targeted pests developed resistance to pesticides, while weakened ecosystems fell prey to unanticipated invasive species. The book closes with a call for a biotic approach to pest control as an alternative to chemical pesticides.

Most of the book's scientific chapters were reviewed by scientists with relevant expertise, among whom Rachel found strong support. She attended the White House Conference on Conservation in May 1962. In 2012, *Silent Spring* was designated a National Historic Chemical Landmark by the American Chemical Society for its role in the development of the modern environmental movement. The academic community by and large backed the book's scientific claims, and public opinion soon turned Rachel's way as well. The chemical industry campaign to deny any wrongdoing backfired, since the controversy greatly increased public awareness of potential pesticide dangers, as well as *Silent Spring* book sales. Pesticide use became a major public issue, especially after the CBS Reports TV special *The Silent Spring of Rachel Carson*, which aired April 3, 1963, was viewed by roughly fifteen million people. The program included segments of her reading from her book and interviews with a number of experts. Reactions from the audience were overwhelmingly positive, and the program spurred a congressional review of pesticide dangers and the public release of a pesticide report by the President's Science Advisory Committee—which validated Rachel's research. This report, the TV program, and Rachel's book together made pesticides a major public issue. Within a year or so of publication attacks on the book and on Rachel had largely lost momentum.

According to environmental engineer and Rachel Carson scholar H. Patricia Hynes, *Silent Spring* altered the balance of power in the world. No one thereafter would be able to sell pollution as the necessary underside of progress so easily or uncritically. Rachel's work was also influential on the rise of ecofeminism and on many feminist scientists. By 1972 the Environmental Defense Fund and other activist groups had succeeded in securing a phaseout of DDT use in the United States (except in emergency cases). Lawsuits were also organized against the government to establish a citizen's right to a clean environment. The creation of the Environmental Protection Agency by the Nixon Administration in 1970 addressed another concern that Rachel had brought to light. Until then, the same agency (the USDA) was responsible both for regulating pesticides and promoting the concerns of the agriculture industry; Rachel saw this as a conflict of interest, since the agency was not responsible for effects on wildlife or other environmental concerns beyond farm policy.

In one of her last public appearances Rachel testified before President John F. Kennedy's Science Advisory Committee. The committee issued its report on May

15, 1963, largely backing her scientific claims. Following the report's release, she also testified before a US Senate subcommittee to make policy recommendations.

Though she received hundreds of other speaking invitations, she was unable to accept the great majority of them. Her health was steadily declining due to having breast cancer, and her treatment left Rachel with only brief periods of remission. She spoke as much as she was physically able, including a notable appearance on the *Today* show and speeches at several dinners held in her honor. In late 1963 she received a flurry of awards and honors: the Audubon Medal (from the National Audubon Society), the Cullum Geographical Medal (from the American Geographical Society), and induction into the American Academy of Arts and Letters. Weakened from breast cancer and her treatment regimen, Rachel became ill with a respiratory virus in January 1964. She died of a heart attack on April 14, 1964, in her home in Silver Spring, Maryland. A variety of groups ranging from government institutions to environmental and conservation organizations to scholarly societies have celebrated Rachel's life and work since her death. Perhaps most significantly, Rachel was posthumously awarded the Presidential Medal of Freedom. A $.17 Great Americans series postage stamp was issued in her honor the following year.

In 2007, *Courage for the Earth: Writers, Scientists, and Activists Celebrate the Life and Writing of Rachel Carson* (Mariner) was released as a centennial appreciation of Rachel Carson's brave life and transformative writing. It contained thirteen essays by prominent environmental writers and scientists. Rachel's work had a powerful impact on the environmental movement. *Silent Spring*, in particular, was a rallying point for the fledgling social movement in the 1960s. The activism that Rachel's work inspired is at least partially responsible for the beginnings and evolution of the grassroots ecology movement.

4.89 RUTH PETERSSON BANCROFT (1908–2017)

Dry-plant specialist and landscape gardener who created the Ruth Bancroft Garden in Walnut Creek, California

Ruth Petersson was born to Swedish immigrants in Boston, Massachusetts, in 1908. Her mother was a schoolteacher and her father was a Latin professor. While Ruth was still a baby, her family moved to Berkeley, California, where her father was offered a job at the University of California, Berkeley. As a child she was an avid reader. Her favorite book was Sibylle von Olfers's *The Root Children*, a German children's book about anthropomorphized plant children who bloom in spring and return to the earth in fall. Fascinated by nature, Ruth explored the undeveloped hills of Berkeley, examining wildflowers and digging up small plants to replant in the family's backyard. Her early garden included a collection of irises she received from Sydney B. Mitchell, the founder of the American Iris Association, and Carl Salbach, an iris breeder.

In 1926, Ruth enrolled in the University of California, Berkeley, and majored in architecture—one of only two women students in the program. Following the Wall Street crash of 1929 even male architecture students struggled to find jobs, and female architects were rare. Uncertain that she could get work as an architect during the Great Depression, Ruth changed her major and graduated with a teaching degree. She saw that a teaching career offered greater job opportunities. She said, *None of the men could get architecture jobs, and of course there were very few girls studying it then. So I decided to go into teaching, which was safe*. She graduated with a teaching certificate in 1932 and taught home economics for eight years at a school in Merced, in the San Joaquin Valley, California.

In the mid-1930s, Ruth met her future husband, Philip Bancroft Jr., and they married in 1939. Ruth moved with her husband to his family's farm in Walnut Creek, in the East Bay region of the San Francisco Bay Area, about 16 miles east of the city of Oakland. In the late nineteenth century, Ruth's husband's grandfather Hubert Howe Bancroft had started a 400-acre fruit farm there, which produced walnuts and Bartlett pears. The farm operated until the late 1960s, when the land was rezoned for residential use, and most of it was sold to developers. The trees, sick with a fungal disease called blacklime, were dying and cut down, and the soil was dry and bare. There Ruth planted a large garden around the family house.

Her interest in different plant groups evolved over time to include bearded irises, roses, herbs, alpine plants, perennials, and more. Fascinated by succulents, she clipped articles about the drought-resistant plants but she did not acquire her own until the 1950s, when she purchased a few hybrids at the estate sale of Glenn Davidson, a furniture seller and plant breeder. These succulents, named *Aeonium* 'Glenn Davidson' after him, were the first dry plants in her collection, which expanded to include agave, aloe, echeveria, and cacti. She grew her plants in pots in lath houses and greenhouses around her house, then transplanted them to mounds of soil around her home.

Ruth, her husband, and their children moved into the main home on the Bancroft farm about 1954, when Philip Bancroft Sr. died. In 1971, Ruth's husband inherited 3 acres of empty land, which he gifted to his wife. Then age sixty-three, Ruth used it to expand her garden for her large collection of succulents, which had outgrown their space. The plot of land had only a single well.

In a 1999 interview filmed for *Martha Stewart Living*, Ruth said, *I thought it seems foolish to plant things that need so much care in the way of constant watering. . . . And in our climate, it seemed more appropriate to plant things that needed less water*. This inspired the xeric (habitat containing little moisture) landscape that ultimately emerged.

A view of part of the Ruth Bancroft Garden. *ruthbancroftgarden.org*

The Ruth Bancroft Garden is now a 2.5-acre public dry garden containing more than 2,000 cacti, succulents, trees, and shrubs native to Africa, Australia, California, Chile, and Mexico. It includes important collections of aloes, agaves, yuccas, and echeverias.

It is at 1552 Bancroft Road in Walnut Creek, California, and has become an outstanding example of a water-conserving garden. There is a central pond for the garden and undulating mounds to break up the flat landscape.

In 1976, Ruth added a folly, an art nouveau gazebo. She transplanted the best specimens of her succulent and cactus collection into the ground, using moss rock as planting beds. By trial and error, Ruth discovered how to display succulents in the landscape and how to protect tender plants from winter rains and the occasional hard frost. She created dynamic planting combinations by using contrasting textures, forms, and colors.

In 1972 an unusually cold winter destroyed most of Ruth's garden. She began replanting, using custom wooden frames to protect tender plants from frost. Her first *Aeonium* 'Glenn Davidson' plant was among the plants to survive the freeze and still grows in the garden today. As with everything else, Ruth paid attention to what plants thrived and what did not, and she kept detailed records. She did not just want to make things look attractive; she wanted to learn. The soils at Walnut Creek are heavy clay, the water very alkaline, and the summers hot and the winters cold. These conditions require special plants, and Ruth became an expert on those that could survive the harsh conditions.

Ruth Petersson Bancroft died on November 26, 2017, nearly three months after celebrating her 109th birthday. She is remembered as a talented, determined dry plant specialist and is yet another example of a woman with no formal horticultural training whose fascination with a specific type of plant—in her case succulents and cacti—resulted in her becoming an expert in her field.

4.90 NELVA WEBER (1908–1990)

Landscape architect who wrote extensively about landscape design

Nelva Weber at Avedon Studio in New York City. Creator: Arthur Avedon.
Division of Rare and Manuscript Collections, Cornell University Library

Born in Arrowsmith, Illinois, Nelva received her BA in English from Wesleyan University and later a BFA in landscape architecture and a MA in plant ecology from the University of Illinois in 1935. That year she moved to New York City. She worked with architect C. C. Combs, and there she worked on the Palisades Parkway. She moved on to work with the architecture firm Shaw, Maess & Murphy, and after several other jobs, she was employed by the New York City Parks Department, where she worked on site designs for the city's parks.

Nelva opened her own landscape architecture practice in 1945, focusing on public and residential work in the northeast. In 1970 her husband, architect Joseph Sammataro, joined her practice as a drafting, administrative, and planning associate. Nelva was always known professionally by her maiden name, Weber.

Drawing on her education in plant ecology, her approach to landscape design was to focus on the elemental nature of the garden. Her simple plans, typical of the transitional years between the Country Place era and the postwar decades, concentrated on smaller gardens and emphasized the use of varied plant material and form while introducing some modern features. Nelva's public projects include designs for the campuses of Illinois Wesleyan University and Bard College, New York; Purnell School, New Jersey; Tree of Life Arboretum at Hancock Shaker Village, Pittsfield, Massachusetts; Saint Andrew's Episcopal Church Memorial Garden, New Providence, New Jersey; and the First Congregational Church, Litchfield, Connecticut.

Nelva's residential clients included designing the private estates of Mary Rockefeller, fashion designer Oscar de la Renta, comedian Gary Moore, and dancer Arthur Murray, and the Walter Howe Estate Garden in New Jersey.

A view of the patio with outdoor furniture at the Gleason Garden, ca. 1960–1967, designed by Nelva Weber; it was anonymously featured in her 1976 book *How to Plan Your Own Home Landscape*. Photograph by Molly Adams. *Smithsonian Collections*

Her landscape plans were published in a 1954 book, *Landscaping Plans for Small Homes*, edited by Ralph Bailey and published by the American Garden Guild. During her career she was generally referred to by her surname —*Weber*.

Nelva maintained an active practice, ran workshops, and wrote extensively on landscape architecture and design. She published articles in *Landscape Architecture* magazine, produced a column for the *New York Times* on landscape and horticulture from 1945 through to the 1970s, and penned the book *How to Plan Your Own Home Landscape: How to Organize Your Outdoor Space and How to Utilize It for Maximum Pleasure and Minimum Maintenance All Year Round*, published by Bobbs-Merrill in 1976.

Nelva Weber died in 1990 from complications due to Alzheimer's disease at the Rose Haven nursing home in Litchfield, Connecticut. She was eighty-one years old.

4.91 JULIA JANE SILVERSTEIN RIES (1909–2005)

The first woman licensed in Colorado as a professional landscape architect, Julia, or "Jane" as she was later known professionally, specialized in preserving and restoring historical gardens and sites.

Jane was born in 1909 in Denver, Colorado, to Harry S. and Eva W. Silverstein. She attended public school and applied to Harvard University but was not accepted because Harvard took only male students at the time. Instead, she went to the Lowthorpe School of Landscape Architecture for Women in Groton, Massachusetts. Jane wanted to go there because many professors who taught landscape architecture to men at Harvard also taught classes to women at Lowthorpe. She graduated in 1932 and went on to do further studies at Colorado University, the University of Denver, and the Rhode Island School of Design.

Jane began her professional career in 1933, when she was hired by Denver-based landscape architecture firm McCrary, Culley and Carhart to work on planting

Julia Jane Silverstein Ries.

designs for Colorado University. Two years later she opened her own office in Denver, focusing on urban residential designs for both small and large homes. During WWII Jane served in New York in the Women's Reserve of the US Coast Guard as an officer working on port liaison and property surveys. She ended the war with the rank of lieutenant. After the war she briefly held a job as a landscape architect for the New York firm Skidmore, Owings & Merrill before returning to Denver in 1947 and reopening her own practice. She worked under her birth name for the first few years of her professional career. In 1953 she married Henry F. Ries, a Colorado insurance actuary, and then, from 1961 onward, she used Jane Silverstein Ries as her professional name.

Jane was active in working to preserve Colorado's urban past. Her projects, which numbered more than 1,000, also showcased her signature style—formal but livable, easy to maintain, and integrating native and specimen plants. Projects included an art moderne (also known as American moderne or modernist) house for General Electrics, the Herb Garden and the Scripture Garden for the Denver Botanic Gardens, gardens at the Colorado Governor's Mansion, and gardens at the Molly Brown House Museum in Denver. In addition to her residential work, her commissions included federal housing projects and civic, academic, and religious buildings, including the urban renewal redevelopment of Larimer Square in Denver.

In the 1960s, Jane worked to establish a Colorado licensing authority for landscape architects. After the state's Landscape Architect Registration Act passed, in 1968 she became the third person and the first woman to be certified as a licensed landscape architect in Colorado. Jane gained a reputation for plantings that diverged from the most common planting plan in Denver of front and back lawn plus foundation plantings and a flowering border. Inspired by the walled gardens of Boston's Beacon Hill, which she had admired during her Lowthorpe years, she designed gardens that were slightly formal yet intimate, often featuring native plants that did not require great amounts of water.

In 1965, Jane was elected a fellow of the American Society of Landscape Architects (ASLA). She was also a member of the ASLA's Rocky Mountain chapter (now the Colorado chapter) and became its first president. She was given the Community Service Award by the American Institute of Architects' Denver chapter. In 1990 she was inducted into the Colorado Women's Hall of Fame. In 1983 the ASLA's Colorado chapter established the Jane Silverstein Ries Award to honor members showing exceptional awareness of the importance of land stewardship in the Rocky Mountains. In 1997 the JSR Foundation was created by ASLA and formalized as the charitable arm of the American Society of Landscape Architects' Colorado chapter, with a mission to continue Jane's legacy.

Today, the JSR Foundation recognizes and supports sustainable and innovative projects and programs that conserve, improve, and enhance built and natural environments. The foundation offers scholarships, grants, educational opportunities, events, and programs that make the spirit of places endure in the Rocky Mountain region. It also administers the Jane Silverstein Ries Award. Jane inaugurated the foundation's lecture program. In 1992, 737 Franklin Street, Denver, where Jane lived and kept an office for many decades, was designated a Denver landmark.

Jane was ahead of her time with her philosophy of incorporating native plants and materials into her designs and built her projects to reflect, preserve, and restore the natural landscape. She was a strong voice in issues of land use and fought to conserve prairie, mountain landscapes, wildlife, and urban spaces. Jane never formally retired, but in 1989 she became a senior adviser to the firm Land Mark Design, which had been founded by former colleagues and associates.

Jane Silverstein Ries died on July 6, 2005. Earlier that same year, she had been honored with the prestigious American Society of Landscape Architects Medal in recognition of her lifetime of achievements in her profession. The JSR Foundation is her main legacy, and a hardy boxwood cultivar, *Buxus microphylla* 'Julia Jane', is named for her.

4.92 THALASSA CRUSO (1909–1997)

Television presenter, author, and newspaper columnist, Thalassa was called the Julia Child of Horticulture.

Thalassa Cruso. *digitalcommonwealth.org*

Thalassa was born in 1909 in London, England, the daughter of Henry and Mildred Cruso. Her family were all keen gardeners, and she spent many happy hours in the family greenhouse and out in the countryside seeking unusual plants. She trained in archeology and anthropology at the London School of Economics and took an honors diploma in 1931. After her marriage in 1935 to archeologist Hugh O'Neill Hencken, she went with him to his native Boston. He became curator of European archaeology at the Peabody Museum of Harvard University. In 1940 they found a house in Chestnut Hill, a village 6 miles west of downtown Boston, Massachusetts. Thalassa said, *It was old farm property and every scrap of goodness had been taken out of the soil*. So she mulched relentlessly and put vegetables in the front lawn. She continued: *There were some things I muddled that I'm still cross about*.

Seven years later, she and Hugh bought another century-old house in Marion, southern Massachusetts. This time the gardens were the attraction. She wrote, *It was lunacy. The house was gloriously unsuited and in bad shape. The garden had gone to pieces and the pond was utterly overgrown. But I could see the traces of what had been. It got to me. I couldn't bear seeing how hard the plants were trying.*

While her children were growing up, Thalassa was rising through the ranks of the exclusive Chestnut Hill Garden Club. She helped set up amateur competitions and question-and-answer sessions. As a result, the germ of an idea of a TV show was formed in Thalassa's mind.

The original inspiration for her show *Making Things Grow* came during a visit to her brother in England. She recalled, *We would watch the BBC TV gardening programs and complain about how bad they were. And I had watched and admired the cook Julia Child on TV, and suddenly I thought: I could do that with plants*. She took the concept to WGBH in Boston, and the resulting television show—a fifty-four-part series—was produced from 1966 to 1969. It was syndicated and shown on about 150 stations across the USA. Her television producer said of Thalassa, *She is the first person who taught me what it means to be educated. The lady is a genius. Her special way of looking at everything is inexhaustible*. On one program she saw a snail. *Ha! There's the little brute*, she exclaimed. Cautioning squeamish viewers to avert their eyes, she raised a flower pot on high. The pot came crashing down unceremoniously onto her worktable and the snail was no more. WGBH in Boston was inundated with telephone calls and mail from delighted viewers.

Julia Child was a contemporary whose cooking show had been launched earlier by WGBH and had a similar personality and attitude to Thalassa's. Both women came across as amusing, commonsense experts with a down-to-earth, no-nonsense presence. Julia once said, *Thalassa Cruso is a remarkable woman. I like the idea of teachers on television whose whole life isn't TV, who do other things. I have enjoyed her programs. They are very down to earth.*

Thalassa had no formal horticultural training. She said, *I have never studied it, and there is so much I don't know. I'm afraid I'll make some terrible mistake*. And yet, she was still able to write a successful gardening column for the *Boston Globe* for twenty-two years. Thalassa's first book, *Making Things Grow Indoors: A Practical Guide for the Indoor Gardener*, was published in 1967 by Alfred A Knopf. It sold 250,000 copies in hardback and was updated and republished in 1992. It was aimed at the novice gardener, and its success was due to her forthright advice as a no-nonsense amateur who developed her advice from her own personal experiences. In addition to *Making Things Grow Indoors* in 1969, Thalassa wrote *Making Things Grow Outdoors* in 1971, *To Everything There Is a Season* in 1973, and *Making Vegetables Grow* in 1975.

She often appeared on the *Tonight Show* with Johnny Carson and taught him (and her listeners) practical gardening tips, including how to make compost from eggshells in a cupboard.

Opening title card for PBS's 1960s gardening program *Making Things Grow* with Thalassa Cruso. *growingwithplants.com*

Through her books, TV appearances, and newspaper articles, she became a trusted, unofficial advisor to her public on gardening matters. *People stop me on the street,* she once said, *and ask what to do with their African violets*. She didn't believe in modern technology or horticultural mystery. *The idea that it is necessary to possess a mysterious power in order to grow good plants is ridiculous*, she wrote in her book about houseplants. If a plant was not thriving, she thought nothing of telling her viewers and readers to throw them unceremoniously on the rubbish heap. She advised, instead, her audience in 1971: *If a plant is unbelievably tatty, dispose of it without the least feeling of guilt*. She also wrote, *Indoor horticulture can be immensely rewarding if you have fun with your plants and refuse to allow them to take over your life.*

She admitted that she was often called a *plant nut* and she agreed. But, she said, *I don't bow and worship my plants. They are there to please me. I please them so that they will please me*. Thalassa owes her success to being in the right place at the right time, just when the medium of television was able to reach millions. Through her humor and enthusiasm, via the mediums of TV and print, Thalassa was able to bring the love of gardening to millions.

She died at age eighty-eight in 1997 at an Alzheimer's center in Wellesley, Massachusetts. She had helped fan American interest in household plants and gardening through her infectious, witty style to become the best-known expert on gardening in America through the '60s and '70s. Her persona was founded on giving forthright advice as a no-nonsense amateur who developed her knowledge from her own personal experiences. Having had no formal horticultural training, Thalassa is another example of a woman forging a successful career through sheer determination and enthusiasm.

4.93 RACHEL LAMBERT "BUNNY" MELLON (1910–2014)

Immensely wealthy horticulturist, gardener, philanthropist, and art collector who designed and planted a number of significant gardens, including the White House Rose Garden

Rachel Lowe Lambert, nicknamed Bunny by her mother, Rachel Parkhill Lowe, was the eldest child of Gerard Barnes Lambert, president of the Gillette safety razor company and a founder of Warner-Lambert. Bunny's paternal grandfather, chemist Jordan Lambert, was the inventor of Listerine, which was later marketed by her father. Bunny attended Miss Fine's School, Princeton, New Jersey, and the Foxcroft School, Middleburg, Virginia. Her parents divorced in 1933, and both subsequently remarried. Bunny married Stacy Barcroft Lloyd Jr. in Philadelphia in 1932. Lloyd served in the Office of Strategic Services during WWII. They divorced in 1948.

Rachel "Bunny" Mellon at Oak Spring (her Virginia farm) amid the herb topiaries she popularized (shown here are common myrtles). *Oak Spring Garden Foundation*

Bunny and her husband had become close friends of banking heir and art collector Paul Mellon and his first wife, Mary Conover, who died of an asthma attack in 1946. After Bunny divorced Lloyd, she and Paul got together and were married on May 1, 1948. Together the couple collected and donated more than a thousand works of art, mostly eighteenth- and nineteenth-century European paintings, to the National Gallery of Art in Washington, DC, and established the Yale Center for British Art. The couple also had an equestrian interest and bred and raced thoroughbred horses. Their horse, Sea Hero, won the 1993 Kentucky Derby. Bunny maintained homes in Antigua, Nantucket and Oyster Harbors, and Cape Cod; two apartments in Paris; and a townhouse in New York City. Her main residence, Oak Spring Farms, was a 4,000-acre estate in Upperville, Virginia.

Bunny shunned the limelight and seldom gave interviews. In a rare 1969 *New York Times* article, she opined that nothing should be noticed. Although this remark was made in reference to garden design, it has frequently been taken to encapsulate her attitude toward personal privacy. Having had no formal training in horticulture, Bunny read widely and made contributions to several landmark gardens. Her interests in gardening were first cultivated while watching gardeners from the landscape architectural firm Olmsted Brothers as they tended her family's New Jersey home. She amassed a large collection of horticultural books and eventually came to be regarded as an authority on American horticulture.

The White House Rose Garden after Bunny's landscaping, looking northwest. *Jack Boucher, Library of Congress's Prints and Photographs division*

Her interest in gardening led to Bunny designing landscapes for many of the Mellons' properties, including the French-inspired gardens of their Oak Spring Farms estate. Her work was strongly influenced by two French gardeners, André Le Nôtre (1613–1700) and Jean-Baptiste de La Quintinie (1626–1688). A longtime friendship with the Kennedy family was initiated by a 1958 visit to Oak Spring Farms by Jacqueline Kennedy, whom she later advised on fine arts and antiques during the Kennedy White House restoration. In 1961, then president John F. Kennedy asked Bunny to redesign the White House Rose Garden. She created more open space for public ceremonies and introduced American species of plants, as well as *Magnolia × soulangeana*. She next began to work on the White House's East Garden, but her work was interrupted by President Kennedy's assassination in

1963. After his funeral, for which Bunny arranged the flowers, Lady Bird Johnson (see 4.96) asked her to resume her work on the White House grounds.

With Jacqueline Kennedy having left the White House, she asked Bunny to design landscapes for the Kennedy home in Martha's Vineyard, the John F. Kennedy Presidential Library, and River Farm, the headquarters of the American Horticultural Society. In France, Bunny created a landscape design for the home of Hubert de Givenchy and assisted with the restoration of the Potager du Roi (the kitchen garden) in Versailles.

On November 10, 2014, items from Mellon's collection of paintings, jewelry, furniture, and decorative objects were auctioned at Sotheby's in New York for a total of $158.7 million, including *Untitled (Yellow, Orange, Yellow, Light Orange, 1955)* by Rothko, which sold for $36.5 million, and another Rothko that went for $39.9 million. Three of her most important paintings, two by Rothko and one by Richard Diebenkorn, were sold privately before the Sotheby's auction for a reported $250 million. Proceeds from the sales benefited the Gerard B. Lambert Foundation, a charitable entity established by Bunny in memory of her father.

A view of part of the Oak Spring Garden. *Oak Spring Garden Foundation*

Among many honors, Bunny was awarded the Royal Horticultural Society's Veitch Memorial Medal (1987) and the Henry Shaw Medal from the Missouri Botanical Garden, awarded since 1893 and named for the garden's founder. This medal honors those who have made a significant contribution to the Missouri Botanical Garden, botanical research, horticulture, conservation, or the museum community. Bunny also received the American Horticultural Society Landscape Design Award for her work on many significant and historic gardens.

Described as a resilient centenarian, a bout with cancer and ongoing macular degeneration slowed her activity, and she was reluctantly forced to give up gardening by 2011. On March 17, 2014, Rachel Lambert "Bunny" Mellon died at her Upperville, Virginia, home of natural causes. She was 103 years old.

An appreciation of her garden design work was published by Vendome Press in 2018. Written by Linda Holden and photographed by Roger Olly, it was titled *The Gardens of Bunny Mellon*.

The first book to focus on all the public and private gardens that Mellon designed, *The Gardens of Bunny Mellon* (Vendome, October 2018), is published with the cooperation and endorsement of the Oak Spring Garden Foundation. *vendomepress.com*

4.94 ALICE RECKNAGEL IREYS (1911–2000)

Landscape architect whose notable clients included the Brooklyn Botanic Garden and what is now the Mount Vernon Hotel, Museum, and Garden

Alice was born in Brooklyn, New York, to Harold S. and Rea Estes Recknagel. Her father was an insurance industry attorney. The townhouse in Brooklyn Heights that Alice grew up in had been occupied by her family since the 1830s, and she would live there her entire life. She became interested in gardening as a child by working with her grandfather at a family farm in Green Harbor, Massachusetts. Her interest developed further as a result of a program at the Brooklyn Botanic Garden funded by the Burpee seed company. She recalled in an interview not long before her death: *The Burpee Company provided the seeds, and after we planted them and followed their growth, we were allowed to take the plants home.*

She went to school at the Packer Collegiate Institute in Brooklyn and then on to the Cambridge School of Architecture and Landscape Architecture, which was then affiliated with Smith College. Although the Cambridge School ordinarily admitted only women holding a BA degree, Alice persuaded school founder Henry Atherton Frost that her Packer diploma was the equivalent of a junior college degree and so secured admission, graduating in 1935.

Alice then started working around New York in collaboration with other landscape architects. These commissions ranged from public housing projects to lakeside plantings for the 1939 New York World's Fair.

Alice married Henry Tillinghast Ireys III in 1943. They had three children—Catherine, Anne, and Henry—and for a period after their births, Alice cut back on her landscaping work. By 1947 she had set up her own office in her Brooklyn

Alice Recknagel Ireys. Unknown photographer. *American Horticultural Society*

townhouse. She traveled to England and France and worked in seventeen states, but it was her native Brooklyn, with its botanic garden, that commanded her attention and affection during her lifetime. Over the course of a long career, she designed more than a thousand projects.

Alice became known for designs that bridged the late-nineteenth-century ideal of gracious, formal estate and the twentieth-century concern for modest residential landscaping and enhanced public spaces, especially catering for the explosion of small suburban and town gardens that followed WWII. She borrowed elements such as terraces and parterres from large-scale landscaping and modified them for more limited acreage, emphasizing such features as serpentine walkways that created an illusion of a larger space than existed. She focused on the simple pleasures of walking around flower beds, sitting under the dappled shade of a tree, or dining with friends on a terrace.

Alice spent much of the period from the late 1950s to the early 1980s teaching at the Landscape Design Schools run by the National Garden Clubs. For the Brooklyn Botanic Garden, she designed both the Mae L. Wien Cutting Garden and Helen's Garden of Fragrant Plants (now named in her honor the Alice Recknagel Ireys Fragrance Garden). The latter was designed specifically for the visually impaired as a memorial to a blind woman named Helen Goodhart Altschul. All visitors are encouraged to rub the fragrant or pleasingly textured leaves of the plants between their fingers. There are four sections in the garden, each with a theme: (1) plants to touch, (2) plants with scented leaves, (3) plants with fragrant flowers, and (4) kitchen herbs.

Designed by Alice Recknagel Ireys in 1955, the Fragrance Garden was the first garden in the whole of the United States to be built for the visually impaired, where visitors are encouraged to touch and smell the plants that grow in raised beds to allow easy access for those in wheelchairs. *Daderot*

The garden is wheelchair accessible, and all planting beds are at an appropriate height for people in wheelchairs. A fountain provides a calming sound and a place to wash one's hands after touching the various plants. Since then, this has been widely imitated by designers concerned with making public gardens accessible to people with disabilities. As a lecturer and designer at the Brooklyn Botanic Garden for more than fifty years, Alice considered the garden her true home.

In Manhattan, Alice's public work can be seen in the colonial-style garden behind the Mount Vernon Hotel Museum and Garden, the former Abigail Adams Smith Museum on East 61st Street, a 1799 carriage house that became a popular hotel on the East River in New York City.

In the mid-1960s, following her husband's death, Alice began writing books, aiming them at amateur gardeners rather than professional landscapers like herself. In the first of her four books, *How to Plan & Plant Your Own Property*, published by M. Barrows & Company in 1967, she defined garden design, saying that it should *produce a living functional picture as well as a beautiful one*. She also wrote *Small Gardens for City and Country*, published by Prentice Hall in 1978, and two books published in 1991 for W. Atlee Burpee: *Designs for American Gardens* and *Garden Designs*, which included her popular planting plans originally published in Burpee catalogs.

These last two books had come about after Alice began working with the Burpee seed company in the 1980s. It was her job to design specialized gardens that Burpee customers could purchase as a package that included the plans, plus all needed seeds and plant materials. Alice's summation of her long career was this: *If you do well in people's gardens, they keep coming back*. But she could speak her mind, bluntly telling one client to remove a row of azaleas because *it looks like motel planting*.

During her lifetime, Alice also amassed many honors and awards, including in 1978 being elected a fellow of the American Society of Landscape Architects (ASLA). In 1991 the American Horticultural Society gave her its highest honor, the Liberty Hyde Bailey Award. She received other awards from the Garden Writers Association (part of the American Public Gardens Association) and the Brooklyn Botanic Garden. In later years, Alice inspected large gardens from the vantage of a golf cart, using a walking cane as a pointer. She admitted at that time, *At night when I can't sleep, I think about my different jobs and what fun they all were*.

Alice Recknagel Ireys worked up to her death, dying in Brooklyn in 2000 at age eighty-nine. To commemorate such an amazing woman, a documentary about Alice, *The Living Landscapes of Alice Recknagel Ireys*, by the Brooklyn Botanic Garden, was released that same year. The commemorative Alice Recknagel Ireys Fragrance Garden at the Brooklyn Botanic Garden can be found at 1000 Washington Avenue in Brooklyn.

4.95 MARIE CLARK TAYLOR (1911–1990)

American botanist, the first woman to earn a science doctorate at Fordham University, and was the head of the botany department at Howard University from 1947 to her retirement in 1976

Marie was born in Sharpsburg, Pennsylvania, in 1911. She graduated from Dunbar High School in Washington, DC. She earned her BS (1933) and MS (1935, botany) at Howard University. In the late 1930s and early 1940s, she taught at Cardozo High School, a historically Black high school in Washington, DC. During that period, she enrolled in the doctoral studies program at Fordham University, where she was a member of the Scientific Research Society's Sigma Xi. In 1941 she became the first woman of any race to receive a scientific doctorate from Fordham when she received her PhD in botany, cum laude. Her dissertation, examining plant photomorphogenesis (the influence of light on plant growth), was titled "The Influence of Definite Photoperiods upon the Growth and Development of Initiated Floral Primordia." In this work, Marie focused her efforts on defining how long a period of light per day was needed to induce flowering (a photoperiod) for three plant varieties: scarlet sage (*Salvia splendens*), cosmos (*Cosmos bipinnatus*), and "Orange Flare" cosmos (*C. bipinnatus* 'Orange Flare'). As she explained, *These experiments were planned to discover the influence of definite photoperiods of six, ten, and sixteen hours upon the inflorescences that develop from floral primordia exposed to these photoperiods.* The fact that plants could be grown under electric lights was a relatively recent discovery at that time, and it opened up new opportunities to test plant growth in controlled experiments. Marie wrote, *The majority of the experiments with seed-plants have been devised to show how certain plants might be forced into earlier bloom. There is definite need for precise records showing the influence of photoperiodism*

upon the development of flowers and fruits. For home gardeners, information such as this is useful in choosing plant species and determining where to site plants to achieve optimum performance. For nurseries, growers, and seed companies, this study (and other later ones) provided essential information to these industries.

After serving in the Army Red Cross in New Guinea during WWII, she joined the botany department at Howard University in 1945. She succeeded Charles Stewart Parker as chair of the botany department in 1947, a position she held until her retirement in 1976. During her tenure the department expanded, and Marie was involved in the design and construction of a new biology building on the Howard University campus, the botanical greenhouse laboratory on the rooftop of the Ernest E. Just Hall Biology Building. An auditorium there is named in her honor. In 1948 she married Richard Taylor, whom she had met while they were both serving in New Guinea.

In 1956, Marie compiled a list of instructional films for teaching botany, including titles on life cycles, physiology, conservation, cytology, seed dispersal, and bacteriology. She also taught a summer science series for the National Science Foundation, designed for biology teachers to make use of botanical materials for their courses to illustrate cell life. These summer classes also developed her teaching methods, where she emphasized the use of microscopes to study living cells. She was awarded multiple grants in the 1950s and '60s to run institutes on botany. In a 1958 article she estimated that *by 1960 about 42,000 participants will have attended NSF Institutes, representing about 30% of the 140,000 junior and senior high school science and mathematics teachers in the country*. During the mid-1960s, President Lyndon B. Johnson asked her to expand her work overseas, bringing her teaching style to an international level. She traveled as far away as India, and her passion for botany has had a significant effect on the teaching and development of science programs, as well as on scientists, across the world.

In a 1965 paper published by the American Biology Society titled "Live Specimens," she commented on the poor state of biology education. She wrote,

> *Eighty to eighty-five percent of the teachers of high school biology are unacquainted with the most easily available and most versatile specimens for dynamic instruction in "aliveness!" Having never studied living plants, many are handicapped in designing the requisite laboratory investigations into life that characterize the newest trends in biology instruction.*

Ray Hill, a former student and fellow professor, in a letter he wrote to Marie when she retired in 1976, said,

Like plants that disperse seeds from year to year, of which some germinate and thrive locally and others are carried by various vectors to far-away places, you have dispersed students annually from the botany department at Howard throughout the United States and the World. . . . So many of the seeds you have dispersed are germinating, and will continue your work for generations to come.

Marie died on December 28, 1990, at Walter Reed Army Medical Center in Washington, DC. According to her former colleague and civil rights activist Margaret Strickland Collins, she was a *powerhouse who worked tirelessly to improve teacher training in the sciences*. Her achievements in the fields of botany and science education are remarkable, especially considering the barriers that she had to overcome as an accomplished Black woman in a field that, at the time, had few Black people and even fewer Black women.

4.96 LADY BIRD JOHNSON (1912–2007)

She worked tirelessly for conservation and the environment and broke new ground by interacting directly with Congress. More than 200 laws related to the environment were passed during the Johnson administration, many of which are credited to her support and work. Her true legacy is the outstanding work that she did to beautify the nation, including being instrumental in promoting the Highway Beautification Act.

Lady Bird Johnson gives a keynote speech at a White House conference on natural beauty.
Library of Congress

Claudia Alta "Lady Bird" Johnson was named Claudia after her mother's brother Claud. During her infancy her nursemaid, Alice Tittle, said that she was as *pretty as a ladybird*. Opinions are divided about whether the name refers to a female bird or a ladybird beetle. The nickname virtually replaced her first name for the rest of her life. Her father and siblings called her Lady, and her husband called her Bird.

She developed her lifelong love of the outdoors as a child growing up in the tall pines and bayous of East Texas, and she marveled as the wildflowers bloomed each spring. She was well educated for a woman of her era and was a capable manager and a successful investor. After marrying Lyndon Johnson in 1934, when he was a political hopeful in Austin, Texas, she used a modest inheritance to bankroll his congressional campaign and then ran his office while he was away, serving in the US Navy.

Lady Bird served as second lady from 1961 to 1963, when her husband was vice president, and was first lady of the United States from 1963 to 1969 as the wife of President Lyndon B. Johnson. She worked tirelessly for conservation and the environment and broke new ground by interacting directly with Congress. More than 200 laws related to the environment were passed during the Johnson administration, many of which are credited to her support and work. Among the major legislative initiatives she actively supported and campaigned for were the Wilderness Act of 1964, the Land and Water Conservation Fund, the Wild and Scenic Rivers Program, the 1965 Highway Beautification Act, and many additions to the National Park system.

As first lady, she employed her own press secretary and was a keen advocate for beautifying the nation's cities and highways. Lady Bird and her husband had driven many times from their home in Texas to Washington, DC, and had been frustrated by the increasing number of ugly junkyards and billboards along the way. In his State of the Union address in 1965, President Johnson addressed the issue by saying that *a new and substantial effort must be made to landscape highways to provide places of relaxation and recreation wherever our roads run*.

Lady Bird began her campaign to get the highways clear of billboards and that junkyards along interstate or primary highways were removed or screened. She actively encouraged scenic enhancement of roadsides by filling them with green landscaping and wildflowers. *Public feeling is going to bring about regulation*, she told reporters, *so you don't have a solid diet of billboards on all the roads*. The power, influence, and fierce lobbying of the billboard industry was a tough match for the White House, and the battle to pass the Highway Beautification Act was fierce. President Johnson told his cabinet and staff members: *You know I love that woman and she wants that Highway Beautification Act*. When it looked as if the bill might not pass, he exclaimed, *By God, we're going to get it for her*.

She became the first president's wife to advocate actively for legislation when she was instrumental in promoting the Highway Beautification Act (HBA), which was nicknamed *Lady Bird's Bill*. *Ugliness is so grim*, she once said. *A little beauty, something that is lovely, I think, can help create harmony which will lessen tensions*. She believed that beauty can improve the mental health of a society, and her determination to make the United States a more beautiful place became her passion.

Getting on the subject of beautification is like picking up a tangled skein of wool, she wrote in her diary on January 27, 1965. *All the threads are interwoven—recreation and pollution and mental health, and the crime rate, and rapid transit, and highway beautification, and the war on poverty, and parks—national, state and local. It is hard to hitch the conversation into one straight line, because everything leads to something*. Later she was to remark, *Even in the poorest neighborhoods you can find a geranium in a coffee can, a window box set against the scaling side of a tenement, a border of roses struggling to live in a tiny patch of open ground. Where flowers bloom, so does hope*.

She started a beautification project called the Society for a More Beautiful National Capital (later expanded nationwide), which improved the landscape in DC by planting millions of flowers, many of them on National Park Service land alongside the roads around the capital. During her Society for a More Beautiful National Capital campaign Lady Bird wrote,

> *Take the small triangles and squares with which Washington abounds, now quite barren except for a dispirited sprig of grass, and maybe a tottering bench, and put shrubs and flowers in them, through the volunteer help of neighborhood associations or business firms (it would take some cutting of red tape to do that); perhaps have a volunteer committee of landscape architects to draw up plans, so that we can have continuity and good taste and a wise choice of plants*.

As a direct result of her support and efforts, Washington gained hundreds of landscaped parks, and thousands of daffodils, azaleas, and dogwood trees were planted during Lady Bird's tenure that endure to this day.

In one of her last meetings with the Society for a More Beautiful National Capital, Lady Bird talked of the accomplishments:

> *Over the past three years, the people in this room have produced nearly two and a half million dollars to take steps toward making this nation's*

> *capital more livable and more beautiful. Not only is your handiwork enjoyed by the three million people who live and work in this city, it can be seen also by seventeen million visitors who come here each year, and our work has inspired other cities across the country.* She told the group: *This has been one of the most lovely springs I can remember in Washington's history. It has also been one of the most poignant and grave. That fact underscores the urgency of improving our environment for all people.*

She worked extensively with the American Association of Nurserymen to protect wildflowers and enthusiastically promoted planting them along highways. She created the Jacqueline Kennedy Garden and the Children's Garden on the White House South Lawn and traveled more than 100,000 miles during forty Discover America trips, in which she went whitewater rafting, hiking, and camping, walking the beaches and exploring ancient forests to prompt interest in, and support for, the national parks. She traveled nationally to raise awareness of parks and scenic areas, came out against adding dams to the Grand Canyon, and wrote letters and spoke for the preservation of the California redwoods and other historic sites.

On her seventieth birthday, in 1982, Lady Bird and actress Helen Hayes founded the National Wildflower Research Center to protect and preserve North America's native plants and natural landscapes. She donated funding and 60 acres of land in East Austin to establish the organization. It later moved to South Austin and was renamed the Lady Bird Johnson Wildflower Center in her honor. The center became part of the University of Texas at Austin, guaranteeing its permanent place in the national landscape.

For fifty of the major initiatives related to conservation and beautification, President Johnson thanked his wife on July 26, 1968, for her dedication by presenting her with fifty pens used to sign these laws. She also received a plaque that read, *To Lady Bird, who has inspired me and millions of Americans to try to preserve our land and beautify our nation. With love from Lyndon*. For twenty years she spent her summers on the Massachusetts island of Martha's Vineyard, renting the home of Charles Guggenheim for many of those years. She is recorded as saying that she had greatly appreciated the island's natural beauty and flowers.

On August 27, 1969, President Richard Nixon dedicated a 300-acre grove of redwood trees as the Lady Bird Johnson Grove due to her efforts as first lady toward preserving national resources for Americans. The grove is just north of Orick, California, and is part of Redwood National Park. She was awarded the

Presidential Medal of Freedom by President Gerald Ford on January 10, 1977. The citation for her medal reads:

> *One of America's great First Ladies, she claimed her own place in the hearts and history of the American people. In councils of power or in homes of the poor, she made government human with her unique compassion and her grace, warmth and wisdom. Her leadership transformed the American landscape and preserved its natural beauty as a national treasure.*

In 1995 she received an honor award from the National Building Museum for her lifetime leadership in beautification and conservation campaigns.

She had led a campaign to clean up Austin's Town Lake in Texas and add trails to its shoreline. Following her death, Austin mayor Will Wynn's office said it was a *foregone conclusion that Town Lake is going to be renamed* in honor of Lady Bird Johnson. The lake was renamed Lady Bird Lake on July 26, 2007.

In April 2008 the Lady Bird Johnson Memorial Cherry Blossom Grove was dedicated in Marshfield, Missouri. The dedication took place during the city's annual cherry blossom festival. She had been supportive of the rural community and their initiative to plant ornamental cherry trees.

On October 22, 2012, the United States Postal Service announced the issue of a souvenir forever stamp sheet honoring Lady Bird Johnson as a tribute to her legacy of beautifying the nation's roadsides, urban parks, and trails. Five of the six stamps feature adaptations of stamps originally issued in the 1960s to promote planting in public spaces.

She has been ranked in surveys by historians as one of the most highly regarded of all the American first ladies, and her greatest legacy is the tireless work that she undertook to improve America's landscape and environment.

4.97 MADALENE HILL (1913–2009)

Known to many as the Grand Dame of Herbs, Madalene blazed a path so that many who followed her could also grow her little plants.

Madalene was born in Rock Island, Texas, in 1913. Her maternal grandparents had settled in the area as rice farmers. But at age three she moved with her mother and younger brother to Kansas to live with relatives. Being the eldest of thirteen children, she developed a strong work ethic and left high school at age sixteen to help support the family. She worked for the Federal Land Bank in Wichita just as the Great Depression hit and times got hard for the farmers in the Midwest. When WWII broke out, Alice went to work at the Brown Shipbuilding Company in the payroll department. After the war ended in 1945 she worked for IBM, being the first female office manager there from 1949 to 1951.

In 1951, Madalene married Jim Hill, who was a keen gardener and cook. In 1957 they both moved to land purchased near Cleveland, Texas; Jim's plan was to grow gladioli on a commercial scale to sell to florists. After two years of preparation, they planted 200,000 gladioli corms. Madalene had grown up using herbs such as dill and sage, and they were always a part of her cooking, so as they prepared for their gladioli experiment they grew herbs and vegetables for their own use. At that time sources for herb plants and for herb seeds were scarce. In 1957, Madalene joined the Herb Society of America, the second member to join from Texas. She was then able to exchange seeds with other members, although the variety of herb plants available was still very limited.

Madalene and Jim saw that there was a growing interest in herbs, especially ones such as cilantro and chives. Because of this they started to grow and sell herbs

Madalene Hill. Unknown photographer. *Round Top Festival Institute* at their property, which they named Hilltop Herb Farm. With the farm's remote rural location, they started on a small scale and opened a small café to feed hungry customers with herb-flavored lunches. This led to the creation of a restaurant business in 1967 that attracted customers from near and far. Madalene began to lecture and write about herbs as well as travel and communicate with other herb enthusiasts to learn more about herbs and to collect different varieties. In 1968, along with a friend, Rexford Talbert, she cofounded the branch called the Herb Society of America, South Texas Unit, based in Houston.

By the early 1980s the variety of herbs available to the public in America was greatly increased, and their business was expanding. Then disaster struck on two fronts. First, in 1982 Jim passed away, and in 1983 Hilltop Herb Farm was destroyed by a December tornado. Madalene, along with daughter Gwen, rebuilt it. In addition, to supplement their income and with their experience of catering, they opened a restaurant in Houston. However, this was not the moneymaking enterprise that they had envisaged. In 1987, when Madalene was seventy-four years old, she decided to retire, and they decided to get out of the restaurant business and sell the farm altogether.

Instead, Madalene and Gwen produced a classic book, *Southern Herb Growing*, published by Shearer Publishing in 1987, and started lecturing around the country on the qualities of herbs.

In 1993, Madalene and Gwen moved into the 1902 Menke House, one of the historical structures at the Round Top Festival Institute in Texas. This was a 200-acre site that pianist James Dick founded for concerts and study. Gwen became director of food services at the institute, and Madalene became a full-time volunteer as curator of the Susan McAshan Gardens. This had been named for the founder of the Houston Arboretum & Nature Center. Always the consummate gardener, Madalene brought along many of her potted herbs and set about creating new gardens to enhance the grounds and provide fresh herbs for the institute kitchen.

During her tenure the gardens expanded to include a wonderful array of rare plants, large herb collections, and theme gardens, such as the Terrace Gardens, Sun-Shade Garden, Fruit Tree Garden and Beethoven's Woods, Cloister Garden, Mediterranean and Wall Gardens, Cultivated Grasses Garden, Medicinal Cacti, Pharmacy Garden, and several more. The Pharmacy Garden is dedicated in her honor. Madalene served as herbalist in residence.

The view entering the Roman ruins in the McAshan Herb Gardens at Festival Hill, on the campus of the Round Top Festival Institute in Round Top, Texas. The brown building to the left is the Menke House, a 1902 Gothic Revival structure moved to Festival Hill from nearby Hempstead. The building is used for food service and meetings. *rock-oak-deer*

With a strong work ethic, Madalene began each day at 5:00 a.m. with her research and writing, then had breakfast and was ready to greet volunteers by 9:00 a.m. Her gardens have evolved into one of the outstanding gardens in the United States and attract visitors and plant researchers from far and wide. Though she never went to college to study, teachers, herbalists, and gardeners across the country consulted Madalene as an authority for information about herbs and other plants. Gardens were named in her honor, and she received many awards and medals for her achievements. However, she said that her greatest honor was *to have been the facilitator for the introduction of culinary herbs and herbs for the landscape to so many through the years. These small fragrant plants have changed the lives of so many.*

Madalene has been credited with introducing herbs such as Mexican mint marigold, Hilltop oregano, Arp rosemary, Madalene Hill doublemint, and Newe Ya'ar sage to the Texas and American markets. The rosemary Hill Hardy was named in her honor by a fellow herb grower.

Whenever she would autograph her book, she would write the saying *Grow Where You Are Planted*. In her ninety-five years, she did just that and became an inspiration for her family, friends, coworkers, and gardeners across Texas and the United States and around the world. Always the enthusiastic educator, she led seminars across the country, emphasizing herbs as living links between past and present. Herbs, she told a newspaper in 2005, *are among the oldest cultivated plants in the world. Herbs are still growing wild in some areas. Some natural hybridizing has occurred, but basically these are the same plants that our ancestors knew and used.*

The Herb Society of America (HSA) is dedicated to promoting the knowledge, use, and delight of herbs through educational programs, research, and sharing the experience of its members with the community. Lois Sutton, HSA board president, said, *Madalene was an entrepreneur, a plantsman, a mentor, an exacting teacher, a gardener, an unending font of garden descriptions from her travels around the world and the history of how herbs came to Texas*. Madalene served as the Herb Society of

America president from 1986 to 1988. In 1994 she became a founding member of the Herb Society of America Pioneer Unit, based in Round Top. The American Horticultural Society recognized Madalene in 2006 for extraordinary and dedicated efforts in the field of horticulture. The Knot Garden at the National Arboretum in Washington, DC, was dedicated to Madalene by Houston benefactors Maurice and Susan McAshan in the 1980s. The Arbor Gate in Tomball dedicated its Madalene Hill Herb Garden in 2005.

Madalene continued to write for respected national publications and always wrote for the newsletter of her beloved Pioneer Unit of the National Herb Society into her nineties. She penned at least two articles every month: usually a book review and an informative article about an herb she had researched. Madalene Hill died in Round Top on March 4, 2009, after a brief illness. She was a grand ninety-four years old.

4.98 ELISABETH CAREY MILLER (1915–1994)

A self-taught garden designer and plants woman who created a spectacular garden outside Seattle, Washington

Elisabeth was born in Montana, where her father was a government agent for the Kalispel tribe, an Indigenous people of the Northwest Plateau, in Washington State. She went to school on the reservation and was taught and shared the Native American respect for the land.

She was captivated by the beauty and variance of the indigenous plants of the region and was taught a rain dance, which she sometimes performed in later years for visitors at her Highlands home when Seattle had been rainless for too long. History does not record if she was successful in producing downpours to relieve the drought. Elisabeth attended the University of Washington, majoring in art. Later she married attorney Pendleton Miller, and they purchased 5 acres of land in 1948 situated at 79 Olympic Drive, Shoreline, Washington, in the Pacific Northwest. The property had expansive views over Puget Sound and the Olympic National Park peninsula.

Local architect Daniel E. Lamont designed their home with an exterior of natural materials, including rustic, hand-split, clear red cedar (*Thuja plicata*) sidings complemented by soft-fawn-, buff-, and peach-toned sandstone walls. The ranch-style design of the house provides a subtle backdrop to the surrounding garden. Early development in the garden included the acquisition and placement of native stone, as well as numerous weathered logs and stumps. Over the course of time, hundreds of tons of stone and logs have since been added to the grounds as decorative, natural accents.

Outcropping of stone provided unique planting locations for a wide variety of alpine plants. The arrangement of these elements provides a unique northwestern US feel to the garden today. Elisabeth's travels to Japan and China influenced her initial plant selection and her design of the garden, combined with an appreciation for the native western North American flora. Although she had no formal horticultural training or education, Elisabeth had a natural feel and talent for appreciating garden design, plant selection, and location of plantings. Older trees and shrubs show careful and artful pruning, accentuating shapely branch structures. A canopy of native conifers composed of Douglas fir (*Pseudotsuga menziesii*), grand fir (*Abies grandis*), western hemlock (*Tsuga heterophylla*), and western red cedar (*Thuja plicata*) rise high above the garden floor, providing shade for a tapestry of woodland plants.

Using skills that she had acquired as an art major, Elisabeth arranged plants on the basis of texture, form, and color of their foliage, bark, and flowers. Composed garden vignettes formed the structure of a bed, with new plantings radiating out from these compositions. Many of Elisabeth's early compositions form the main features of the garden today. Her business adviser, Frank Minton, said, *She loved to get her hands in the dirt and garden. She told me: If the entire world could have been paved over with concrete, my family would have seen more of me.*

As a self-taught gardener, Elisabeth found rare and unusual plants both challenging and rewarding to cultivate. Through careful soil preparation, extensive research, and trial and error, she successfully grew many garden treasures, several for the first time in North America. Among the plants that she was first to cultivate in the USA were *Hakonechloa macra aureola* (golden Japanese forest grass), *Blechnum chilense* (Chilean hard fern), and *Lysichiton camtschatcensis* (Asian skunk cabbage).

Elisabeth founded the Rhododendron Species Foundation and belonged to several other gardening groups. She was a popular lecturer and helped select the plantings in Freeway Park, Seattle; oversaw plantings along the Lake Washington Ship Canal; and helped landscape and plant traffic islands throughout Seattle. She helped establish the University of Washington Center for Urban Horticulture, which opened in 1984 and is part of the University of Washington Botanic Gardens. It includes a 16-acre landscaped site with buildings and gardens and the 74-acre Union Bay Natural Area, which provides publicly accessible wildlife habitat and an outdoor laboratory for University of Washington research. Along with her husband, Pendleton, Elisabeth established her namesake ornamental plant library in the center. She also endowed a chair in her husband's name at the University of Washington Law School.

Elisabeth Carey Miller died in 1994 at age seventy-nine, and the garden in Shoreline, Washington, was left in her will to become a botanical garden and serve as a resource for the horticultural community. Continuing her vision, the garden collections today still focus on new, rare, and unusual plants, in addition to experimentation and the evaluation of plants best suited for the climate of the maritime Pacific Northwest. The Pendleton and Elisabeth Carey Miller Charitable Foundation was established to continue the philanthropic activities that they so generously supported during their lifetimes.

4.99 JANET MEAKIN POOR (1929–2017)

Plant conservationist and landscape designer Janet was a driving force behind saving and conserving our planet's botanical heritage.

Janet Meakin Poor

Janet was born Janet Meakin Lee in Cincinnati, where she grew up. Her education after high school included study at the University of Cincinnati. Much later she took courses at Triton College in River Grove, a village in Cook County, Illinois, and at the University of Wisconsin–Madison to earn a degree in landscape design and horticulture. She married Edward Poor in Cincinnati in 1951 and moved with him to Chicago in 1957. Job transfers later took the family to several other midwestern cities before a return to Chicago in 1967. It wasn't until then that Janet developed a serious interest in plants and gardening.

In the late 1960s she started a landscape design business, initially designing gardens for friends. As the business grew so did her reputation, and she later got involved in larger projects, including some commercial work. Little did she know that she had launched a career for herself that would lead her to the forefront of plant conservation and landscape design with a fine reputation locally, nationally, and internationally. In the late 1960s, Janet became a member of the Chicago Botanic Garden and in 1978 was appointed to the woman's board, leading to joining the board of directors in 1980. She served as board chair from 1987 to 1993.

A view of part of the garden at Filoli. *filoli.canto.com*

For more than twenty years, beginning in 1980, Janet chaired the Botanic Garden's Research Committee, now known as the Science and Education Committee. She worked on the Buildings, Gardens, and Visitor Experience Committee and was later named an honorary woman's board member and was an honorary life member. In all her appointments she focused on conservation, research, and the value of plant diversity. In addition to her skills as a landscape architect, Janet was important as a driving force behind saving and conserving the earth's botanical heritage. She headed an ambitious program to collect seeds from the world's endangered plants, encouraging the Chicago Botanic Garden into its participation in the international Millennium Seed Bank Project (now called the Millennium Seed Bank Partnership). The project involves seeds of the world's rarest and threatened plants being collected, preserved, and stored, some of them in Glencoe, on Chicago's North Shore. The project is the largest plant conservation program in the world. There are more than 100 partnerships worldwide, including the UK, Australia, Mexico, Chile, Kenya, China, Jordan, Mali, Malawi, Madagascar, Burkina Faso, Botswana, Tanzania, Saudi Arabia, Lebanon, and South Africa.

Janet was a longtime supporter of the California-based Center for Plant Conservation. She was a board member there for thirty-two years and was known for her recognition of the important role that gardens can play in preventing plant extinction. Its president and CEO, John Clark, once said of Janet: *I think it's her understanding of people that led her to care about plants. . . . The reality is that plants are central to our quality of life on this planet, and she got that. . . . She's just been incredibly generous with her resources and her time.*

Janet was the editor of two books: *Plants That Merit Attention, Volume I: Trees*, published by Timber Press in 1964, and *Plants That Merit Attention, Volume II: Shrubs*, also published by Timber Press, in 1966. She began her first book with her belief that there are no perfect plants. Her view was that nature needs diversity in its flora, especially in trees. Diversity, she believed, makes for a stronger garden, a stronger landscape, and a stronger planet.

Janet was vice president of the Garden Club of America and chair of Open Days 1989–2000, a showcase of hundreds of American gardens by the national organization the Garden Conservancy. She was an advisor to the Filoli Center, now called Filoli Historic House & Garden, near San Francisco—a country house set in 16 acres of formal gardens surrounded by a 654-acre estate in Woodside, California. Now owned by the National Trust for Historic Preservation, Filoli is open to the public. The site is both a California Historical Landmark and listed on the National Register of Historic Places.

Janet also served on the awards committee at the Winterthur Museum, Garden, and Library in Delaware; as an advisor to the McKee Botanical Garden in Vero Beach, Florida; as a board member with the American Horticultural Society; and as a member of the advisory council of the United States National Arboretum, an appointment by the US secretary of agriculture.

The Janet Meakin Poor Research Symposium at the Chicago Botanic Garden was created to highlight the increasing need for a cooperative international plant conservation, particularly to encourage efforts to better understand the impact of climate change on plants. Internationally recognized experts discuss global strategies for plant conservation through science and education. Janet also played a major role in the development of the new Daniel F. and Ada L. Rice Plant Conservation Science Center at Chicago Botanic Garden, which provides laboratories and teaching facilities for more than 200 PhD scientists, land managers, students, and interns. The Chicago Botanic Garden has achieved a leading conservation role both nationally and internationally under Janet's inspiration, enthusiasm, and leadership. Janet's many awards include

Chicago Botanic Garden Horticulture Society Medal
Catherine H. Sweeney Award from the American Horticultural Society
Hutchinson Award from the Chicago Horticultural Society
Creative Leadership Award and Medal of Honor from the Garden Club of America
American Horticultural Society Book Award, for her book on shrubs

Janet Meakin Poor died in 2017. Upon her death, Chicago Botanic Garden board chair Bob Finke wrote in a note to staff, board members, and other garden associates upon hearing of her death:

> *Unquestionably, Janet was one of the principal drivers of the* [Chicago Botanic] *Garden's current place as a global leader across horticulture, plant science conservation research and education.* [She was] *one of the pillars upon which our garden rests. Her dedication to every aspect of the garden, and especially to horticulture and conservation, and her insistence on excellence in everything the garden does, was unmatched.*

Chicago Botanic Garden has established the Janet Meakin Poor Scholarship Endowment Fund, which supports the Plant Biology and Conservation Program in partnership with Northwestern University. Janet was a leader in establishing the science programs at the garden; she recognized that growing a new generation of plant scientists and conservation advocates was essential to saving plants, people, and the planet.

4.100 ELIZABETH *"LIZ"* CHRISTY (1945–1985)

Founder of the urban community garden group Green Guerrillas, which improves abandoned open spaces and works to establish community gardens in New York City, and now all over North America

Educated at Columbia University, New York University, and the New School, Liz's interests ranged from art and urban planning to botany, agronomy, and landscaping. During New York City's financial crisis, abandonment of the plots had left the city with vacant, rubble-strewn lots. Littered with trash and rats, they became centers for drug dealing and abuse, prostitution, and places to strip down stolen cars and sell their parts. Rather than seek a positive use for the land, the city's answer to the problem was to spend thousands of dollars enclosing the lots with cyclone fencing. Frustrated with government ineptitude, in 1973 Liz and a band of like-minded activists calling themselves the Green Guerrillas began taking over abandoned lots on Manhattan's Lower East Side to tidy up the neglected land and create gardens there for the benefit of the local community. They started their first garden on the corner of Bowery and Houston Streets in the Bowery, where a few months earlier two people had been found frozen to death in a cardboard box.

One of Liz's early recruits was Bill Brunson. He said, *You could not have picked a more unlikely place to start a garden. At the time, there were still all these men lined up along the Bowery drinking wine and panhandling. To put a garden there—in what was probably the ultimate slime spot in the city—that was unheard of*. Armed with bolt cutters and pickaxes, they saw themselves as a strike force to liberate the

Liz Christy (*foreground*) in 1975, at a ceremony renaming the Bowery Houston Community Garden as the Liz Christy Community Garden. The Liz Christy Community Garden is the oldest community garden in New York City. *Donald Loggins, Cultural Landscape Foundation*

A view of part of the Liz Christy Community Garden at the corner of Bowery and Houston Streets, New York City. *Donald Loggins, Cultural Landscape Foundation*

crumbling landscape around them and find a practical use for them. Liz lived on Mott Street, on the Lower East Side of Manhattan, and together with other volunteers spent much of 1973 removing trash, adding topsoil, installing fencing, and otherwise beautifying the abandoned lot. She spearheaded the creation of the Bowery Houston Community Farm Garden, working with the Green Guerrillas, the community activist group that she had helped start.

The Green Guerrillas threw seeded Green-Aids—balloons or Christmas tree ornaments stuffed with peat moss, fertilizer, and wildflower seeds—into fenced-off lots and along highways and street borders across the five boroughs. They also held training sessions and set up phone lines so that people could call to find out where to get free plants and trees. Amos Taylor, another early Green Guerrilla, recalls: *It was a form of civil disobedience. We were basically saying to the government, if you won't do it, we will.* The activity was, to many bureaucrats, illegal. Although the Guerrillas initially got permission to clean the lots, the city later accused them of trespassing and threatened to banish them off the land. Liz's response was to instigate a media blitz, and she brought in TV cameras to show how they transformed the lot, creating soil with nothing but sifted rubble and compost. The public outcry of approval and support that followed made the city back down, and it offered them a lease. On April 23, 1974, the city's office of Housing Preservation and Development approved the site for rental as the Bowery Houston Community Farm & Garden for a fee of $1 a month. In its second year of existence, this forerunner of today's urban community gardens won its first Mollie Parnis Dress Up Your Neighborhood Award.

The garden also has a wildflower habitat, a grape arbor, a grove of weeping birch trees, fruit trees, a dawn redwood, vegetable gardens, berries, herbs, and hundreds of varieties of flowering perennials. It is divided into individual areas designed and tended by the volunteer garden members; general maintenance is shared. It is a peaceful oasis open to all to sit in, relax, and enjoy. In addition to the many visitors, it has benefited the many local volunteers, who enjoy the introduction to and learning about nature and gardening, the physical exercise, the fresh air, and the satisfaction of helping their community. Many volunteers have been introduced to the joys of gardening and the outdoors by working on this and other Liz Christy inspired projects.

The garden was renamed the Liz Christy Community Garden in 1986 to honor its founder. It was the inspiration for people to create similar plots in other neighborhoods in all five New York boroughs and then all over the USA. Soon the Green Guerrillas were running workshops and planting experimental plots to learn how a wide range of plants could be grown in hostile conditions. The garden became a site for many plant giveaways, where plants grown on-site or donated from nurseries, professional horticulturists, and local gardeners were given to new gardens all over the city.

By 1976 their efforts were beginning to win over government officials, including Brooklyn congressman Fred Richmond, who pushed through a federal program to support urban gardening. In Brooklyn, the first demonstration project was set up through Cornell University's Cooperative Extension Service. It was so successful that a national program was funded with $3 million and was expanded to include fifteen other cities. Between 1974 and 1981, Liz hosted the *Grow Your Own* radio program in New York City, covering such topics as urban forestry, community gardens, community design and planning, and the environment.

Liz provided technical assistance and training for approximately 700 community gardens in New York City and helped create similar programs in many other cities. She developed the Citizen Street Tree Pruners course with the city's Parks Department and instituted public education programs on urban tree care.

Her numerous awards include the Municipal Art Society Award for Urban Improvements, the Parks Council Award for Community Service, the US Environmental Protection Agency Region II Award, and the American Forestry Association Urban Forestry Award. She worked as the first director of the Open Space Greening Program, part of the New York City government's Council on the Environment, a position she held until her tragically early death at just forty years old. Volunteers and visitors were often living in overcrowded urban areas with few social amenities, and they benefited from the many positive aspects of the gardens.

Liz was the first director of the Council on the Environment of New York City's Open Space Greening Program and the first winner of the American Forestry Association's Urban Forestry Award. She was an important frontrunner of community gardening in the United States. The thousands that have been created still bring a number of important benefits to neighborhoods across the country. Liz, through her determined efforts creating and encouraging community gardens, has introduced countless people to the joys of gardening.

Liz takes a moment of reflection. *Donald Loggins, Cultural Landscape Foundation*

Appendixes

APPENDIX A:

Index of the 100 Biographies

4.1 Martha Daniell Logan (1702–1779)
4.2 Eliza Pinckney (1722–1793)
4.3 Jane Colden (1724–1766)
4.4 Elizabeth Lamboll (1725–1760)
4.5 Margaret Tilghman Carroll (1742–1817)
4.6 Lady Jean Skipwith (1748–1762)
4.7 Frances "Fanny" Allen Penniman (1760–1834)
4.8 Almira Hart Lincoln Phelps (1793–1884)
4.9 Catharine Parr Traill (1802–1899)
4.10 Mary Riggs Collins (1818–1852)
4.11 Jane Loring Gray (1821–1909)
4.12 Susan Hallowell (1835–1911)
4.13 Annie Linda Jack (1839–1912)
4.14 Buffalo Bird Woman (ca. 1839–1932)
4.15 Emma Homan Thayer (1842–1908)
4.16 Theodosia Burr Shepherd (1845–1906)
4.17 Frances "Fannie" Griscom Parsons (1850–1923)
4.18 Mariana Griswold Van Rensselaer (1851–1934)
4.19 Alice Morse Earle (1851–1911)
4.20 Clara Eaton Cummings (1855–1906)
4.21 Katherine Olivia "Kate" Sessions (1857–1940)
4.22 Elizabeth Gertrude Britton (1858–1934)
4.23 Helena Rutherfurd Ely (1858–1920)
4.24 Mabel Osgood Wright (1859–1934)
4.25 Alice Eastwood (1859–1953)
4.26 Mary Vaux Walcott (1860–1940)
4.27 Frances Theodora Parsons (1861–1952)
4.28 Edith Wharton (1862–1937)
4.29 Louisa Boyd Yeomans King (1863–1948)
4.30 Harriet Risley Foote (1863–1951)
4.31 Hulda Klager (1863–1960)
4.32 Margaret Clay Ferguson (1863–1951)
4.33 Frances Benjamin Johnston (1864–1952)
4.34 Clara Bryant Ford (1866–1950)
4.35 Margaret Neilson Armstrong (1867–1944)
4.36 Jennie Foster Butchart (1868–1950)
4.37 Mattie Edwards Hewitt (1859–1956)
4.38 Ellen Biddle Shipman (1869–1950)
4.39 Mary Agnes Chase (1869–1963)
4.40 Josephine Tilden (1869–1957)
4.41 Martha Brookes Hutcheson (1871–1959)
4.42 Beatrix Cadwalader Farrand (1872–1959)
4.43 Rose Standish Nichols (1872–1960)
4.44 Grace Tabor (1873–1973)
4.45 Nellie Beatrice Osborn Allen (1874–1961)
4.46 Marian Cruger Coffin (1876–1957)
4.47 Louise Beebe Wilder (1878–1938)
4.48 Lester Gertrude Rowntree (1879–1979)
4.49 Isabella Preston (1881–1965)
4.50 Marian "Daisy" Hubbard Fairchild (1889–1962)
4.51 Anne Ethel Spencer (1882–1975)
4.52 Helen Morganthau Fox (1884–1974)
4.53 Mary Gibson Henry (1884–1967)
4.54 Florence Bell Robinson (1885–1973)
4.55 Marie Selby (1885–1971)
4.56 Lilla Leach (1886–1980)
4.57 Elsa Rehmann (1886–1946)
4.58 Ganna Walska (1887–1984)
4.59 Rose Ishbel Greely (1887–1969)
4.60 Elizabeth Lord (1887–1976) and Edith Schryver (1901–1984)
4.61 Annette Hoyt Flanders (1887–1946)
4.62 Caroline "Carrie" Coroneos Dormon (1888–1971)
4.63 Ruth Bramley Dean (1889–1932)
4.64 Ethel Zoe Bailey (1889–1983)
4.65 Emma Lucy Braun (1889–1971)
4.66 Alice Orme Smith (1889–1980)
4.67 Florence Yoch (1890–1972) and Lucile Council (1898–1964)
4.68 Louise Klein Miller (1890–1967)
4.69 Marjorie Sewell Cautley (1891–1954)
4.70 May Petrea Theilgaard Watts (1893–1975)
4.71 Edith A Roberts (1881–1977)
4.72 Wanda Kirkbride Farr (1895–1983)

Supplementary Index

APPENDIX B:
Visiting the Featured Gardens

Gardeners are usually generous people. They love to share their knowledge, and sometimes their plants, with other enthusiasts. Many are happy to open their gardens to the visiting public, but before planning a visit to any of the gardens mentioned in this book that are open to the public, you should always check their websites to see if there are times when the owner opens it to the public, and plan your visit accordingly. Of the gardens mentioned in this book that are open to visits by the public, some of them are open every day in the year except Christmas Day, while others open only on specific days, and some are open only by appointment.

Some gardens are still in private hands and not available for visits by the public. Always check opening times for any garden you intend to visit, if possible. Not all gardens have their own website, but typing in a search ending in the name of the garden or alternatively *Gardens to visit in . . .* can often provide the necessary information, sometimes listed by local authorities or local tourist information offices.

The Garden Conservancy's Open Days program is worth checking. Local garden clubs are often a good source of information about gardens in their area open to the public—for instance, the garden clubs of Virginia and Maryland publish booklets listing all public and private gardens that are open, and the Pennsylvania Horticultural Society has a mailing list of 130 garden clubs in their region. The website www.gardenvisit.com is a good source, as is culturetrip.com, which lists the most-beautiful public gardens in the United States. Forbes's website, www.forbes.com, includes the article "13 Ways to Enjoy the Most Beautiful Gardens in the United States Year-Round."

APPENDIX C:
About the Cultural Landscape Foundation

Note: The following copy has been obtained from the Cultural Landscape Foundation website. For further information, please visit it at: tclf.org.

A nonprofit established in 1998, the Cultural Landscape Foundation® (TCLF) connects people to places. TCLF educates and engages the public to make our shared landscape heritage more visible, identify its value, and empower its stewards. TCLF achieves this mission through the ongoing development of its four core programs:

What's Out There®, North America's largest and most exhaustive database of cultural landscapes;
Pioneers of American Landscape Design®, an in-depth multimedia library inclusive of video oral histories chronicling the lives of significant landscape architects and educators;
Landslide®, an ongoing collection of important landscapes and landscape features that are threatened; and
The Oberlander Prize, a biennial prize in landscape architecture that includes a $100,000 monetary award and two years of public engagement activities.

Cultural landscapes are landscapes that have been affected, influenced, or shaped by human involvement. A cultural landscape can be associated with a person or event. It can be thousands of acres or a tiny homestead. It can be a grand estate, industrial site, park, garden, cemetery, campus, and more. Collectively, cultural landscapes are works of art, narratives of culture, and expressions of regional identity. There are primarily four types of cultural landscapes, although any given landscape may fall under more than one typology:

Designed Landscapes
Ethnographic Landscapes
Historic Sites
Vernacular Landscapes

Why are cultural landscapes important?
Cultural landscapes are a legacy for everyone. These special sites reveal aspects of our country's origins and development, as well as our evolving relationships with the natural world. They provide scenic, economic, ecological, social, recreational, and educational opportunities helping communities to better understand themselves.

Why is it important to protect cultural landscapes?
Neglect and inappropriate development put our irreplaceable landscape legacy increasingly at risk. Too often today's short-sighted decisions threaten the survival and continuity of our shared heritage. It is everyone's responsibility to safeguard our nation's cultural landscapes. The ongoing care and interpretation of these sites improve our quality of life and deepen a sense of place and identity for future generations.

The Cultural Landscape Foundation (TCLF) is a 501(c)(3) nonprofit organization that provides people with the ability to see, understand, and value landscape architecture and its practitioners in the way many people have learned to do with buildings and their designers. A gift to TCLF is tax deductible to the extent allowed by law and will ensure TCLF's programs and ongoing initiatives collectively tell the stories of our nation's rich landscape heritage.

APPENDIX D:

About the Author

Stefan White was born into a garden-loving family. The family home in the Midlands area of England had a 4-acre plot landscaped by one of Britain's most prominent landscape architects, Percy Kane. Sadly, the garden has been recently broken up, and there are now six houses where there was previously a large vegetable and fruit garden, a 100 ft. greenhouse, a putting green, a rose garden, and an ornamental pool.

Stefan began his business career as a management trainee with Cadbury, one of the world's largest chocolate and food companies. Appointed to the managerial sales staff, he moved to London to manage sales and marketing. He left after six years to study business administration in Boston, Massachusetts, to prepare for an entrepreneurial career.

Returning to England, he saw a gap in the giftware market: gifts for men. He designed and developed a wide range of desk accessories, wall décor, and home accessories decorated with the sports golf, polo, horse riding, sailing, and fishing. The gifts were manufactured by craft companies in England to his exclusive designs and sold in thirty countries in high-end department stores, gift shops, specialty stores, online retailers, and mail order catalogs. His biggest market was the USA, and he established a distribution warehouse, administration, and sales facility in Rhode Island. The company, Hurley Style, became a world leader in its field. After forty-five years as owner he decided to retire and sold his company to one of his suppliers. He has visited ninety-seven countries to date. In retirement, inspired by his love of fine food and wine, he was appointed by Britain's oldest guide to prestigious hotels, Signpost, as their hotel inspector for London and the southeast of England.

This book and his career as a public speaker started one peaceful, gloriously warm summer day twenty-four years ago on the river Thames in southern England. A friend owns a splendid mahogany and brass riverboat called an Edwardian Gentleman's Luncheon Launch. It seats eight for a meal on the aft deck, and he was invited to join a party for lunch. After an enjoyable lunch (and perhaps rather too much champagne and chablis), another guest said that she was having trouble finding speakers for her local garden club. In the heat of the moment, Stefan told her that he would be happy to give them a talk. The next morning she telephoned to advise that she had booked him in for an evening two months ahead. He had always been interested in garden history, and there was a particular tale that he had read about a very underappreciated, pioneering English plant hunter, avid collector of curiosities, and gardener to the royal family in the sixteenth century, John Tradescant. He thought that this would make an interesting story and a talk. He rapidly researched and developed it, and later, as his career as a horticultural historian grew, he created a number of other garden-themed talks, which he gives to garden clubs and horticultural societies in England. He has lectured at universities, at the Royal Horticultural Society, and to leading societies and special interest groups, including a private member group in the House of Commons in the UK Parliament. Stefan has also written two books on the roles of women in American history, three booklets on the history of golf, and one on appreciating wine.

Author Stefan White during one of fifty-six cruises he has undertaken as guest lecturer

His invitation to become a speaker on cruise ships started in 2007 and began with his enrichment talks. In 2011 he graduated from a course developed by a southern English speakers agency specifically designed for training destination lecturers, and now specializes in port and destination talks while also offering his portfolio of thirty-eight entertaining and informative enrichment talks covering a wide range of subjects encompassing history, the arts, the Mediterranean Sea, the history of golf, conservation, climate change, and, his specialty and focus, gardening history and horticulture. Stefan is a member of the Royal Horticultural Society and, in 2019, was elected a member of the prestigious Royal Historical Society.

Stefan purchased a portion of the manor house and garden in a Thames-side village about 40 miles west of London in 1972 and has recently celebrated fifty years of residence there.

His garden consists of part of the original walled estate of the Elizabethan manor house. Among its features are a number of mature trees, including two enormous Thuja plicata cedars, beech, horse chestnut, yew, pine, and magnolia. There are lawns and flower beds containing shrubs and perennials and annual flowers. The vegetable patch features eight large raised beds inspired by the early settlers' gardens in the USA. One of these is devoted to growing eight types of herbs, others to growing runner beans, French beans, broad beans, potatoes, beetroot, lettuce, spinach, rocket, carrot, and broccoli. Two of the raised beds are devoted to growing Cucurbitacae pepo, the vegetable marrow from the family that includes pumpkins and zucchini. Stefan is the founder and life president of the Hurley Curcurbitacae Club, a horticultural society devoted to breaking the world's record weight for a marrow, currently standing at 256 pounds, 9.8 ounces. Stefan admits that the club's members have never really threatened the world record, but members do enjoy a very active social life.

The gateway into the author's home, Manor House, Hurley, UK, in 1945, when the house was requisitioned by the US Army as Station Victor, undertaking secret interpretation of signals from agents in occupied Europe. *OSS archives*

APPENDIX E:
About the Artist

As noted in the introduction, there are images of nearly all of the 100 heroines of horticulture whose brief biographies appear in chapter 5. Sadly, many of these are old photographs, some dating from the very early days of photography, and the quality of them makes them impossible to reproduce on the printed pages of this book.

It was felt that a portrait of every one of the 100 heroines was important to provide an overview of their work and personality and that, where a painting or photograph was of poor quality, it could be used by a competent artist as the basis for creating a pen-and-ink line drawing.

After an intensive search, an artist was located who had the talent and interpretative skills to create the required images. Pablo Jose Martinez was born on May 22, 1997, in Caracas, Venezuela. From an early age he showed artistic talent, and he focused this on pen-and-ink line drawings. At age seventeen he began to work independently with portraits and murals in Caracas. He began his higher studies in graphic design in 2017 at the Rodolfo Loero Arismendi Industrial Technology University Institute in the city. As well as local clients, his commissions spread globally and, using the internet, he began to sell illustrations in digital format to clients around the world.

APPENDIX F:
Acknowledgments

I am grateful to those copyright owners who have given permission for their material to be used. Some of the material comes from secondary and tertiary sources. I have tried to locate the original author/photographer/artist and make the appropriate acknowledgment. In some cases the sources have proven obscure, and I have been unable to track them down. In these cases, I would like to hear from the copyright owners and will be pleased to acknowledge them in future editions.

Sources of research material include the Library of Congress; the Smithsonian Institute, the National Museum of Natural History Library; Harvard Library; Wellesley College Archives; the Garden Museum, London; John D. Rockefeller Jr. Library; the Colonial Williamsburg Foundation; the Estate of Anthony Huxley; Cambridge University Library; Vassar

College; the British Library; National Portrait Gallery, London, archives and collections; Cornell University; Royal Botanical Gardens, Kew; the Metropolitan Museum, New York; and many other museum and university archives.

Please also see appendix C, which acknowledges the Cultural Landscape Foundation as a source of images for this book and outlines the objectives of this very worthwhile organization which seeks to preserve North America's horticultural heritage.

I also wish to thank Caroline Seebohm, a published author of gardening books whom I met by chance while I was acting as guest lecturer on a cruise ship. She was very helpful in reviewing my proposal and advising on the structure of the book. Fiona Fieldhouse, a next door neighbor and another published author for reviewing my draft manuscript and providing insightful critique and comments; Lucy Melzer and Val Read for editing and formatting the book; Ian Robertson of Schiffer Publishing for editing the book into printable form; and my wife, Erica, for her help with proofreading and editing, and particularly for her continued patience and support over the six-year period of researching and writing the book. I hope you think that it has been a worthwhile journey.

Stefan White, December 12, 2022